Algorithms
and
Their Computer Solutions

Algorithms
and
Their Computer Solutions

Lucio Artiaga
Wichita State University

Lloyd D. Davis
University of Tennessee at Chattanooga

Charles E. Merrill Publishing Company
A Bell & Howell Company
Columbus, Ohio

The Merrill Mathematics Series

Erwin Kleinfeld, Editor

International Standard Book Number: 0–675–09151–9

Library of Congress Catalog Card Number: 71–181581

1 2 3 4 5 6 7 8 9 10–78 77 76 75 74 73 72

Printed in the United States of America

To our wives, Maria and Barbara

Preface

This book is intended as a text for an introductory course in a computer science program. The major intent of the writers is to show the student how to find algorithms, that is, problem-solving procedures, that can be implemented by computers. As soon as the student has an elementary knowledge of the way a computer works, he is introduced to a series of problems from widely different fields. In each case he is shown in detail how to derive an algorithm to show the problem and how to program the algorithm in FORTRAN for use with a computer. On occasion, the reader will be unfamiliar with the subject matter of certain problems. This should not deter the reader from working through each problem. It is the firm conviction of the writers, based on experience, that the reader will learn that he can program in areas in which he is not an expert.

The book is divided into three parts. Part I deals with computers and FORTRAN, Part II takes up algorithms and Part III contains applications. Twenty complete programs are included. We hope that this will be the starting point of a library of programs. In order to make such expansion easier, the concepts of subroutine and subalgorithm are emphasized. The reader is encouraged to find new algorithms by modifying those set down here.

The only prerequisites for reading this book are high school algebra and a willingness to work through the exercises. We believe that programming is an art that can be mastered by students in any discipline.

We wish to thank the members of the mathematics departments at the University of North Carolina at Charlotte, the University of Tennessee at Chattanooga, and Wichita State University for their help in preparing this book. Special thanks are due to Miss Susan Willett, who has very patiently helped with the typing and proofing.

Contents

PART III

Algorithms
and
Their Computer Solutions

Part I

Chapter I

1. BRIEF HISTORY OF COMPUTING DEVICES

Mankind has used computing devices almost as long as counting. In fact, the word "calculating" comes from the latin word "calculi" meaning pebbles which were used by the early Romans for counting. The general opinion is that the first calculator was the abacus. The abacus, a device in which stones or pebbles are strung on wires suspended within a rectangular frame, first appeared in China about the sixth century, B.C.

In 1642, at the age of nineteen, the French mathematician Blaise Pascal invented what is believed to be the first adding ma-

Photo 1

Blaise Pascal's Arithmetic Machine. (Courtesy IBM.)

chine. This machine, which worked much as do modern adding machines, was made with ten-toothed counter gears. When the counter gear was moved from 9 to 0, a small side tooth advanced the next counter gear by one, taking care of the "carry" in addition.

In 1671, Gottfried Wilhelm Leibnitz started working on an adding machine which was completed in 1694. The basic difference between this machine and Pascal's was that besides addition, multiplication could also be performed by using repeated addition.

C. X. Thomas extended the ideas of Leibnitz and built the *arithmometer* which could perform all four basic arithmetic operations. The invention won Thomas a Legion of Honour medal from the French government in 1820.

In 1812, Charles Babbage, at the age of twenty, became interested in the European calculators and started his own independent work. Over the next fifty years, with support from friends, the English government, and his own inheritance, he worked with two machines, the difference engine and the analytical engine. With the difference engine, Babbage planned to construct mathematical tables for use in navigation. Before this machine was completed,

Photo 2

Charles Babbage's Difference Engine. (Courtesy IBM.)

however, Babbage abandoned it and devoted his effort to a new project, the analytical engine. The analytical engine conceptually was a prototype of modern computers. Babbage expected his machine to have a memory for storing information, control, arithmetic unit, input by punched cards, and output in the form of type setting. It mattered not how conceptually brilliant Babbage was, for the technology of the eighteenth century could not produce the engine gears and parts to the required tolerances. The analytical engine was unfortunately therefore never completed.

An early development in calculator capabilities was the invention of the punched card. Dr. Herman Hollerith was an employee of the United States Government and was involved in the counting of the 1890 census. Dr. Hollerith devised a 3″ by 5″ card into which he punched holes in a prearranged code. To assist in tabulation he constructed a machine with probes capable of testing any of the possible 240 holes. When a card was punched, the probe would go through the hole making contact with a mercury pool. This completed an electrical circuit which caused a tally by moving the index on a specified dial. Thus the results of a day's work could be found by reading the dials at the end of the counting period. Dr. Hollerith was very successful and eventually started his own company. This company eventually became part of International Business Machine Corporation.

Photo 3

Herman Hollerith Electrical Tabulator. (Courtesy IBM.)

In 1937, George Stivitz started to work on a sequentially automatic digital computer. At the meeting of the American Mathematical Society in Hannover, N.H., in 1940 he presented his partially automatic computer for complex numbers which was built at Bell Telephone Laboratories. In 1942, Stivitz produced the air relay interpolator, a special purpose computer with input on tape, capable of performing linear operations. Bell Laboratories built a series of these computers and enhanced the state of art in computer construction through their technological advances.

At about the same time Stivitz was working on his computer ideas, Howard Aiken began what was to be the first fully automatic computer. This computer, called Mark I or Automatics Sequence Control Calculator, was built by IBM and finished in 1944. Fifty feet long and weighing nearly five tons, Mark I could add and subtract in .3 seconds and multiply and divide in about 4 and 11 seconds, respectively. Mark I, although electromechanical rather than electronic, was a milestone in computing and remained in use until the early 1960s.

A group of professors at the University of Pennsylvania began in 1943 to investigate the possibilities of using electronic tubes in calculators instead of the traditional gears and electromechanical relays. Under the direction of John Mauchly and G. P. Eckert, the University of Pennsylvania designed a computer, ENIAC (for

Photo 4

Magnetic Core Plane Section. (Courtesy IBM.)

Electronic Numerical Integrator And Calculator). Finished in 1946, ENIAC had no moving internal parts and was considered the first electronic computer ever built. With nearly 1800 vacuum tubes and weighing 30 tons, ENIAC could add 5000 numbers a second. Although ENIAC was useful in constructing ballistic tables, it was given instructions by wiring certain appropriate circuits together. These wires had to be changed for each type of problem to be solved; this made the ENIAC rather inflexible and difficult to re-program.

At this stage of affairs, Arthur W. Burks, Herman H. Goldstein, and John von Neumann wrote a monumental paper entitled "Preliminary Discussion of the Logical Designs of an Electronic Computing Instrument." It is believed that this was the first paper delivered in which the ideas of a stored program computer were introduced. The authors called a computer a machine and recommended two different types of memory, one in which to store numbers and the other to store orders. They said, however, that if the orders (instructions) are written in numerical control and if the machine can distinguish between a number and an order, then the same memory can be used to store both numbers and orders (stored program). Furthermore, they claimed that there must be a device which could execute an order stored in memory; this device is now called control.

Using von Neumann's ideas, a group of professors from the University of Pennsylvania developed EDVAC, Electronic Discrete Variable Automatic Calculator. Started in 1945, EDVAC was important because it used binary arithmetic, contained internal circuitry for converting decimal numbers to binary, and used a stored program. About 1949, the EDSAC, Electronic Delay Storage Automatic Computer, was completed at the University of Cambridge by Morris B. Wilkes. EDSAC contributed, in addition to the stored program idea, that of using an accumulator register for arithmetic purposes and the concept of program counter. In 1946, under the direction of von Neuman himself, the Institute for Advanced Studies started to build a computer, the IAS. Completed six years later, the IAS computer had, in addition to the ideas of the EDVAC and EDSAC, the following features: memory addresses, conditional transfers, parallel arithmetic, and overlays of computation with input and output.

In 1951, the Digital Computing Lab at MIT finished the WHIRLWIND I, to be used as an aircraft simulator. Containing 5000 vacuum tubes and over 11,000 semi-conductor diodes, it could perform additions in three millionths of a second. The principle innovation was the use of magnetic core memory allowing for 1024 words of data programs.

The UNIVAC I, Universal Automatic Computer, was produced by Remington Rand. First delivered in 1951, it was the first commercially available computer produced. Smaller than previous computers and able to add in two millionths of a second, over forty UNIVAC I's were produced.

During the years 1946–1960, 4,000 IBM 604 Electronic Calculators were produced, delivered, and installed. The program was entered by using wires in a plugboard. Incorporating the 604 with an accounting machine, IBM developed the Card Programming Calculator, whose program was stored in cards. A very flexible machine, this was the first general purpose computer to be manufactured in quantity.

Photo 5

Three Generations of Circuity, Tubes, Transistors and Solid Logic Technology, Showing the Relative Changes. (Courtesy IBM.)

Photo 6

50,000 SLT Transistors Can Be Placed in a Thimble. (Courtesy IBM.)

In the middle and late 1950s, computer architecture and construction changed radically. The bulky and unreliable vacuum tube was replaced by the small, reliable, and cheaper transistor. Computers were dramatically reduced in size; reliability of error-free performance improved from good to excellent; speeds of execution increased from tens of thousands of operations per seconds to hundreds of thousands per seconds and even faster. The overall improvement due to the transistor and other features was so impressive that the terminology "first and second generation computers" evolved. First and second generation computers referred to vacuum tube and transistor type construction, respectively.

This same period saw computer programming take giant steps. Originally, these computers were programmed in machine language with numeric operation codes and absolute addresses. To handle these bookkeeping chores and free the programmers from the associated nuances, assembly languages were developed by computer manufacturers and their associated computer users. Higher level languages, like FORTRAN, COBOL, ALGOL, etc., relieved programmers from their machine dependence and allowed them to think, work, and program in terms of procedures, formulae, and statements. FORTRAN, for example, was developed in 1957 by IBM for the IBM 704. John Backus directed the project which initially required forty man-years to complete. FORTRAN, *FORMULA TRANSLATION*, allowed programmers to write programs in mathematical type notation which was reasonably easy for most programmers. The contribution of these languages cannot be overestimated as they allowed the users of computers to more efficiently, effectively, and speedily make use of their computer resources.

About 1964, computer manufacturers again made a dramatic change in both hardware equipment and programming. Transistors were miniaturized until it took nearly fifty thousand to fill a thimble. Circuits were made with processes called "solid logic technology." Core memories were increased in capacity. Input and output devices were made faster, more flexible, and more error free. Instruction times were measured in billionths of a second. Higher level languages were improved and expanded. Programs to assist computer operators in their duties were made more sophisticated. These programs, called *monitors* or *supervisors*, allow smooth flow of jobs through the computer reducing of operator setup, stop, and intervention times and increasing of the total amount of work done by the computing systems. This era, characterized by the solid logic technology and operating programs or systems, was called the *third generation*.

Photo 7

IBM System 370 Model 165. (Courtesy IBM.)

2. ABACUS

The abacus we are going to demonstrate is the simplified Japanese version known as *Soroban*.

The Soroban consists of:

(1) A rectangular wooden frame.
(2) Some vertical rods made of bamboo or some other light material.
(3) A horizontal wooden strip pierced by the rods.
(4) Some perforated beads (counters) which slide on the vertical rods. (see Figure 1.)

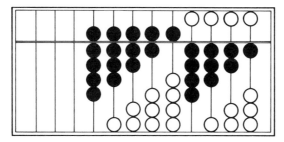

Figure 1

Each vertical rod (from now on called "vertical") holds five counters, one counter on the upper part of the rod, above the horizontal strip (from now on called the "strip") and four counters below the strip. The counters take their assigned values (active) when they are moved towards the strip; when they are moved away from the strip we say they are in the neutral position. We shall denote by ○ a counter in neutral position; ● shall denote active counters.

Numbers are placed in the abacus according to the decimal system of numeration. For convenience the strip has a small black dot to indicate the unit rod and to the left of this rod and every third rod the strip has black dots to indicate 1,000 positions, 1,000,000, etc. The value assigned to the counter on the upper part of a row is five. The value assigned to each counter on the lower part of a rod is one. Each rod contains a digit, its value being the total value of the counters on the rod. Figure 2 contains examples of the following: (*a*) represents 23, (*b*) represents 51, and (*c*) represents 246.

Addition, subtraction, multiplication, and division can be performed with an abacus. Before we can describe how these opera-

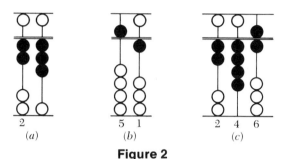

Figure 2

tions are performed, we need to introduce some notation:

↑   means "push up" one or more counters.

↓   means "push down" one or more counters.

The words "push up" and "push down" will be abbreviated to "up" and "down," respectively.

◒ means a counter has been used in addition.

◐ means a counter has been used in subtraction.

The student should try to push up counters with the right thumb and to push down counters with the right index finger.

2.1   Addition

(*a*)   Add two one-digit numbers.

Example 1.   4 + 1 = 5

We observe that the four counters on the unit-rod have been used to represent 4. In trying to add to this rod we find there are no counters left. Therefore we down counter 5 and down the four unit counters. This is simplified by saying "one clears 4 and brings down five." (Figure 3.)

Example 2.   3 + 2 = 5

We observe that we have used three unit counters in placing number 3, leaving a total of one unused counter in the unit rod. However, since the total is five, we down counter five and down

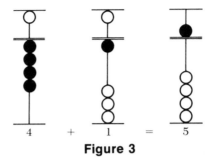

Figure 3

the three unit counters. We simplify this by saying "2 clears three and brings down counter 5." (Figure 4.)

These two examples have in common that the two numbers to be added are complementary to five. Therefore, they "clear" to each other and bring down a five counter. Hence we have the following rules:

> 1 clears 4, brings down 5
> 2 clears 3, brings down 5
> 1 clears 9, brings up 10
> 2 clears 8, brings up 10
> 3 clears 7, brings up 10
> 4 clears 6, brings up 10
> 5 clears 5, brings up 10

and the converse of the above rules holds.

Example 3.   7 + 4 = 11

One mentally thinks 7 clears 3 up 10. Therefore, up one counter

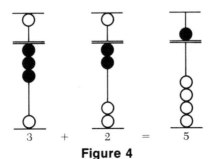

Figure 4

on the tenths (i.e., next rod to the left of the unit rod), and down 3 counters on the unit rod. (Figure 5.)

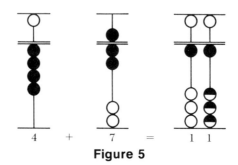

Figure 5

(*b*)   Adding numbers with two or more digits.

With the abacus, addition is always performed from left to right.

Example 1.   36 + 48 = 84

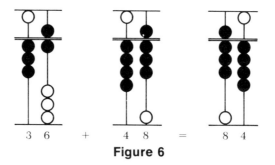

Figure 6

We think as follows: (Figure 6)

>   4 clears one down 5.
>   8 clears two up 1, (one next rod).

Example 2.   72 + 49 = 121

We think as follows: (Figure 7)

>   4 clears 6, up one on next rod.
>   9 clears 1, up one on next rod.

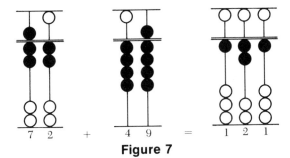

Figure 7

2.2 Subtraction

We shall use the following rules:

(i) $5 - 1 = 4$, one clears 5, up 4.
(ii) $5 - 2 = 3$, two clears 5, up 3.
(iii) $5 - 3 = 2$, three clears 5, up 2.
(iv) $5 - 4 = 1$, four clears 5, up 1.
(v) $10 - 1 = 9$, one clears 10, down 5, up 4.
(vi) $10 - 2 = 8$, two clears 10, down 5, up 3.
(vii) $10 - 3 = 7$, three clears 10, down 5, up 2.
(viii) $10 - 4 = 6$, four clears 10, down 5, up 1.
(ix) $10 - 5 = 5$, five clears 10, down 5.
(x) $10 - 6 = 4$, six clears 10, up 4.
(xi) $10 - 7 = 3$, seven clears 10, up 3.
(xii) $10 - 8 = 2$, eight clears 10, up 2.
(xiii) $10 - 9 = 1$, nine clears 10, up 1.

Example 1. $18 - 7 = 9$

We think as follows: 7 clears 10, up 3; next, 3 clears 7, up one (next rod).

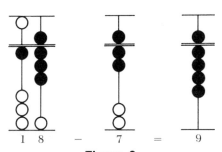

Figure 8

Example 2.   14 − 5 = 9

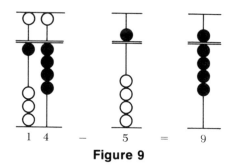

Figure 9

We think as follows: five clears 10, down 5.

Example 3.   137 − 76 = 61

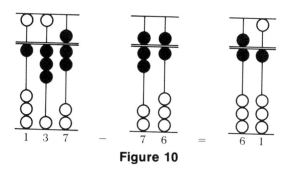

Figure 10

We think as follows: 7 clears 10, up 3, i.e., down 5, down 2; six clears 10, up 4, i.e., 4 clears 6, one up (next rod).

2.3   Multiplication

Recall that, for example, in $23 \times 6 = 138$, 23 is called the "multiplicand," 6 is called the "multiplier," and 138 is called the "product." We shall consider several cases:

(*a*)   The multiplier is a one-digit number.

Example.   23 × 6 = 138

(*i*)   Place the multiplier 6 at the left of the abacus (Figure 11).
(*ii*)   Place the multiplicand three vertical rods to the right of the multiplier (Figure 11).
(*iii*)   Place the decimal point of the product on the rod immediately to the right of the multiplicand.

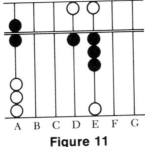

Figure 11

(*iv*) Multiply 3 by 6. The product 18 is placed with the 8 on the vertical rod containing the decimal point of the product, that is, rod F. Note that we have cleared the digit 3 of the multiplicand.

(*v*) Multiply 2 by 6 placing the product 12 starting at one vertical to the left of the decimal point. We have performed the following changes: Up two on vertical E, and up one on vertical D (Figure 12).

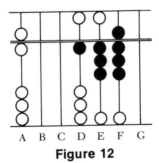

Figure 12

(*b*) Multiplier is a two-digit number:

Example. 7 × 24 = 168

(*i*) Place the multiplier 24 on the left of the abacus (Figure 13).

(*ii*) Place the multiplicand 7 two verticals to the left of 24 (Figure 13).

(*iii*) Place the decimal point of the product on the rod immediately to the right of the multiplicand.

(*iv*) Multiply the 4 on vertical rod B by the seven on the

vertical E. Note that this clears the seven on the multiplicand.

(v) Multiply the two on vertical rod A by seven (keep this number in your memory). The partial product 14 is placed on the vertical rods E and D as follows: 4 clears one, down 5. Up one on next vertical to the left. 168 is obtained as a product. (Figure 14).

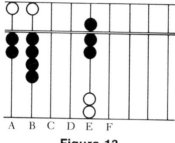

Figure 13

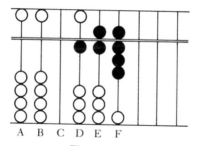

Figure 14

2.4 Division

We shall illustrate the method used in dividing two numbers with several examples.

Example 1.   260 ÷ 4

We proceed as follows: Place the decimal point in some place in the abacus, say at F. Place the divisor 4 in A; place the dividend 260 to the right of the divisor. (Figure 15.) Next proceed as if we were going to use the method of short division, i.e., we think that 4 goes 6 times into 26; place 6 one rod to the right of the divisor. 6 is going to be the first digit of the quotient; multiply 6 by 4, the

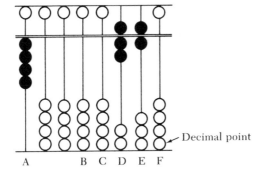

Decimal point

A   B C D E F

Figure 15

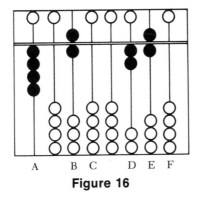

A   B C   D E F

Figure 16

product 24 is subtracted from the first two digits of the divisor. We think: $4 \times 6 = 24$, down 2 in rod D, next we say 4 cancels 5, up one in rod E, getting the following setting: (Figure 17)

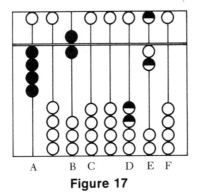

A   B C   D E F

Figure 17

where the symbol ● is used to indicate a counter that just has been used during a partial subtraction. Observe we have obtained 20 as a remainder at the end of the first partial division. Next we think: 4 goes 5 times into 20; place 5 in the rod next to the right of rod B; then we say 4 × 5 = 20; down two in rod E, getting: (Figure 18).

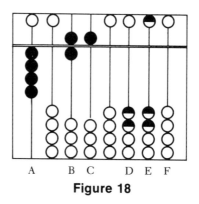

A   B C   D E F

Figure 18

At this point the procedure ends since there are no more counters in the dividend rods. We have: 65 as the quotient which is placed in the B and C rods.

Example 2. 2184 ÷ 84

Place the decimal point in rod J; place the divisor 84 in rods A and B; place the dividend 2184 in rods G, H, I and J. (Figure 19.)

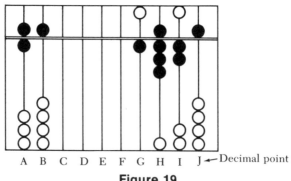

A B C D E F G H I J ←Decimal point

Figure 19

Next, we say: 84 goes 2 times into 218; place 2 in rod D, the first figure of the quotient, then we say: $2 \times 8 = 16$, down 1 in rod G, 6 cancels 10 (down 1 in G), down 5 in H, down 1 in H. Next $2 \times 4 = 8$, down 8 in rod I, obtaining the first partial remainder 504. (Figure 20.)

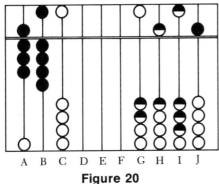

Figure 20

Now, we say 84 goes 6 times into 504; place 6 in rod E, obtaining the second figure of the quotient. Then we say: $6 \times 8 = 48$, 4 cancels 5, up 1; 8 cancels 10 up 2, (next rod). Now we say $6 \times 4 = 24$; canceling the 24 that was in the abacus. We get (Figure 21) 26 as the quotient.

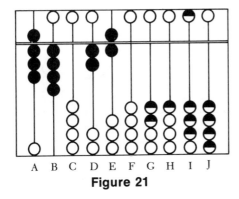

Figure 21

Example 3.   1825 ÷ 65

Place the decimal point in rod J; place the divisor 65 in the rods A and B; place the dividend 1825 in rods G, H, I, and J. (Figure 22.)

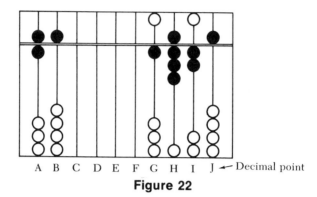

A B   C   D   E   F   G   H   I   J ← Decimal point
Figure 22

Next, we say: 65 goes 2 times into 182; place 2 in rod D, the first figure of the quotient. Then we say: down one in rod G, down 2 in rod H. Next $2 \times 5 = 10$, down 1 in H, obtaining the first partial remainder 525. (Figure 23.)

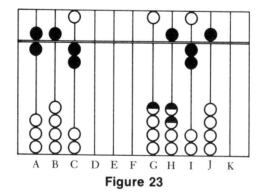

A B   C   D   E   F   G   H   I   J   K
Figure 23

Now we say 65 goes 8 times into 525. Place 8 in rod E obtaining the second figure of the quotient. Then we say: $8 \times 6 = 48$ up 5, up 1 in rod H, 8 cancels 10 up 2, down one in rod H, up two in rod I. Next $8 \times 5 = 40$; down 4 in column I, leaving 5 in rod J as the remainder. We get 28 as the quotient and 5 as the remainder. (Figure 24.)

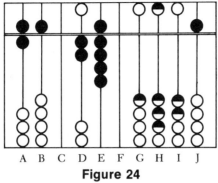

Figure 24

Chapter II

The purpose of this chapter is to introduce the reader to some basic concepts in the art of programming.

1. Algorithm

An *algorithm* is a step-by-step procedure that will solve a specific class of problems.

It is generally characterized by the type of problems to which it applies. Examples are square root algorithm, sorting algorithm, Newton's algorithm, etc.

An algorithm should have the following properties:

Finiteness. Definiteness. Input. Output. Efficiency.

By finiteness we understand that the algorithm must be able to determine after a finite number of steps (although very large) the solution to a specific starting problem or, alternatively, to determine the nonexistence of a solution. Definiteness shall mean that the sequence of steps leading to the solution is clear, unambiguous, and capable of being rigorously followed. Considering input (problem information) and output (results or answers), an algorithm should have zero or more inputs and one or more outputs. Efficiency means that the algorithms yield the desired results without waste or unnecessary effort.

The reader should check the instructions given to perform arithmetic operations with the abacus to see that they constitute an algorithm having the required properties to be an algorithm (i.e., finiteness, definiteness, input, output, and efficiency).

In order to illustrate the above properties of an algorithm we use the following example:

For each value of *a*, *b*, *c*, *d*, and *x* determine the value of

$$y = ax^3 + bx^2 + cx + d. \tag{1}$$

We can proceed as follows:

Step 1.   Get *a*, *b*, *c*, *d*, *x*.
Step 2.   Form $y = ((a \cdot x + b) \cdot x + c) \cdot x + d$.
Step 3.   Obtain *y*.

The above three steps are: definite, since the process will terminate after three steps. There are five inputs: *a*, *b*, *c*, *d*, *x*. There is one output: *y*. The above algorithm is more efficient than a first approach to the problem might be. For if we calculate *y* by

$$y = ax \cdot x \cdot x + b \cdot x \cdot x + c \cdot x + d$$

we would have used six multiplications and three additions instead of three and three, respectively, as it is done in Step 2 above. The above steps are unambiguous, hence this algorithm is also definite.

In attempting to make an algorithm definite, one finds that a natural language, like English, is not always sufficiently rigorous to state the algorithm. The statements of the algorithm tend to be

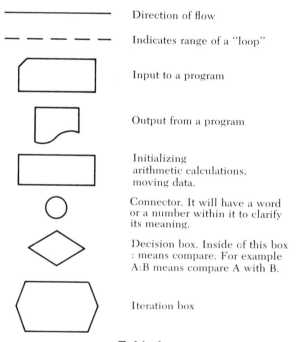

Direction of flow

Indicates range of a "loop"

Input to a program

Output from a program

Initializing arithmetic calculations, moving data.

Connector. It will have a word or a number within it to clarify its meaning.

Decision box. Inside of this box : means compare. For example A:B means compare A with B.

Iteration box

Table I

Algorithm   27

lengthy and wordy in a natural language. Therefore, algorithms will be stated in an algebraically oriented language that should prohibit ambiguity and, by its algebraic properties, encourage brevity.

This algebraically-oriented language may be combined with certain symbols. This representation forms a "flow chart," a device which easily displays the steps of an algorithm as well as the overall relationships of the steps. We shall adopt the symbols given in Table I for use in flow charts.

A flow chart may look like Figure 25.

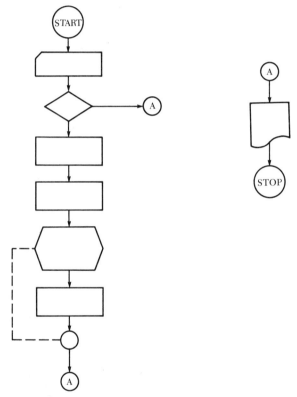

Figure 25

Example

Assume that we wish to compute

$$y = Ax^3 + Bx^2 + Cx + D$$

for different values of A, B, C, D and x. A flow chart to show the necessary steps to compute y might look as in Figure 26.

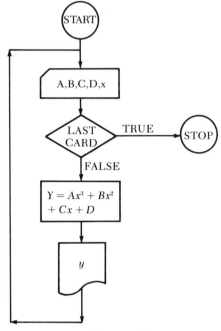

Figure 26

2. COMPUTERS

We are taking a very naive approach to computers.

Computers are to be considered as devices used to implement algorithms in obtaining solutions to various types of problems.

A computer must have:

(1) Input, flow of information into the computer.
(2) Output, flow of information out of the computer.
(3) Arithmetical and logical capability, called "ALU" henceforth.
(4) Control, capable of causing arithmetic and logical decisions to be made and responding to these results according to the algorithm.
(5) Storage.

A block diagram of a computer would look like the following chart. (Figure 27.)

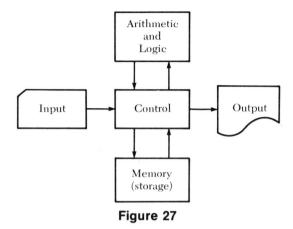

Figure 27

3. MEMORY

Memory, or *storage,* is that part of a computer which is used to "remember" input, output, and the steps required to implement an algorithm.

In a digital computer all the information is stored as sequences of digits. In mechanical devices, gears can be cut with ten states or positions (cogs) corresponding to the decimal numbers 0, 1, . . . , 9. Modern electronic digital computers with ten state devices are expensive to manufacture. This is largely due to an attempt to reduce or eliminate mechanical devices from digital computers. The only devices capable of operating at electronic speeds are at present two-state devices.

These two-state (binary) devices are either electrical or magnetic. That is, current flows in either a clockwise or counterclockwise direction in a circuit. Alternatively, a device is either magnetized in a northerly direction or in a southerly direction.

As an illustration, consider a light as being a two-state device, one state being on, the other state being off (Figure 28).

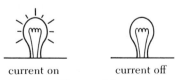

current on   current off

Figure 28

This on-off principle may be used to represent numbers. Suppose that we have four lights, A, B, C, and D. Then we could code numbers using the following table.

A	B	C	D	
OFF	OFF	OFF	OFF	0
OFF	OFF	OFF	ON	1
OFF	OFF	ON	OFF	2
OFF	OFF	ON	ON	3
OFF	ON	OFF	OFF	4
OFF	ON	OFF	ON	5
OFF	ON	ON	OFF	6
OFF	ON	ON	ON	7
ON	OFF	OFF	OFF	8
ON	OFF	OFF	ON	9

Any group of four On, Off words as shown in the table constitutes a *memory position*. For efficiency of operation, computer manufacturers group memory positions into units called *words*. A computer, for example, might have eight decimal positions in a word. This type of computer would allow to encode up to eight digits in a word.

Each word must be easily retrievable. In order that it might be quickly retrieved, each word of memory is given an *address*. This address located the memory word for the ALU (arithmetic logic unit).

Consider for the moment that we have four planes, A, B, C, and D, each of them having six vertical wires and six horizontal wires forming a grid. Arrange these planes, one upon the other, with small distances between each plane (Figure 29). In this way we have constructed 36 positions of memory, each position consisting of a point from each of the four planes. Each of these points is a binary device. Generally, these binary devices are ferrite cores, approximately the diameter of a pencil lead. Each core would have two wires inserted through the center. Collectively it would resemble Figure 29.

We single out for discussion location 41 (hereafter abbreviated loc. 41). This location consists of the binary devices found at the intersection of the vertical four wire with horizontal one wire. If

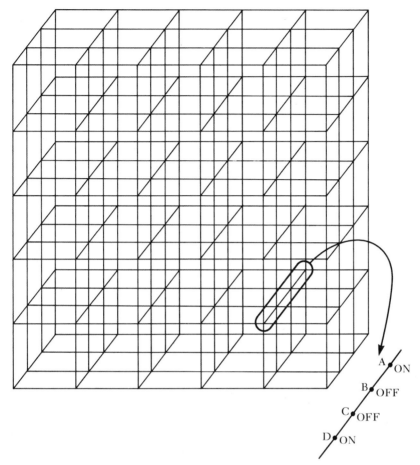

Figure 29

loc. 41 represents a 9, the A and B devices would be energized (magnetized, on).

Assume that we have a computer with words eight positions long. Each word might contain an *instruction*. An instruction is an order which is understandable to the computer and contains an *operation* and some *operands*. As operations we might have addition, multiplication, etc. Operands are quantities to be operated on by the operation. If a word containing eight positions is thought of as being divided into four groups of two positions each, the operation could be found in the first group and the last three groups could be used for operands. Remember that each position may represent a decimal digit by using an appropriate on-off sequence as is shown in the table. For example, the word from loc. 41 through loc. 48 might contain 01 33 49 17. This might be an instruction that adds the quantity located by 33 to the quantity located by 49 and stores the result in 17. The operation is addition, 01; the operands are 33, 49, 17.

Since a word is made up of several positions, it is a common practice to refer to a word by its starting location or address. Assuming an eight position word computer, a word at loc. 33 would include loc. 33 through loc. 40. Computers which make this assumption are called *fixed length word computers.*

4. LANGUAGE AND PROGRAM

The *fundamental language* of a computer is the set of permissible digits and the ways in which they may be combined so that a computer may interpret these digits and act accordingly. The fundamental language understood by a specific computer is called its *machine language.* A *program* is a complete sequence of instructions to carry out the necessary steps to implement an algorithm on a computer. A program is named according to the language used to write it, i.e., machine language program, Fortran program, Algol program, Mad program, etc.

Words in a program are of two types.

Words of the first type are instructions. That is, words are used to instruct the computer to do some specific task. Assume that the instruction is addition and the quantities to be added are 11 and 20. How shall the computer interpret the quantities 11 and 20? One interpretation could be to add 11 and 20 getting 31. This literal approach is restrictive, since this specific interpretation limits the addition to a set of two specific numbers. A better interpretation is to add x and y, where x and y are any two numbers. By varying the values of x and y, one may use the same instruction many times. Therefore, computers would interpret the above 11 and 20 not as quantitative data, but rather as the locations where the data is to be found. In summary, add x and y means the contents of location x are added to the contents of location y.

Writing programs in machine language is a very tedious task. One must decide on the absolute location in which data is to be located. That is, if X is to be used, the programmer must decide to use a location like 35, 743, etc., to hold X. Later, if this location must be shifted, for reasons such as the program has expanded to that location or it is necessary to reorder the variable locations, all references to 35 must be changed to X's new location. Likewise, if it becomes necessary to insert or delete program instructions, it may be necessary to recode large segments. This is because branch locations have shifted and, since we are working with absolute addresses, the instruction must be recoded with a new absolute address. All in all, this type of programming required a lot of bookkeeping and attention to detail.

In order to facilitate the writing of programs, manufacturers have produced language processors. These language processors convert a source program, that is, a program written in a language other than a machine language, into machine language. For example, an *assembler* is a processor which converts machine language-like instructions with symbolic fields into machine language instructions. In assembly language, instead of referring to the location of X or the value of X as 35, one uses X itself to refer to the location of X or the value of X. The context determines the location or value. Therefore, if it is necessary to physically move X in the program deck, none of the instructions involving X need to be changed. The assembler will calculate X's new location for these instructions. Also, instead of remembering arithmetic codes for the instruction operations, assembly language allows the use of "sound alike" or "look alike" symbols called *mnemonics*. For example, instead of remembering that addition has a code of 61 one might remember ADD, instead of 42, MUL, instead of 53, BRN, etc. The introduction of assembly programs relieved the programmer of much bookkeeping and allowed the computer to assume these responsibilities.

Another form of processor is the *"compiler."* A compiler is a program that translates a programmer's source deck into machine language coding where the source language is algebraically or algorithmically oriented. Processors of this type include COBOL compilers, FORTRAN compilers, PL/I compilers, etc. These compilers, named for the language the source program is coded in, have the ability to translate statements like $A = B + C$ or ADD B to C giving A into machine language code. Automatically the compilers allocate storage space for the quantities A, B, and C and generate the machine instructions to do the addition. It is especially important to have the compiler generate machine program instructions for difficult programming problems involving complex arithmetic calculations, iteration control, and decision making. These areas can be difficult enough in an algorithmic language; they can be seemingly impossible in machine language coding.

Now we introduce a very simple machine language. We shall use this language to illustrate some programming techniques.

5. DATAS

DATAS is a machine language capable of being operated in most digital computers. It has a memory capacity of 99 words. Each word contains eight decimal digits. These digits are divided into four groups of two digits each. We shall denote these four groups as D_0, D_1, D_2, and D_3. D_0 shall be used as an operation. D_1, D_2, and D_3 are used to contain the locations of the operands. For example, let D_0, D_1, D_2, and D_3 be 01, 14, 15, and 20. 01 indicates that the operation is addition. The contents of word 14 are added to the contents of word 15, and the result is stored in word 20.

The following are DATAS operation codes:

$01 = \text{ADD}$ 01 D_1 D_2 D_3 means add D_1 to D_2 and store result in D_3

$02 = \text{SUBTRACT}$ 02 D_1 D_2 D_3 means subtract D_1 from D_2 and store result in D_3

$03 = \text{MULTIPLY}$ 03 D_1 D_2 D_3 means multiply D_1 by D_2 and store result in D_3

$04 = \text{DIVIDE}$ 04 D_1 D_2 D_3 means divide D_1 by D_2 and store the result in D_3

$05 = \text{BRANCH}$

If $D_1 = 00$,   05   00   00 D_3, branch unconditionally to location D_3

If $D_1 = 01$,   05   01 D_2 D_3, branch to D_3 if D_2 is negative, otherwise take the next instruction.

If $D_1 = 02$,   05   02 D_2 D_3, branch to D_3 if D_2 is positive, otherwise, take the next instruction.

$06 = \text{HALT}$ 06 00 00 00   Stop at this location.

$07 = \text{READ}$ 07 D_1 00 00   Read into location D_1.

$08 = \text{WRITE}$ 08 D_1 00 00   Write from location D_1.

$09 = \text{SORT}$ 09 D_1 00 D_3 Square root of D_1 and put it into D_3.

$10 = \text{ABS}$ 10 D_1 00 D_3 Absolute value of D_1 and put it into D_3.

In order to read the program into the computer, each word has a two-digit prefix attached to it. This two-digit number is called a *loader*. Its purpose is to place each word in a location specified by the programmer. If the instruction word is to be stored in loc. 21, the loader and instruction would appear as 21 01 10 11 17. The instruction is, of course, to add contents of 10 to contents of 1 and store the result in 17.

Example 1

Consider the problem of adding two numbers and determine the associated input-output.

The program to accomplish this could be as follows:

```
01 07 50 00 00   Read A into 50.
02 07 51 00 00   Read B into 51.
03 01 50 51 52   Add A to B and place result, C, in 52.
04 08 52 00 00   Write C from 52.
```

Example 2

Obtain the square root of 23·100 and print the result. A program to accomplish this follows:

```
01 05 00 00 52   Branch to 52.
50 00 00 01 00   100 loaded into 50.
51 00 00 00 23   23 loaded in 51.
52 03 51 50 10   2300 put into 10.
53 09 10 00 11   √2300 47 put into 11.
54 08 11 00 00   Content of 11 printed.
55 06 00 00 00   Halt.
```

Example 3

Write a program to compute $1 + 2$ and store the result 3. A program to accomplish this follows:

```
01 05 00 00 52   Branch to 52.
50 00 00 00 01   1 loaded into 50.
51 00 00 00 02   2 loaded into 51
52 01 50 51 02   1 + 2 = 3 put into 02
53 08 02 00 00   Content of 02 printed
54 06 00 00 00   Halt.
```

Example 4

Write a program that will read 20 numbers, compute their sum, compute their average, write their sum, and write their average.

A program with comments follows:

```
01 01 40 40 41   places 0 in loc. 41
02 07 42 00 00   read x into loc. 42
03 01 42 41 41   add x to loc. 41 forming Σ x.
```

04 02 43 44 43   subtract 1 from n, getting n − 1, store it back into loc. 43.

05 05 02 43 02   if loc. 43 positive branch to loc. 02 (to read more cards). If loc. 43 is not positive, branch to loc. 06

06 08 41 00 00   write loc. 41 (Σx)

07 04 41 45 46   divide loc. 41 (Σx) by 20, getting the average, store it in loc. 46.

08 08 46 00 00   write average (loc. 46)

09 06 00 00 00   stop or halt

40 00 00 00 00   zero ⎫

43 00 00 00 20   twenty ⎬ Constants used in the program

44 00 00 00 01   one ⎪

45 00 00 00 20   twenty ⎭

Remarks

(a)   instruction in loc. 01 places a zero in loc. 41, which is part of the initialization required in accumulating x in loc. 41

(b)   instruction in loc. 02 reads x into 42

(c)   instruction in loc. 03 adds x to loc. 41, thus building sums of x, that is, Σ x

(d)   instruction in loc. 04 subtracts 1 from loc. 43 which holds initially 20, thus each time that loc. 04 is executed, loc. 43 is decreased by one, getting 19, 18, . . . and eventually 0.

(e)   instruction in loc. 05 tests the value of loc. 43; if this value is positive, it "loops" back to loc. 02 to start again. However, after 20 readings of x loc. 43 will hold a zero and thus, instead of to loc. 02, it will fall through the next statement loc. 06

(f)   instruction in loc. 06 writes Σ x or contents of loc. 41

(g)   instruction in loc. 07 divides Σ x by 20 getting the average in loc. 46

(h)   instruction in loc. 08 writes the average or the contents of loc. 46

(i)   instruction in loc. 09 causes the program to halt

(j)   loc. 40, loc. 43, loc. 44, and loc. 45 contain constants used

(k)   loc. 41, loc. 42, and loc. 46 are used for temporary storage

Exercise

Show that the algorithms used by the abacus have the required properties of algorithms, that is, finiteness, definiteness, input, output, and efficiency.

Chapter III

---

1. FORTRAN

In this chapter FORTRAN is introduced. (Fortran is an abbreviation for FORmula TRANslation). A source program written in FORTRAN is translated by a FORTRAN compiler into an object program. The FORTRAN programming language is oriented towards stating problems which can be solved by algebraic techniques. Hence, FORTRAN is problem oriented rather than machine language oriented. The FORTRAN language uses many of the naming conventions found in the English language in addition to the formula representation of algebra.

This chapter is divided into two sections. In section 1 we include what is now known as *Basic FORTRAN*. We do this so those students studying with a small computer system will have an opportunity to learn sufficient FORTRAN statements to write programs for most of the algorithms in this book. In section 2 we include the remaining statements that can be implemented in larger computer systems.

Section 1 and 2 together constitute the so-called FORTRAN IV language.

1.1 CONSTANTS AND VARIABLES

1.1.1 Numbers

Two types of numbers can be represented in FORTRAN IV: *Integer and Real*.

Integer numbers are those numbers whose representation does contain a decimal point.

Integers may be signed either + or −. If an integer is unsigned, it is assumed to be positive. Each FORTRAN IV compiler places restrictions on the number of digits that an integer may have. Table A.1 of the Appendix gives this information for most computers. Example: 32, 57, −365.

Real numbers are those numbers whose representation contains a decimal point.

Real numbers are internally represented in *floating point* form. Floating point requires that the number being represented has the form $^+.XXXXXXX \cdot 10^{\pm YY}$. The XXXXXXX portion will be called the *mantissa;* the ^{YY} portion will be called the *exponent*. Real numbers may be signed either + or −. If the number is unsigned it is assumed positive. For example:

103.72	would be written $^+.1037200 \cdot 10^{+03}$
−10.3107	would be written $−.1031070 \cdot 10^{+02}$
−.0003127	would be written $−.3127000 \cdot 10^{-03}$

The XXXXXXX part of the real number as well as the YY portion vary in allowable size from one computer compiler to another. The maximum number of digits represented by XXXXXXX is called the *precision* of the real number. Table A.2 illustrates ranges for different compilers. The exponent value YY also varies with the compiler used. Table A.3 gives the permissible range for different computers. FORTRAN IV allows us to use both real numbers and integer numbers as constants, or variables, or a mixture of both.

Let us try to calculate the area A of a circle with radius *r*, using the machine language DATAS. To compute A we use the formula $A = \pi r^2$. In order to compute A we would need to have the value π and also the value *r* stored in the computer's memory. Assuming π is stored in loc. 50 and *r* in loc. 51, A could be computed by multiplying the contents of 50 by the square of the contents of 51 and storing the result in the loc. assigned to A. Thus, we might have a DATAS machine language program consisting of:

03 50 51	52	$\pi \cdot r \to 52$
03 52 51	53	$(\pi \cdot r) \cdot r \to 53$

in which $\to$ means replace quantity on right by quantity on the left. Therefore, according to the program, the result of $(\pi \cdot r) \cdot r$ will be stored in loc. 53 and A might be assigned to loc. 53 for convenience. By varying the contents of 51, which contains *r*, we get a different A. Thus, we see that loc. 51 could be thought of as holding the value of a "variable" *r*. In FORTRAN IV language, the compiler will be allowed to assign a storage location for "variable" *r*. The programmer can use that quantity by referring to its name, *r*, rather than its storage location, loc. 51.

We have the following definition: *Variable* is a symbolic reference (or name) for a storage location.

Example: In the previous example, $A = \pi r^2$, we might have, using $*$ to indicate multiplication,

$$AREA = PI*RADIUS*RADIUS \qquad (1)$$

where PI, RADIUS, and AREA are FORTRAN variables. If the programmer assigns a value to RADIUS and 3.14159 to PI, then the variable AREA will be given a value whenever the calculation (1) is performed. Now, if the programmer changes the value of RADIUS, the value of AREA remains at its previous value until (1) is performed, at which time we would have a new value for AREA.

Each variable has a name entirely made up of alphabetic and/or numeric characters. The first character must be alphabetic. The permissible length of a name varies from compiler to compiler. This information is found in Table A.4. We have seen that in FORTRAN IV there are two types of numbers, integer and real. Hence in FORTRAN IV there are two types of variables, integer and real.

1.1.2 Integer Variable

An *integer variable* is a symbolic representation whose first character is one of I, J, K, L, M, or N.

Valid Examples: KAT, N, M42, JACKY, 134SUE, LLL.

Invalid Examples:
SUE—invalid first character (not I, J, K, L, M, or N)
4K3—invalid name (first character not alphabetic)
INTEREST—name too long for certain compilers; see Table A.4

1.1.3 Real Variable

A *real variable* is a symbolic representation whose first character is alphabetic but not I, J, K, L, M, or N.

Valid Examples: SUE, XT, YBAR, PRINCP, APPLE, C45, YR1968.

Invalid Examples:
NUMBER—invalid first character (must not be I, J, K, L, M, or N)

VARIANCE—name too long for certain compilers; see Table
   A.4

C(12—special characters not allowed, and (is a special character.

5DOG3—name is invalid (first character must be alphabetic).

In summary, we have the following rules pertaining to naming
variables:

(1) Alphabetic or numeric characters only.
(2) Length shall be six (6) or less characters.
(3) First character alphabetic.
(4) First character determines the type of variable.

1.1.4 Constants

A number is considered to be a constant if its numerical representation is used in FORTRAN IV rather than its symbolic representation. To illustrate, assume we wish to write a program to
compute the area A of a circle whose radius is R. The formula is,
as we know, $A = \pi R^2$. We might use PI for the representation of π,
where π is a mathematical constant: A and R are FORTRAN variables. This could be written in FORTRAN IV in two ways:

(*a*) A = PI*R*R. Each of A, PI and R are variables. According
       to the number of significant digits stored in PI, values of
       A are obtained with different degrees of accuracy.
(*b*) Alternatively, A = 3.14159*R*R. In this case, R and A are
       variables, and 3.14159 is a constant.

Example

(*a*) V = .5*G*T*T   G and T are variables.
                        .5 is a constant.
(*b*) V = .5*32.*T*T   T is a variable.
                        .5, 32. are constants.

G and T are variables since we are using their symbolic names,
and .5 and 32. are constants since a numerical representation for
each is used rather than a symbolic name.

We have the following definitions.

A *constant* is a number that is referenced by the number itself
rather than its symbolic reference name. There are two types of constants, integer constants and real constants.

An *integer constant* is any permissible integer (see Table A1) used as a constant.

Valid Integer Constants:

$$
\begin{array}{cc}
-100 & -32130 \\
0 & -25 \\
12357 & 34
\end{array}
$$

Invalid Integer Constants:

10.	No decimal point allowed
−1000.3	No decimal point and not an integer
1,324	No special characters allowed
113245678932143	Integer too long for some compilers

1.1.5 Real Constants

A *real constant* is any permissible number (see Tables A.2, A.3) with a decimal point in which the number is used as a constant.

Valid Real Constants: 100.   0.   37.4   −2.13
1001.32 E + 04 (means 1001.32×10^4 in FORTRAN)   −37.123

Invalid Real Constants:

37	No decimal point
.1000123001423	Too many significant digits for most compilers.
43,213.2	Special characters such as "," not allowed.
132.432 E + 123	$132,432 \times 10^{123}$ exponent 123 too large for most compilers.

1001.32 E + 04 is scientific notation for 1001.32×10^4. Thus we see that the multiplier E + 04 means 10^4 (E indicating exponential). The general form for this notation is $\pm$nnnnnnE $\pm$ YY where nnnnnn is a real number with a decimal point somewhere in the field and YY an integer that indicates the exponent of 10 is used.

In summary, we find that FORTRAN IV has the capacity to use either variables or constants, both with a wide range of permissible values. The specific choice of variable or constant is the responsibility of the programmer. The choice of which parameters are to be variables and which are to be constants is determined by an analysis of the problem.

Exercises

1. Decide whether each of the following symbols represents valid or invalid variables. If it is a valid symbol, is it real or integer? If it is invalid, why is it?

(*a*)	XY	(*b*)	X7	(*c*)	15
(*d*)	J.Y	(*e*)	A B	(*f*)	NUM
(*g*)	4X	(*h*)	X(3(	(*i*)	SOCIALSECURITY
(*j*)	MISTER	(*k*)	XINT	(*l*)	INTEREST
(*m*)	X12Z5	(*n*)	STATE #	(*o*)	V.I.P.
(*p*)	01	(*q*)	ALPHA	(*r*)	13452

2. Construct the appropriate constants.

(*a*) For the value of π (to five digits)

(*b*) 8.75% as a decimal number

(*c*) -1.738×10^{-38}

(*d*) $-.0000000654321$ with no leading zeros

(*e*) $2^{10} - 1$ as an integer

(*f*) Least common multiple of 84, 98, and 36

(*g*) Conversion multiplier to go from miles to inches

(*h*) Conversion divisor to go from tons to pounds

(*i*) 4:45 PM as a decimal number based on a 24-hour military clock where 12:01 AM is 0.01 and 11:59 PM is 23:59

(*j*) Conversion multiplier from cubic meters to cubic yards

1.2 Input, Output

In the solution of a problem, one or more data sources are required. That is, data collected for the problem must be transferred into the *memory* of a computer. This data enters from an external device, such as a card reader, paper tape, console typewriter, etc. It is then stored in the computer memory. Once a problem is solved, the above process is reversed. That is, data representing the solution is displayed on an external device. This data, residing in main storage, must be transferred to external devices such as a console typewriter, a cathode ray scope, a printer, a card punch, etc.

Input is the combined action of the computer and the external devices in storing outside data into the computer memory.

Output is the total process of moving data from the internal memory to an external device.

Information is generally transferred from a written document, such as a report, list, coding pad, etc., to cards by a keypunch machine operated by a keypunch operator. Each card has 80 columns and 12 rows. A sample card is shown in Figure 30.

Characters available in an IBM 029 keypunch are A, B, C, . . . 7, 0, 1, . . . 9, and ,.# @%$* −⁺)¢/&'"=!(?. Characters are represented in a card by combinations of punches in one or more rows. (Figure 30.)

Example: A is 12 and 1, 3 is 3, ! is 11, 2, and 8.

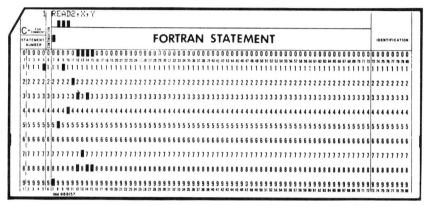

Figure 30

Information going into the computer (input) may be divided into two classes:

(*a*) FORTRAN IV Program
(*b*) Program Data

A FORTRAN IV program is information to the FORTRAN IV compiler. The information given to the FORTRAN IV compiler is called the source program. Source programs are made up of statements. FORTRAN IV has the following statement types:

(*a*) Format
(*b*) Input/Output
(*c*) Control
(*d*) Arithmetic
(*e*) Specification

Each statement may be written on one or more punched cards. In order that the FORTRAN IV compiler can correctly translate each card (or statement), certain rules are made concerning the physical placement of the information on the card. That is, information areas of the card have restricted uses, and any information found in these areas must be of a specified type.

FORTRAN IV source statements use columns 1 through 72 of a card. Columns 73 through 80 of a source statement are not used; a programmer may use these columns for any identification or sequencing purposes he wishes.

Each FORTRAN IV statement may be referenced by other statements by using a statement label.

Label is a number which is used for reference purposes associated with a FORTRAN statement.

A label is also called a *statement number*. If a label is present, it *must be in columns 1 through 5* of the statement card. This label is always a positive integer and may range in value from 1 to 32767. Certain FORTRAN IV compilers have a larger range of permissible values.

FORTRAN IV statements are optionally numbered. In fact, only one class of statements (Format) must be numbered. The statement labels do not have to be in either ascending or descending order. The programmer decides on the values for the statement label. The only restrictions are as follows:

(*i*)   Size.

(*ii*)   It must be a positive integer.

(*iii*)   The same label cannot be used in two or more statements.

1.2.1   Body of Statement

The instruction portion of a FORTRAN IV statement is punched in columns 7 through 72. If a statement required more space than is found on one card, it may be continued onto a second card, provided any non-zero digit is punched in column 6 of each of the following cards. Column number 6 is called the *continuation column*.

Continuation statement is that part of a statement that is punched on a card containing a punch in the continuation column.   (6)

Compilers allow at least four and some as many as nine continuation cards.

Example: 17 FORMAT (75H TODAY IS WEDNESDAY,
           1 TOMORROW IS EXAM DAY   )

The card columns 7 through 72 contain the FORTRAN IV statements. These statements are:

(a)   FORMAT
(b)   INPUT/OUTPUT
(c)   CONTROL
(d)   ARITHMETIC
(e)   SPECIFICATION

These statements will be discussed later.

A sample FORTRAN is included below so that the reader may see various types of statements in use.

```
C   THIS PROGRAM COMPUTES THE SUM OF
C   TWO VECTORS A AND B
C
    11 READ (1,100) N,(A(I),I = 1,N),(B(I),I = 1,N)
C   NEXT STATEMENT PRODUCES WHAT IS KNOWN AS
C   ECHO CHECK. THIS IS GOOD PRACTICE BECAUSE
C   ONE CAN SEE IF THE DATA WAS PROPERLY
    PUNCHED
C
       WRITE (3,102) N,(A(I),I = 1,N),(B(I),I = 1,N)
       DO 10 I = 1,N
    10 SUM = A(I)+B(I)
       WRITE (3,101)
   100 FORMAT (I4,5F4.0)
   101 FORMAT (F6.0)
   102 FORMAT (1X,I4,5F4.0)
       STOP
       END
```

1.2.2 Data

Data processed by the FORTRAN IV object program is the other important data class. This class includes both data entering the computer on order of the FORTRAN IV program (input) and data leaving the computer after being generated, manipulated or transformed by the FORTRAN IV object program (output). This input/output data flow is a form of transformation. That is, the external representation of data, such as punched cards, paper tape, etc., is *transformed* to the internal representation of data in the computer. The reader will note that this process is input; if the order of data *transformation* is reversed, the data flow becomes output.

If information is to be used effectively, it must be organized logically and completely. This organization is influenced, if not determined, by: 1. The manner in which it is to be read or written: 2. The order in which it is processed: 3. The external device on which it is encoded: 4. The physical requirements of sorting, filing, retrieval, and updating.

The largest group of data that we shall consider is a *file*.

> A *file of information* is a group or block of documents that are logically related.

Files can be classified as (a) Application, (b) Device, and (c) Means of referencing.

(*a*) *Application.* A file might be a payroll file, a customer file, an orders file, or other such files as determined by their application. In each of these files, we find that there is some characteristic that would tend to group the information together. In a payroll file, information leading to a paycheck and containing all data pertinent to its preparation would be included. Thus, for all the employees in the payroll file the documents would be logically the same, but individually different.

(*b*) *Device.* Some files are named according to their device types. As device type files, there could be the card input file (card reader), the card output file (card punch), the printer output file, the console typewriter file (information entered or displayed by the console typewriter), magnetic tape files, paper tape files, etc.

(*c*) *Means of Referencing.* Mass information files, such as a disk file, would not satisfactorily classify the file for users of the computer. Thus, other file description methods are used. These methods describe the ways used to find, read, or write the data on that device. There are two principal methods for constructing files, sequential and random. In a sequential technique one starts with first entry, proceeds to the second, on to the third, and so forth. In random organization one may go directly to any entry without knowledge of where the desired items are relative to the starting point.

Therefore, one says that information is on sequential files, random files, and other types called direct or indexed sequential, according to the characterizing quality used to describe the file.

Each file is broken into smaller more manageable pieces of information, called *records*.

> A *record* is a portion of information within a file.

Normally, a record is the amount of information that may be used in a single read or write statement. A record is generally very specific in the application areas.

Within a payroll file, one would find payroll records. A payroll record would contain the information required to compute a paycheck. A payroll record is matched with one person. Information in a payroll record, although similar to other payroll records, is specifically about one employee.

Other records contained within "application" files might be cost records, delivery records, classification of merchandise records, etc.

Like files, records are sometimes classified by the medium in which they appear or are coded. We find card records, print records, paper and magnetic tape records, disk records, etc.

When a program causes the computer to read or write, generally a complete line of print or a complete card is transferred to or from the external device. This means that all 80 columns of the card or 120 (to 132) positions of the printer are logically used even if the positions do not physically contain data. These devices use a *card record* or a print record.

> A *card record* is a complete card.
> A *print record* is complete print line.

Neither card nor print records require that all positions to be used, but rather that these are available. If some positions are not used, they are ignored or filled with blanks. Therefore, when a *read* is issued, an entire card is read; when a *print* is issued, a complete line of print is printed.

Records are also broken down into more manageable units. A payroll record would contain payroll information concerning an employee. This information would include his name, pay rate, state and federal exemptions, social security number, regular and overtime hours, medical and life insurance deductions, etc. This decomposition of a record forms *fields* within the record.

> A *field* is used to describe the specific area used or required by a piece of information within a record.

In FORTRAN IV, any input/output quantity (field) will occupy space on the document (record) on which it is encoded. For example, if the number 3127 occupies columns 6, 7, 8, and 9 of a card, the field position must be accurately defined so that the program can instruct the computer where to access or display the input/output data. To be able to supply information about the position the data has within the record as well as its characteristics, FORTRAN has a field specification.

A *field specification* is the description of the field(s) supplied to the computer by the FORTRAN IV program.

1.2.3　Field Specifications

With only minor exceptions (such as machine limitations or compiler implementations levels), the field specification statement must be provided by the programmer in the FORTRAN IV program. The field specifications are included with a "FORMAT" statement.

A *FORMAT* is the physical arrangement of data within a record, relative to the physical device (card reader, printer, etc.,) on which it is transferred.

We shall next discuss the more important field specifications statements or FORMAT.

A FORMAT STATEMENT is a FORTRAN IV instruction that gives the field specification information to the computer. Its form is:
Statement number FORMAT (field 1, field 2, . . . , field N)

1.2.4　Integer, Format

Integer input/output is handled by the "I format." The Specification for this input/output requires that the numbers processed be integers and that the field width be given. The field width is measured in columns. The number 137 would require at least three columns. However, −137 would require at least four columns as the sign occupies a column position. Therefore, a signed three digit number would require four columns or positions. Although three positions would suffice, if the number were unsigned a programmer might specify I4, I meaning integer and the four meaning that up to 4 columns might be used for the number and its possible sign.

Iw is the format used to read or write integers, where I represents integers and w the column width.

When an input/output document is produced, it usually contains several quantities. The reason is obvious. A card has 80 columns, a printer at least 120. To write only one field on a record would be wasteful. It is desirable to be able to include several fields within a single record. This is accomplished by including, in a single FORMAT statement, a field specification for each input or output variable.

Example

Suppose a card is to be read with M punched in the first three columns, JACK in the next five columns, and KAR in the next three columns. The arrangement of the data is shown below in Figure 31. Note that M, JACK, and KAR are integer variables.

A format that would describe this would be:

FORMAT (I3, I5, I3)

M	JACK	KAR	
XXX	XXXXX	XXX	Ignored
Field 1	Field 2	Field 3	

Figure 31

Note that only eleven columns are specified, with the remaining sixty-nine columns to be passed over in a "read" statement. A "read" statement always reads a whole number of cards.

Remarks

If signed, M will range in value from −99 to 99; if unsigned, M can range from 0 to 999.

JACK being five columns can accommodate unsigned integers from 0 to 99999. Signed numbers may vary from −9999 to 9999. KAR being three columns, KAR has the same range of values as does M.

All integers must be in the extreme right portion of their respective fields. This is called *right justification*. Otherwise, the integer being read will have the blanks to its right interpreted as zeros; thus 7bb for KAR is interpreted as 700 by the FORTRAN program.

1.2.5 Fixed Format. (F Format)

Fixed Format is used to read or write real numbers with a decimal point. Input/output using Fixed Format requires:

(1)   The specification F.
(2)   The field width in columns.
(3)   The numbers of places to the right of the decimal point.

In counting the columns required to express the real number, we should include a column for the decimal point and a column for the sign of the number.

The Fw.d is the principal specification used in input/output of real variables. The integer w is the field width of the real number in columns. The integer d is the number of positions to the right of the decimal point if the decimal point is not punched in the card.

If more than one quantity is found in a card or print record, it is handled by the inclusion of the multiple Fw.d field specifications within a single FORMAT statement.

Example

Consider a card that is to be read as a record. On this card there are five fields denoted by the names A, SAM, SUE, PEACH, and X. A is in columns 1 to 5. SAM has length seven and is in columns 6 to 12. SUE has length eight and is in columns 13 to 20. PEACH has length eight and is in columns 21 to 28. Finally X has length five and is in columns 29 to 33. A has two positions to the right of the decimal point. SUE and PEACH have no digits to the right of their decimal points. SAM and X have one digit to the right of their decimal points. (Figure 32.)

A	SAM	SUE	PEACH	X	
XX.XX	XXXXX.X	XXXXXXX.	XXXXXXX.	XXX.X	Ignored
Field 1	Field 2	Field 3	Field 4	Field 5	

Figure 32

Remark

Note that in the previous two figures, the fields have been separated when in actuality they would be adjacent punched. A format to read the above card might be:

```
     READ    (1,10) A, SAM, SUE, PEACH, X
10   FORMAT (F 5.2, F 7.1, 2F 8.0, F 5.1)
```

A read statement causes an entire card to be processed. Therefore, all 80 columns are examined. Since the FORMAT specified information from column 1 to column 33, the last 47 columns are ignored and passed over.

The ranges of values of the fields described above are:

	Signed		*Unsigned*
A	−9.99 to +9.99	A	0.00 to 99.99
SAM	−9999.9 to +9999.9	SAM	0.0 to 99999.9
SUE	−999999. to +999999.	SUE	0.0 to 9999999.
PEACH	−999999. to +999999.	PEACH	0.0 to 9999999.
X	−99.9 to +99.9	X	0.0 to 999.9

Note that if the + sign is omitted, one column is gained.

1.2.6   X FORMAT

Often, data is not continuously located on a document. That is, data fields do not adjoin. Quite commonly, blanks separate fields. One method to separate data fields is to use the X FORMAT.

wX causes w characters to be ignored on input and w blanks to be formed on output.

Example

Suppose a printer record contains two fields, I and J, separated by 75 blank positions. I is to be printed in the first five columns of a printed page. J is to be printed in columns 81 through 86.

I		J
XXXXX	75 Blanks	XXXXX

Since I and J are both integers, a format that would accomplish this might be:

10   FORMAT (X, I5, 75X, I6)

The X is used in print position one to allow for carriage control (which is described later).

The X FORMAT, wX, shall be used to skip w characters on input or to cause w blanks on output. In output, this format is used for editing purposes, namely, for increasing the readability of the document.

1.2.7 Titling

Generally when a report is to be prepared by the computer, it is desirable to insert *alphameric* (alphabetic or numeric) information into the report. This increases readability and understanding. Imagine a long report with nothing but numbers on it. One would have difficulty knowing what quantity each number represents. To clarify the report, titles are placed wherever appropriate or needed. This is accomplished using the H format.

The H format takes the following form:
Statement Number FORMAT (wH alphameric information) where w is an integer whose value is the length of the alphameric information being transmitted.

Example

12   FORMAT   (17H THIS IS PROBLEM 1)
         or
18   FORMAT   (4H X = , F7.2, 4H I = , I5)

In this message, THIS IS PROBLEM 1, there are 17 letters and spaces. This is conveyed in statement 12 by using 17H.

1.2.8 Principal Input/Output Devices

Card Reader.   Input, either of data or program type, generally is encoded on cards. Cards are easily resequenced. Mistakes may be corrected by repunching the card(s) in error. Cards are easy to handle, moderately easy to check, and very economical. This extensive use of cards makes the card reader a very important device.

Cards are read either by metallic brushes or optical cells. When brushes are used, one brush is provided for each of the eighty columns of the card. The card is rolled so that the card separates the metallic brush above the card from a metallic contact below the card. If the hole is punched in the card, the brush makes contact with the metallic plate, causing an electrical circuit to be made. Thus, the hole is sensed. If there is no hole, no contact is made. Optical cells may be used by providing one for each row, twelve in all. Lights are shined on all rows of a card, and the card is scanned column by column. If a hole is present, the light causes the photo-electric cell to record the hole. Similarly, if no hole is present, the light cannot be sensed by the photo-electric cell. Thus, the presence of a hole or no hole is sensed, thereby processing the card.

Card readers, in a wide variety of speeds, are available for most computers. Speeds vary from two hundred cards per minute to over one thousand cards per minute. An average installation of small to medium size will have a card reader with a card-reading speed of about four hundred cards per minute.

1.2.9 Printer

Output from a program is generally printed on the console typewriter or the line printer. Printers are used for nearly all output results. Printers use a continuous sheet on which answers are printed. The paper is perforated so that it can be torn off to form pages. Each page is approximately 14″ across and 11″ deep. This allows 120 to 144 characters per printed line and about 55 to 60 lines to be formed per page. Characters are printed by hammers striking the appropriate position of a chain of a type bar. A chain, which looks much like a bicycle chain, is made with its character set repeated several times. The type bar slides back and forth; the chain rotates continuously. When a character on the chain or type bar goes by the position in which it is to be printed, the character is sensed. The sensing causes a hammer to swing out, printing the character in the desired position.

Printers are limited in speed largely because of their mechanical nature. However, printers range in speed from two hundred lines per minute to over twelve hundred lines per minute. Most small to medium size computer installations have printers with speeds of six hundred or less lines per minute.

1.2.10 Card Punch

Often the output of a program must be used as input to a second or a third program. That is, the output from program 1 is input to program 2. This means that if the only available output from program 1 is printing, the printed material must be key-punched into cards. This process is tedious and the possibility of inducing errors is great. An alternative to keypunching is having the computer, under the direction of the computer program, punching output directly into cards, thereby reducing the margin of error. Not only are the results more accurate, but the overall time of program execution is shortened. In summary, from time to time, one may punch output data into cards for later use as input. One can produce both printed and punched output if so desired at the same time.

FORTRAN IV uses the first print position of each line to control the printer spacing. If an attempt is made to print certain characters in print position one, then one might get strange results, such as single spacing, a page ejection, etc. Therefore a programmer must be careful to use only this position for control of the printer. Table 1 shows the effects of using print position one.

Table 1

Printer Control

Character	*Effect*
blank	single space before printing
0	double space before printing
+	no space
1	skip the first line on the next page

Another name for printer control is carriage control.

The first character is never printed, but rather causes paper movement to occur.

1.2.11   Input/Output Statements

The input or output (I/O) of all information is caused by the programmer issuing the command READ or the command WRITE. In order that a READ or WRITE can be used, it is necessary to know these things:

(1) Device type—Device on which I/O is performed.
(2) Format number—Format being used to give arrangement of data.
(3) I/O List—Variable names of items to be moved in or out of the computer on the Specified I/O device using the data arrangement associated with the Format number.

The statement to "read" data is

READ (I, J) List

where I is the device number; J is the format number; and List represents the variables to be input on device type I according to format number J. I and J must be integer variables or constants.

The statement "write" data is

WRITE (I, J) List

where I is the device number; J is the format number; and List represents the variables to be output on device type I according to format number J. I and J must be integer variables or constants.

1.2.12   Repeated Scanning

Within a FORMAT statement, parentheses effect repetitions or fields contained within the parentheses grouping. This can be an extremely effective tool for the programmer. However, it must be used with care.

When a set of specifications are to be repeated one can use $n(S_1, S_2 \ldots)$ where n is a positive integer and $S_1, S_2, \ldots$ are full specifications. The repetitive grouping $n(S_1, S_2 \ldots)$ indicates that $S_1, S_2, \ldots$ is repeated n times.

Example

10   FORMAT (F5.0,3(F6.0, 12)) is nearly equivalent to
10   FORMAT (F5.0, F6.0, 12, F6.0, 12, F6.0, 12)

The only difference results when the output list is longer than the total number of field specifications within the Format statement.

When the number of output variables in a list exceeds the number of fields specified, the FORMAT is reused. Reuse starts immediately after the last left parenthesis before the final right parenthesis (i.e., the left parenthesis closest to the first right parenthesis).

Example 1

WRITE (3,10) (X (I), I = 1, 10)
10   FORMAT (2F10.5)

causes five rows to be printed, each containing two quantities. The repeated scanning uses 2F10.5 five times.

Example 2

WRITE (3,11) I,J,(X(K),K = 1.9)
11   FORMAT (2I6/(4F10.0))

causes record containing I and J to be written on one line, and X's to be written on two lines, each with 4 fields, and a third line with only one field.

Example 3

WRITE (3,12) (A(I),I = 1, 15)
11   FORMAT (2F10.0 / 3(F5.1,2F6.2) / F10.0)

causes the two variables to be transmitted by 2F10.0 and the next 13 variables to be output by using the portion of the FORMAT underlined as many times as required.

1.2.13 Device Types

Numbers are assigned to input/output devices by the computer manufacturer or by the programmer. These numbers must then be used to reference the input or output device. For example, if the card reader has assigned to it the number 1, then the programmer would issue a command to read on device 1.

A common assignment of numbers is as follows:

Device Number	Device Type
1	Card Reader
2	Card Punch
3	Printer

Note. The programmer should inquire from the computer center personnel as to the specific device numbers that should be used in the program.

Example

Write a FORTRAN IV program to read from the card reader the following variables: CAT, TABLE, LEMON, SALLY, and JOE, where each variable is described in the following table:

Variable	Card Columns	Decimal Point in Column
CAT	1–5	4
TABLE	6–12	10
LEMON	20–25	none allowed
SALLY	40–48	48
JOE	50–56	none allowed

In addition, we wish to output on the printer the same variables with the following arrangement:

Variable	Printer Column	Decimal Point in Column
JOE	4–10	none allowed
LEMON	11–16	none allowed
CAT	21–25	24
SALLY	31–39	39
TABLE	41–47	45

A FORTRAN IV program that would accomplish this is:

```
      READ (1,11) CAT, TABLE, LEMON, SALLY, JOE
      WRITE (3,12) JOE, LEMON, CAT, SALLY, TABLE
   11 FORMAT (F5.1,F7.2,I6,14X,F9.0,I7)
   12 FORMAT (3X,I7,I6,4X,F5.1,5X,F9.0,1X,F7.2)
      END
```

Remarks

(a) Note that the device type of 1 in READ statement indicates use of the card reader.

(b) 11 in the READ statement indicates that the FORMAT statement number is 11.

(c) CAT, TABLE, LEMON, SALLY and JOE is the list used in the READ statement.

(d) FORMAT 11 calls for 5 variables to be input from the card. The arrangement is given in Table II. FORMAT 11 is made to agree with that arrangement. Note that there are 14 blanks (14X) between third and fourth data items in the list. Also two variables are integer variables, and three are real variables.

(e) Similar comments apply to the WRITE statement and on FORMAT 12.

(f) Use of the END statement is required in all FORTRAN IV programs to indicate the end of the source program.

1.2.14 Repeated Fields

When field formats are repeated within a FORMAT statement, it is convenient to use the *repeated field* specification. This takes the form mQ where m is an integer and Q is any valid field specification.

Example 1

```
   10 FORMAT (2I3, 4F7.2) is equivalent to
   10 FORMAT (I3,I3,F7.2,F7.2,F7.2,F7.2)
```

Parentheses may be inserted to cause repetition of field specifications.

Example 2

```
  100 FORMAT (I3,F7.2, 3(F5.2, F4.3)) is the same as
  100 FORMAT (I3,F7.2, F5.2, F4.3, F5.2, F4.3, F5.2, F4.3)
```

1.2.15 Slash

The slash is used within a FORMAT statement to cause records with possibly different data arrangements to be read or written by a single input/output statement using a single FORMAT statement. That is, two or more cards with possibly different formats may be read with a single READ statement. Similarly, two or more printer lines may be written using a single WRITE statement. To understand how the slash is used, consider the following examples.

Example 1

Suppose these variables X, Y, Z are to be read from card 1 in cols. 1–10, 11–20, 21–30, respectively, and variables T and U are to be read from a second card in cols. 25–30 and 41–50, respectively. Assume each variable on the first card has two decimal places, and each variable on the second card has one decimal place. A program sequence might be:

```
      READ (1,10) X, Y, Z, T, U
10    FORMAT (3 F10.2/24X, F6.1, 10X, F10.1)
```

Both cards using the FORMAT described above would be read by a single READ statement.

Example 2

As an example of the use of the / in a WRITE statement, consider the following statements, where b indicates a blank

```
      WRITE (3, 21) X,Y,Z
21    FORMAT (21HbbbbTbbbbbbbbYbbbbbbbZbbb/3F8.2)
```

If X = 10.32, Y = −3.01 and Z = 127.31 then the above statements would cause the printer to output the two lines:

```
bbbTbbbbbbbbYbbbbbbbZ
10.32   −3.01   127.31
```

Example 3

(*a*)   WRITE (3, 101) I,J
    101   FORMAT (I5,/,I8)

causes I and J to be printed on separate lines like

I

J

(*b*)　　　WRITE (3, 102) I,J
　　102　FORMAT (I5,///,I8)

causes I to be printed, two blank lines, and then J.

I

J

Note. n slashes in-between field specifications causes n − 1 blank lines.

Example 4

Suppose we wish three blank lines between successive lines of output. A WRITE statement and FORMAT might be

　　WRITE (3, 20) X, Y, T, U
20　FORMAT (10X, 3F12.3, ///)

This would cause three blank lines after printing X, Y, T and U. If statement 20 were

20　FORMAT (///, 10X, 3F12.3)

three blank lines would be formed before printing.

Note. n slashes at the beginning or end of a format causes n blank lines to be written or, in the case of a READ, n cards to be ignored.

1.2.16　E Format

When working with scientific calculations, the programmer is often confronted with a wide range of values, especially for output variables. In order to facilitate input/output of this type, FORTRAN IV provides the E format. The general form is

$$E \; w.d$$

where w is the width of the field in columns, d is the number of digits following the decimal point.

In the E format, a number is printed as ± 0.XXX.X E±YY, known as the *exponential form*.

The following table indicates various combinations of variable values, formats, and printed representations.

A	Format	Printed Value	
3.71	E10.3	0.371E 01	
−3.71	E10.3	−0.371E 01	
3.71	E 8.2	0.37E 01	insufficient field width
−3.71	E 8.2	0.37E 01	to print sign when needed
37.12	E 8.2	0.37E 02	insufficient field width
−37.12	E 8.2	0.37E 02	to print sign when needed
−37.12	E10.3	−0.371E 02	
−37.12	E13.6	−0.371200E 02	

Seven columns of space are needed for sign, decimal point, exponent field, and initial 0. The programmer normally adds seven to the necessary d to get the field width w.

1.2.17 Character Fields — A Format

When data is to include non-numeric characters, the I, E, and F format will not be suitable for input/output. If this information is not manipulated, the H format is used. However, if this non-numeric information is to be processed, a special format must be used for input/output.

The general form is

Aw

where A indicates alphameric information (alphabetic, numeric and special characters) and w is the field width in columns.

On input the alphameric data is converted character by character, into an internal form, where each character has its own internal representation. If the number of characters w to be read is larger than the number of characters x stored in a variable, then the x characters on the right side of the word are input and stored while the leftmost w−x are ignored. If the number of characters w is smaller than or equal to x, then the w characters are read and stored with blanks being used on the right as necessary to fill the word out to x characters.

On output the data is converted from internal character form to external alphameric form. If w in the A format is greater than x, the number of characters in a variable, the data is right justified and filled in the extreme left w−x columns with blanks. If w is less than or equal to x, the w characters of the extreme left in the variable are output, and the remaining characters are ignored.

Assume, as an example, that x = 4. We have the situation presented in the Table III. The B's indicate blank spaces.

Table III

Data	Input Internal	Aw	Aw	Output Internal	Data
A123	A123	A4	A4	XYZW	XYZW
A1234B6	34B6	A4	A3	XYZW	XYZ
A1	A1bb	A4	A6	XYZW	bbXYZW

Exercises

1. A card has three names written on it, V, X, and Y in columns 10–15, 20–25, and 40–47, with each number having a decimal point two places from the end. Write the necessary statements to read this card and print the numbers in E Format using your own choice for print positions.

2. Four cards are punched, each containing two data items in columns 40–45 and columns 70–75. Write the necessary FORTRAN statements that will read these four cards in integer form and print them on one line of the printer starting in column 10 with two spaces between each field.

3. Write the necessary FORTRAN statements that will write the following information on the printer on a new page, double spacing between the first and the second lines and single spacing between the second and the third lines.

Line 1   JOHN J JONES
Line 2   CSC 100, SECTION 1
Line 3   PROBLEM ONE . . PRINTING EXERCISE

4. Write the necessary FORTRAN statements that will read a card into appropriately named variables when the card has the form:

cols. 1–6   Identification number
cols. 8–11   Named abbreviated to four alphabetic positions
cols. 12–17   Priced in dollars and cents
cols. 18–22   Quantity in stock
cols. 23–25   Factory number where products are stored (numeric field)

cols. 26–30   Quantity sold last year
cols. 31–35   Quantity sold the year before
cols. 36–40   Quantity sold two years ago
cols. 41–48   Information that is not to be read
cols. 79–80   Departmental code

5.   An employee payroll card used in the weekly payroll has the form

Social Security number	9(9)	cols.	1–9
Name	A(21)	cols.	10–30
Pay rate	9.99	cols.	31–34
Hours worked	99.9	cols.	35–38
Previous pay total	99999.99	cols.	39–46
Previous Fed. tax total	9999.99	cols.	47–53
Previous State tax total	999.99	cols.	54–59
Previous Soc. Sec. total	999.99	cols.	60–65
Number of dependents	99	cols.	66–67
Hospitalization	99.99	cols.	68–72
Life insurance	99.99	cols.	73–77
Clock number	999	cols.	78–80

where 9 indicates numeric information, A indicates alphabetic information, and . is a decimal point. A(9) and A(21) indicated 9 numeric digits and 21 alphabetic characters.

Write FORTRAN statements to read this card and assign the values to appropriately named variables. (Hint: In order to read the alphabetic, use the AW FORMAT for one or more variables, and break up the social security field into several if the nine digit field is too large for your computer.)

6.   Construct FORTRAN statements that will produce on the printer the Christmas tree design:

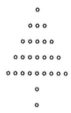

7.   Construct, using FORTRAN statements on the printer, a

rectangle which has top and bottom consisting of 12 dashes, sides 5 I's, and containing the statement A(I) = J.

```
    - - - - - - - - - -
I                   I
I                   I
I    A(I) = J       I
I                   I
I                   I
    - - - - - - - - - -
```

8. Given the number A, signed, 7 digits long with two to the right of the decimal point, using FORTRAN, produce a line double spaced from the previous containing 10 spaces, A = ± XXXX.XX, and finally overstrike the number for emphasis.

9. Write a FORMAT statement that will read an integer field from columns 1–3 of first card and any number of subsequent cards with one number in columns 6–10 and a second number in columns 16–20, each of the form X.XXX.

10. Write the FORTRAN input/output and FORMAT statements to read column 1 in alphabetic mode, and then put the alphabetic character in both A format and I format starting in columns 10 and 30 of the print line. (Hint: Allow the field for integer to have nine or ten columns.)

11. Assume that a magnetic tape record is to be read using a FORTRAN FORMAT description. If the record contains five fields of form XXXXX XXX, ten fields of form XXXX, and four groups of alternating form XXXX and XX XXXX, write the appropriate FORMAT statement.

12. The card

12345678931

is input with the statements

    READ(2,25) I,J,F
25 FORMAT (2I4,F5.3)

State the stored values of the variables I, J, and F.

13.   Indicate how many lines of print will be generated with the following statement.

FORMAT(1X,2I3//2(F3.2,2I3),6F4.2)

14.   Find the errors in the following statements.

WRITE I,J,F
FORMAT (2F3.2,F4.5)

15.   Find the errors in the following statements.

READ I,F,TWO
FORMAT (1X,12H THERE ARE)

16.   Write the necessary statements to get as an input the message

TODAY IS SUNDAY
TOMORROW
I MUST GO TO WORK

leaving two blank lines between each printed line.

1.3   Arithmetic Statements

In this section, we introduce the *arithmetic statements,* also called *expressions.* These statements provide the means to formulate meaningful algebraic expressions. The operations that will be discussed are as follows: addition, subtraction, multiplication, division, and exponentiation. Certain "unary" operations and functions also will be considered.

1.3.1   Arithmetic Operations

The arithmetic operations used in Fortran IV with the symbols used to represent them are:

(*a*)   ADDITION, represented by the symbol +.
(*b*)   SUBTRACTION and NEGATION, represented by the symbol −.
(*c*)   MULTIPLICATION, represented by the symbol °.
(*d*)   DIVISION, represented by the symbol /.
(*e*)   EXPONENTIATION, represented by the symbol °°.

Example

A+B   ADDITION of A and B.
A−B   SUBTRACTION of B from A.

A*B   MULTIPLICATION of A and B.
A/B   DIVISION of A by B.
A**B   A raised to the power of B.
−B   NEGATION of B (Unary operation).

An *arithmetic expression* is any meaningful combination of variables and operations.

In order that arithmetic expressions be meaningful, an order of preference, i.e., a hierarchy, between operations is assumed. That is, if several operations are present in an arithmetic expression, they are executed in the following order of preference:

> EXPONENTIATION, first.
> NEGATION (unary operation), second.
> MULTIPLICATION and DIVISION, next.
> ADDITION and SUBTRACTION, last.

When the arithmetic operations are of the same order of preference, the computations are performed from left to right.

Examples

(a)   A+B*C−D**2+E/F

Computations are performed as follows:

STEP 1. $A+B^*C-D^2+E/F$

STEP 2. $A+(B \cdot C)-D^2)-\left(\dfrac{E}{F}\right)$

STEP 3. $\left(\left(\left(A+(B \cdot C)\right)-D^2\right)-\left(\dfrac{E}{F}\right)\right)$

(b)   N+1**2

STEP 1. $N+(1^2)$

(c)   A+E/F*G

STEP 1. $A+\left(\dfrac{E}{F}\right)^*G$

STEP 2. $A+\left(\left(\dfrac{E}{F}\right) \cdot G\right)$

(d)   −B+4

STEP 1.   (−B)+4   Note: (−B) is the negative of B.
STEP 2.   ((−B)+4)

(*e*)   E/F/G

STEP 1. $\left(\dfrac{E}{F}\right)/G$

STEP 2. $\dfrac{\left(\dfrac{E}{F}\right)}{G}$ which is algebraically equivalent to $\dfrac{E}{F \cdot G}$

(*f*)   A/B*C

STEP 1. $\left(\dfrac{A}{B}\right)$*C   Division is performed first since * and / are of the same order.

STEP 2. $\left(\left(\dfrac{A}{B}\right)\cdot C\right)$ which is equivalent to $\dfrac{A \cdot C}{B}$

Parentheses are used to indicate a preferred order of computation. Parentheses are always used in pairs. Expressions inside parentheses are evaluated first. If parentheses are written within parentheses, the innermost quantities are evaluated first, as is customary in algebra.

Examples

(1)   (A+B)*(A+B)   means $(A + B)\cdot(A + B)$
(2)   (A+B)**2   means $(A + B)^2$
(3)   (A+B)/(C−D)   means $\dfrac{A + B}{C - D}$
(4)   A/(B+C/(D+E/F))   means $\dfrac{A}{B + \dfrac{C}{D + \dfrac{E}{F}}}$

Note that without the parentheses, the above examples would be interpreted as:

(1) $A + B\cdot A + B$
(2) $A + B^2$
(3) $A + \dfrac{B}{C} - D$
(4) $\dfrac{A}{B} + \dfrac{C}{D} + \dfrac{E}{F}$

Note that the number of left parentheses must be the same as the number of right parentheses. The expression $(A + B*(C + D)$ is invalid as there is a missing right parenthesis.

Modes.   If all variables and constants in an arithmetic expression are real, then the expression is said to be of *real mode*. Similarly, if all variables and constants in an expression are integers, then the expression is said to be of *integer mode*. Whenever an arithmetic expression contains real and integer variables and constants then the expression is said to be of *mixed mode*.

Basic Fortran does not permit mixed mode expressions; however, some compilers do allow mixed mode. (Check with your computer center.)

1.3.2. Substitution Statement

A substitution statement has the form:

$$V = Exp.$$

where V is any variable name and Exp. is any arithmetic expression.

The equality symbol, =, in the statement V = Exp. means: The value of the expression Exp. is stored in the variable V. As a consequence of the storing of a value in V, the previous quantity residing in V is destroyed.

Example

AREA = 3.14159*R*R
TSEC = TMIN*60.
SPACE = .5*G*T**2.

Note. If the quantity on the left hand side of the = symbol must be preserved, one can do the following:

(1) TEMP = V
(2) V = EXP

after the statement has been executed, in order to use the initial V, one must use the variable TEMP.

We can use the above procedure to interchange the value of the variables A and B.

TEMP = A
A = B
B = TEMP

Remarks

(*i*) If the substitution statement

$$A = J$$

is executed for

$$J = 2$$

then 2. is stored in A since A is a real variable.

(*ii*) If the substitution statement

$$J = A$$

is executed for

$$A = 3.4$$

then 3 is stored in J since J is an integer variable. Thus the decimal part of A is disregarded, i.e., A is *truncated*.

Note. (i) and (ii) do not contain *mixed mode* variables. Mixed mode applies only to the arithmetic expression (right side) of the substitution statement.

1.3.3 Library Functions

FORTRAN IV provides in a "library" the more common arithmetic and trigonometric functions. These functions are square root, absolute value, truncation, float, fix, logarithm, exponential, sine, cosine, arctangent, and the hyperbolic tangent.

Suppose that we want to know the distance between two points, *P* and *Q*. We can compute this distance if we know their coordinates. Assume these to be (*a*, *b*) and (*c*, *d*), respectively. Then the distance is given by the formula

$$\sqrt{(a - c)^2 + (b - d)^2}$$

The substitution statement that will perform this calculation is

$$DIST = SQRT((a-c)**2+(b-d)**2)$$

where DIST is the variable that will contain the value for the distance between P and Q. SQRT is the library function for $\sqrt{}$.

These library functions are retrieved from the library as follows:

Name (arithmetic expression) where Name stands for one of the following:

SQRT   is used for obtaining the square root of an expression.

ABS   is used for obtaining the absolute value of a real expression.

IABS   is used for obtaining the absolute value of an integer expression.

AINT
INT   is used for obtaining the truncation of an expression.

FLOAT is used for obtaining the conversion from integer to real.

IFIX   is used for obtaining the conversion from real to integer.

ALOG   is used for obtaining the logarithm to the base e of an expression.

EXP   is used for obtaining e raised to the power of an expression.

SIN   is used for obtaining the sine of an expression.

COS   is used for obtaining the cosine of an expression.

ATAN   is used for obtaining the arctangent of an expression.

TANH   is used for obtaining the hyperbolic tangent of an expression.

SIGN   is used for transfer sign of argument$_2$ to argument$_1$ for reals.

ISIGN is used for transfer sign of argument$_2$ to argument$_1$ for integers.

and "expression" stands for any permissible arithmetic expression.

Remarks

AINT   truncates the expression and is used as a real value.

INT   truncates the expression and is used as an integer value.

FLOAT   converts an integer variable to a real value.

IFIX   converts a real variable to an integer to an integer value.

SIN,COS   require the expression to be given in radians.

ATAN   computes the arctan in radians.

Exercises

1. Construct FORTRAN expressions that are equivalent to the following mathematical expressions:

(a) $a^2 + b^2$

(b) $\dfrac{a^2 - b}{c + d}$

(c) $\dfrac{(x + y) + (3y - x)}{y}$

(d) $\dfrac{4R^3}{3}$

(e) $\sqrt{p(p - a)(p - b)(p - c)}$

(f) $\dfrac{n^2(n-1)^2}{4}$

(g) $A + \dfrac{B}{C + \dfrac{D}{E+F}}$

(h) $1/2gt^2 + v_0 t + s_0$

2.   Choose suitable variable names and construct FORTRAN arithmetic statements:

(a) $v = 1/2gt^2$, where v is velocity, g is acceleration due to gravity, and t is time in seconds.

(b) $I = Prt$ where I is simple interest for principal P at interest rate r per period for t periods.

(c) $s = 4\pi r^2$. Surface area S of a sphere of radius r.

(d)   The integer sum of first n integers is $\dfrac{n(n+1)}{2}$.

(e) $n!$ n factorial which is the product of the first n integers.

(f)   (Stoke's Law)

$$v = 2/9 \ r^2 g \ (\rho - \rho_0)/\eta$$

where r, g, ρ, ρ_0, and η are all real variables.

(g)   The equation of a standing wave may be written as

$$y = [2A \cos 2\pi \ ft] \cos 2\pi x/\lambda$$

where A, f, t, x, λ are real numbers.

(h)   The intensity level of a sound wave is defined by

$$B = 10 \log I/I_0$$

where I is the intensity, and I_0 is an arbitrary reference intensity (for example, 10^{-15}).

(i)   The magnetic induction B at a point is defined as

$$B = F/qv\sin \phi$$

where q is the charge, v its velocity, ϕ the angle between v and the direction of the magnetic field, and F is the force.

(j)   For two resistors in parallel

$$R = R_1 R_2 \ / \ (R_1 + R_2)$$

where R_1 is the resistance of resistor 1, R_2 is the resistance of resistor 2, and R is the resistance equivalent to the two in parallel.

3. Write FORTRAN arithmetic statements to compute the following:

(a) $\sin(a^2 - b^2)/(c - d)$
(b) $\log |x - y\sin(x^2 - y^2)|$
(c) $\arctan(x - y^2)/y^2$.

1.3.4 Subscripted Variables

On occasion, a programmer has need to manipulate multiple data as if the data items were a single variable. For example, suppose we have to compute the average of N numbers $A, B, C, \ldots, K$; we could think of these numbers as if they were a single item by associating with each one of them as index as follows:

A becomes the first element, B becomes the second element . . . , and K becomes the Nth element. We then rename $A, B, C, \ldots, K$ by calling them $X_1, X_2, \ldots, X_N$, that is, X_1 represents A, X_2 represents $B, \ldots$, and X_N represents K. Now the problem can be restated to find the average of N numbers, $X_1, X_2, \ldots, X_N$. We can develop this idea still further as follows: put $X(1) = X_1, X(2) = X_2, \ldots, X(N) = X_N$. Next find the average of the numbers $X(1)$, $X(2), \ldots, X(N)$. The set $X(1), X(2), \ldots, X(N)$ is called a *vector* or an *array*. The use of $X(1), X(2), \ldots, X(N)$ instead of $A, B, \ldots, K$ is called the *indexing* or *subscripting* of the set $\{A, B, \ldots, K\}$, and $\{X(1), X(2), \ldots, X(N)\}$ is called an *indexed* or *subscripted* variable X.

The example introduced above involves one subscript. FORTRAN IV provides for multiple subscripts. A two dimensional array is called a *matrix*.

An example of a 7 by 10 array is

$$A(1,1)\ A(1,2) \ldots A(1,10)$$
$$A(2,1)\ A(2,2) \ldots A(2,10)$$
$$\cdot \qquad \cdot \quad \ldots \quad \cdot$$
$$A(7,1)\ A(7,2) \ldots A(7,10)$$

$X(1)$ contains left and right parentheses. Parentheses are special characters and are not permissible characters for use in a variable name. Therefore subscripted variables require a naming statement. The naming statement gives the variable name and the maximum number of elements which the array might have. This statement is called the DIMENSION statement.

The form of a DIMENSION statement is:

DIMENSION v1(sl,s2,s3), v2(tl,t2,t3), . . . , vN(X1,X2,X3)

The v1,v2, through vN are names of indexed sets.

In FORTRAN IV, these indexed sets are called "arrays." An array may be single indexed, double indexed or triply indexed at the programmer's option. The $s1$, $s2$, $s3$ are positive integer constants specifying the maximum value of the index. In FORTRAN IV these constants, in reference to an array, are called *subscripts*. The number of subscripts in an array is called the *dimension* of the array. A single element of an array is called a *subscripted variable*.

Example

(*a*)   DIMENSION X(10)
(*b*)   DIMENSION   A(7,10)
(*c*)   DIMENSION I(2,45), X(20)

Remarks

In example (a) a one dimensional variable X is named with a maximum of ten elements.

In example (b) a two dimensional real variable A is named with a maximum of 7 rows and 10 columns for a total of 70 elements.

In example (c) a three dimensional integer variable I is named, with a maximum of two planes, 4 rows, and 5 columns for a total of 40 elements; also a one dimensional variable X is named with a maximum number of 20 elements.

The naming of subscripted variables must follow the same rules as the naming of any other variable. That is, if the subscripted variable name begins with I, J, K, L, M, or N, then the subscripted variable is an integer array; otherwise, the subscripted variable is a real array.

A permissible subscript can be of the following types:

(*a*)   Integer constant   Example 7
(*b*)   Integer variable   Example I
(*c*)   Integer constant*Integer variable   Example 7*I
(*d*)   Integer variable ± Integer constant   Example J−3
(*e*)   Integer Constant*Integer variable ±
         Integer constant   Example 5*J−3

where Integer variables and constants are positive.

Exercises

1.   Indicate which of the following expressions are invalid if used as subscripts.

(a)   III
(b)   1+L
(c)   X
(d)   I+.5
(e)   2*I−3
(f)   I*J
(g)   I−5
(h)   3*I+5
(i)   −7
(j)   0
(k)   I?3+2
(l)   M

2.   Assume that X has been dimension $x(100)$ and Y has been dimension $Y(5,100)$. Write a FORTRAN statement to compute

(i) $A = X_{17} + \log (Y^2_{3.17} + 1)$
(ii) $Y_{5.100} = Y_{1.100} + Y_{2.100} + Y_{3.100} + Y_{4.100}$
(iii) $SP = X^2_1 + X^2_2 + X^2_3$.

1.3.5   Statement Function

The library functions, such as SIN, ALOG, and SQRT, are extremely useful. Many times the programmer wishes that he had the ability to use functions of his own naming and for his own specific purposes. By means of the *arithmetic statement function,* FORTRAN provides the programmer with an ability to name functions, describe arithmetic calculations in terms of these named functions and use them in a way similar to the way in which library functions are used.

The general form of the arithmetic statement function is

$$name(arg_1, arg_2, \ldots) = f(arg_1, arg_2 \ldots)$$

where *name* is the variable name to be used when invoking the function; arg_1, arg_2 . . . are the dummy arguments of the arithmetic function; and $f(arg_1, arg_2, \ldots)$ is the calculation to be performed expressed as an arithmetic expression involving arguments arg_1, arg_2, . . . , other functions and constants.

To use the arithmetic statement, the programmer must describe or name the statement using dummy variables. Then, when he needs to use the function, he invokes it by using the name of the function and arguments in an arithmetic expression. There must be only one naming for each function, but once named, it can be invoked or used as often thereafter as needed.

Example

(*a*)   SUM(X,Y,Z) = X+Y+Z
(*b*)   QUAD(A,B,C) = −B+SQRT(B°B−4.°A°C)/(2.°A)
(*c*)   POLY(T) = A°T°°3+B°T°°2+C°T+D
(*d*)   DER(X,DEL) = POLY(X+DX)−POLY(X)

The above are examples of the naming of functions. Now if one programs

(*a*)   Z = X+SUM(A,B,3.)

then X+(A+B+3.) is calculated and stored in Z. The dummy arguments A, B, and 3. replace X, Y, and Z, respectively, in the function SUM.

(*b*)   QUAD(A,B,C)°°2   causes

$$\left(\frac{-b+\sqrt{b^2-4ac}}{2a}\right)^2 \text{to be calculated}$$

Variables A, B, and C replace dummy variables A, B, C, respectively.

(*c*)   If DER(e,H) is used in an expression, then

$$[a(e+h)^3 + b(e+h)^2 + c(e+h) + d] - [ae^3 + be^2 + ce + d]$$

is calculated.

Notice that using DER causes POLY, another arithmetic function, to be invoked as poly is used in describing DER. Also observe that POLY has argument T and constants A, B, C, and D.

Arithmetic statement descriptions must follow any specification instructions and precede the first executable statement.

1.4   Control

The flow of a program is normally sequential. That is, suppose I is the statement being executed. Under sequential control the next statement to be executed is I + 1, i.e., the one that follows I. Invariably, if the programmer wishes to alter this normal flow, some branching techniques must be provided.

On occasion a program must be able to make decisions. According to the decision made, an appropriate transfer of control must be chosen; for example, suppose y is to be computed using the following formulas:

(i) $y = x^2 - 2x + 2$ whenever $x \leqslant 5$.
(ii) $y = x^2 - 20x - 5$ whenever $x > 5$.

In order to compute y, one must know whether $x \leqslant 5$ is true or $x > 5$ is true. Hence, a decision must be made. Once a decision has been made, the program must switch control (branch) to that particular area of the program which computes y using either (i) or (ii).

1.4.1 IF Statement

The IF statement or, more specifically, the Arithmetic IF, is the FORTRAN IV workhorse for decision making. The IF statement transfers control based on the outcome of an arithmetical comparison.

The form of the IF statement is:

$$\text{IF (exp) } N_1, N_2, N_3$$

where

exp is any valid FORTRAN IV arithmetical expression
N_1, N_2, N_3 are three statement numbers, not necessarily distinct.

If exp is negative, program control transfers to N_1, the first branch, and if exp is zero, program control transfers to N_2, the second branch. If exp is positive, program control transfers to N_3, the third and last branch point in the IF statement.

For example, the statement

IF (B*B−4.*A*C) 10,13,13

would transfer control to the statement number 10 if $B^2-4AC<0$ and would transfer control to statement number 13 if either $B^2-4AC = 0$ or $B^2-4AC>0$. Although the exp is evaluated, the value is not retained anywhere for the programmer to use.

Example

Let y be given by

(1) $y = x^2 + 3x + 2$ if $x \leqslant 5$
(2) $y = x^2 + 20x - 5$ if $x > 5$.

This might be coded as

IF(X−5.) 10, 10, 28
10Y = X°X+3.°X+2.

—

—

—

28Y = X°X+20.°X−5.

Now, if X<5, the expression X−5. will be negative, and the first branch, 10, shall be taken where Y is evaluated according to (1). If X = 5, the expression X−5. is zero, and the second branch, 10, will be taken. Finally, if X>5, then X−5. is positive, and the third branch, statement numbered 28, will then be taken where Y is evaluated according to (2).

Assume that in the above example once the value of y has been computed, the variable y is used in a subsequent statement. For example, the program below uses the computed value of Y in the statement D = Y/2.

IF (X−5.) 10, 10, 28
10   Y = X°X+20.°X−5.
28   Y = X°X+20.°X−5.
     D = Y/2.

We find that for X>5., say 6., the IF statement sends us to 28, where Y is set equal to 6.°6.+20.°6.−5. or 36+120−5 = 151. Next, D is set equal to Y/2. or D = 75.5. However if X<5., say 4., then the IF statement sends control to statement 10 where Y is equated to 4.°4.+3.°4.+2. = 16+12+2 = 30. After statement 10 has been executed, control is passed, sequentially, to statement 28 to execute Y = X°X+20.°X−5., since this statement follows 10. Thus, it recomputes Y, storing in Y the value 4.°4.+20.°4.−5. = 16+80−5=91. What has happened? The program found the value Y to be 30 for X = 4. Next, it continued into a statement which recomputed Y to be 91 and stored the 91 in Y, erasing our previous value of 30. Normally, this is not what we should want to do! If control is sent to 10, FORTRAN IV provides a means for the program to jump over the statement 28. The "GO TO" statement is generally used in this case:

1.4.2   GO TO n

The general form of a "GO TO" statement is:

$$GO\ TO\ n$$

where n is an integer corresponding to some statement number.

The GO TO statement transfers control to statement number n.

In this way the normal sequential flow of the program is broken. Using the GO TO we now have:

```
     IF (X−5) 10, 10, 28
10   Y = X*X+3.*X+2.
     GO TO 31
28   Y = X*X+20.*X−5.
31   D = Y/2
```

Now, if X = 4., program control goes to statement 10, computes Y = 30, and jumps to statement 31 setting D = 15., thus skipping statement 28. The reader can verify that for X>5., say X = 6., the sequence is correct.

1.4.3 Pause Statement

This statement has the form

$$PAUSE$$
$$PAUSE \ N$$

where N is an unsigned integer constant with 1 through 5 digits.

After this statement, the computer waits until the operator causes the program to resume execution, restarting with the statement immediately following the PAUSE statement.

This statement may be used to provide time for the computer operator to change paper, reload cards, or other machine housekeeping chores. One use of the PAUSE statement is to allow the operator to successively run data through the program. This is done by allowing the operator all the time necessary to rebuild his data for a new pass through the computer. However this practice is increasingly being discouraged by computer centers as waiting on operator intervention wastes computer time. The local computer facilities must be investigated by the student to see if he might be able to use this statement.

Example

```
5    READ (1,3) X, Y, Z
     IF (X) 11, 10, 10
10   T = (X+Y+Z)**2
     WRITE (3,4) X, Y, Z, T
     PAUSE
     GO TO 5
11   ---------
     ---------
```

One sees that after the PAUSE statement the program will go back to 5, the READ statement. Thereby, the programmer may see his results on the printer output, alter his X or Y or Z, and reload the card reader. After the operator restarts the machine, the program will again execute for a new set of data.

1.4.4 STOP

STOP N

where N is an unsigned integer constant. This statement causes the execution of the object program to terminate. This is a convenient method of terminating program control and provides a smooth transition from one program to the program immediately following.

1.4.5 END

END is a *non-executable* statement that is used to define the physical end of the source program. This instruction causes the FORTRAN compiler to cease looking for more source cards and to assume that it now has a completed source deck for compilation purposes. This statement acts as a "bookend" to the source program and generates no object coding. It must not be confused with the STOP statement. STOP does cause coding to be generated, is executable, and allows the computer to cease operations. To reiterate, END is the last card for each FORTRAN source program and for all subprograms.

1.4.6 DO Statement

Suppose that there are 25 cards to be read, each card containing an observation X. We wish to read each X, square it, and then print the value X^2. Since there are 25 X's to be squared, and 25 X^2's to be printed, we might employ a *loop* to the problem. (The word "loop" is suggested by the circuit below.) The loop might start with the variable I having an initial value of one. Each time an X is processed we increment I by one. I is tested against the terminal value of 25 after each X is processed. If I equals 25, 25 data cards have been processed and the loop is terminated; otherwise, the process of reading, squaring, writing, incrementing I by 1, and testing must continue. In a flow chart this would look like Figure 33.

A program to accomplish this might be:

```
      I = 1
50    READ (2,10)X
      XX = X*X
```

```
        WRITE (3, 20)XX
        IF (I−25) 80, 100, 100
80      I = I+1
        GO TO 50
100     ......................
```

The above technique uses only the GO TO statement, IF statement, and a substitution statement. The loop in this example is straight forward and not complicated. More complicated situations easily arise. Loops involve considerable programmer thought and occur with amazing frequency. For such reasons, FORTRAN IV is equipped with the means of simplyfying loops and their implementation. This is accomplished with the *DO statement.*

The form of a "DO statement" is:

DO statement number L = I, J, K

where

Statement number is the number of the statement which is the *terminus* of the DO loop.

L is an integer variable called index

I, J, K are positive integer constants or variables. The last quantity K is optional. If K is missing, it is assumed to be equal to one.

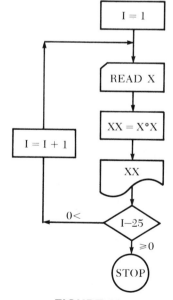

FIGURE 33

The DO statement is interpreted as follows:

    (1)   Set the integer variable L equal to the value of I.

    (2)   Perform all statements down through and including the statement number found in the DO statement.

    (3)   Increment L by K. (That is, add the value of K to L and place the sum back to L.)

    (4)   If L is less than or equal to J, proceed to step 2.

    (5)   If L is greater than J, go to the statement immediately following the statement number given in the DO statement.

The collection of statements between the DO statement itself and the terminus of the loop is called the "range" of the DO-loop. Note all DO-loops are processed at least once regardless of the relative magnitude of the variables used as initial and final values.

Example

    (*a*)   DO 25 I = 1, 10, 1

This statement sets I equal to 1. Next, all the statements through and including statement 25 are executed. Add 1 to I, getting I = 2. Test I against 10, as I is less than 10, execute again all statements through and including 25. Continue for I = 3, 4, . . . , 10. Eventually I equals 10, and when it is incremented by 1, its value is 11. Since 10 is the upper value of the DO-loop, and I exceeds this value, the program transfers control to the statement following statement 25. Note that the same results would be obtained if the DO statement were written as:

DO 25 I = 1, 10

    (*b*)   DO 100 JACK = 3, 30, 2

This statement sets JACK to the value 3. Process all the statements through and including 100. Next, the value of JACK increases by the value of K, 2. Process all the statements through and including statement 100. Eventually JACK will become 31. Since JACK = 31 exceeds 30, which is the upper value of the DO loop, the program transfers control to the statement following statement 100.

    (*c*)   Write a program to compute the sum of the first 100 integers. After the sum is computed, print the result. A program that would do this might be:

```
      ISUM = 0
      DO 5 I = 1, 100
5     ISUM = ISUM+1
      WRITE (3,4) ISUM
4     FORMAT (I4)
      STOP
      END
```

(*d*) Write a program that will read three numbers A, B, and C; compute their sum, write the result. Repeat this process for a total of N times. A program that would do this might be:

```
C     A CARD WITH C IN COLUMN ONE IS TREATED
C     AS A COMMENT BY THE COMPILER
C     AND IS NOT PROCESSED
C     READ N
C     READ A, B, C, COMPUTE
C     D = A+B+C, AND WRITE D:
C     REPEAT FOR A TOTAL OF N TIMES
      READ (1,5) N
5     FORMAT (I4)
      DO 10 IT = 1, N
      READ (1,6) A, B, C
6     FORMAT (3F8.3)
      D = A+B+C
10    WRITE (3,7) D
7     FORMAT (F10.3)
      STOP
      END
```

Restrictions in the Use of DO Loops. In general, control cannot be passed into the interior of a DO loop from outside the DO loop. Suppose we have a program containing the statements:

```
      GO TO 50
      .....................
      .....................
195   DO 81 I = 1, 108
      .....................
49    X = 0.0
50    X = X+L
      .................
      .................
51    IF (X−80.) 52, 52, 100
```

52   GO TO 49

....
....

81   N = 3*I+4
100   STOP
      END

The statement GO TO 50 outside the above DO loop is in error.
However, the statement 52, GO TO 49 is not in error since both
statements 49 and 52 are inside the DO loop.

Note that control may be passed from a statement within a DO
loop to outside the DO loop at any time. In the above example,
if X is greater than 80, control is passed to statement 100 which is
outside the DO loop.

DO loops can be entered only by sequential statement execution or by transfer control directly to the DO statement. In the
above example the DO statement is 195 DO 81 I = 1, 108. The DO
loop would be entered either by GO TO 195, or by the normal
sequential method, that is, after executing the statement immediately before statement 195.

The integer variable controlling the loop may not have its
value modified within the DO loop. Suppose we have:

DO 81 I = 1, 108

....

80   I = I+5
81   N = 3*I+4

Statement 80 is not permissible as this would modify the value of
the integer variable controlling the DO loop. To accomplish the
same task, one could write:

DO 81 I = 1, 108
J = I

....
....

80   J = J+5
81   N = 3*I+4

Note that statement 81 is valid in the examples as the variable
I is on the right side of the statement and hence is not changed
except by the DO statement itself.

DO loops may not end on a transfer-of-control statement such
as IF, GO TO, etc. The examples below indicate the necessity
for this restriction.

DO 10 I = 1, N

5

_____

....

....

10   GO TO 5

causes control to be taken over by the inside sequence 5, . . . , 10 with never any way to properly change I.

DO 20 I = 1, N

....

....

20   GO TO 50

....

....

50

_____

causes control to exit from the loop to statement 50, automatically voiding the loop on its first operation.

3   DO 10 I = 1, N

....

....

10   IF (X) 3, 3, 15

....

....

15

_____

The IF statement, by sending control to statement 3, would reset I to 1, never allowing it to complete its indexing to N. Yet there is no other way of continuing the loops indexing of I from 1 to N.

In summary, DO loops have the following restrictions:

(1) Control cannot be transferred from outside a loop to the inside.
(2) Control can only enter the DO loop at the DO statement from either sequential or transfer.
(3) The index cannot be modified anywhere inside the loop.
(4) The index is modified automatically by the loop itself.
(5) The loop cannot end on a transfer statement.

In order to bypass restrictions on the ending of a loop, FOR-

TRAN IV provides a dummy statement, the CONTINUE statement. The general form of a CONTINUE statement is:

CONTINUE

A CONTINUE statement is a coding device used mainly to sidestep restrictions imposed on the DO loop. Recall that a DO loop cannot end or terminate on an IF or on a GO TO statement. Since many DO loops would normally end with an IF statement which is illegal, the IF statement may be followed with a CONTINUE statement. The statement number of the CONTINUE statement would be the statement number found in the DO loop.

Example

```
       S = 0
       DO 100 I = 1, 1000
       READ (1,2) X
       S = S+X
       IF (S-200) 100, 100, 105
100    CONTINUE
105    WRITE (3,7)
2      FORMAT (F4.2)
7      FORMAT (F5.2)
       STOP
       END
```

This program reads X (as many as perhaps 1000) and adds each X to S. As long as $S \leq 200$, the program transfers to 100, which is the end of the DO loop. Control is sent back to the DO statement, which increments I by 1 and tests I to see if I is still less than or equal to 1000. This continues until S is greater than 100, in which case control is passed beyond the CONTINUE statement to statement number 105.

Example

Write a program to find the smallest of 50 numbers. This can be accomplished with the following program.

```
       READ (1,2) X
2      FORMAT (F4.2)
       SMLL=X
       DO 11 I=1, 49
       READ (1,2) X
       IF (X-SMLL) 10, 11, 11
10     SMLL=X
```

11 CONTINUE
    STOP
    END

In this program, the first X is read and used as a candidate for SMLL. We read 49 more X's. If any new X is smaller than SMLL, we place X into SMLL. The CONTINUE statement forms a convenient end for the DO loop. In either case, whether or not X is smaller than SMLL, control reaches 11, which is a non-executable statement. Control goes back to the DO statement resetting I to I+1. Control continues through the steps of the DO loop until I exceeds 49, at which time control passes to the statement following statement 11.

1.4.7 The Computed GO TO Statement

The form of the Computed GO TO statement is:

GO TO $(n_1, n_2, \ldots, n_m), I$

where $n_1, n_2, \ldots, n_m$ are statement numbers, not necessarily different, and I is a positive integer variable. If I is 1, control goes to the executable statement whose number is n_1. If I is 2, control passes to statement numbered n_2; if I = m, control passes to statement numbered n_m.

Example

GO TO (11, 3, 4, 12, 11, 4) JSET

If the integer JSET is equal to 1 or 5, control goes to statement 11.
If the integer JSET is equal to 2, control goes to statement 3.
If the integer JSET is equal to 3 or 6, control goes to statement 4.
If the integer JSET is equal to 4, control goes to statement 12.

In this example it is required that JSET not be 7 or greater, as only six options are provided for JSET.

Example

Suppose a factory ships four types of products. These four products, called 1, 2, 3, and 4 have prices associated with them of 2.00, 3.00, 1.75, and 4.00 dollars per item, respectively. The type of product, number of items, and the company to whom the product was shipped is encoded in a punch card. The factory wants to know at the end of each day the number and value of each type shipped and the accumulated value for all four items. A card is punched so that the item type 1, 2, 3, or 4 is punched in column 1, the number of items in the shipment in columns 2 through 7, and the name and address in the remaining 73 columns. All cards are read, values computed, sums accumulated, and results printed. The last card, a dummy card, would have a 5 punched in column 1.

A program follows that will accomplish the above calculations.

```
1       FORMAT  (I1,F6.0)
        V1 = 0
        V2 = 0
        V3 = 0
        V4 = 0
        N1 = 0
        N2 = 0
        N3 = 0
        N4 = 0
2       READ  (1,1) ITYPE, QUAN

        M = QUAN
        GO  TO  (10,20,40,100,1000) ITYPE
10      V1 = V1+QUAN*2.00
        N1 = N1+M
        GO  TO  2
20      V2 = V2+QUAN*3.00
        N2 = N2+M
        GO  TO  2
40      V3 = V3+QUAN*1.75
        N2 = N2+M
        GO  TO  2
100     V4 = V4+QUAN*4.00
        N4 = N4+M
        GO  TO  2
1000    WRITE  (3,6) N1, N2, N3, N4, V1, V2, V3, V4
6       FORMAT (4I54F6.2)
        STOP
        END
```

1.4.8 Nested DO Loops

Suppose that we want to write a program that will generate the first N numbers and will compute the value of the expression

$$\text{ISUM} = \sum_{I=1}^{N} K(I) \quad \text{where } K(I) = (I+1) + (I+2) + \ldots + (I+N)$$

as notation

$$\sum_{I=1}^{N} K(I) = K(1) + K(2) + \ldots + K(N)$$

Using the FORTRAN IV statements a first approach to the writing of a program could be:

STEP 1. A section of a program to compute K(I) for a fixed I would be

```
      DIMENSION K(100)
10    K(I) = 0
      DO 20 J = 1, N
20    K(I) = K(I)+(I+J)
```

Note that statement 10 "initializes" K to zero for accumulation purposes. In statement 20 for fixed I, J varies from 1 to N, hence computing (I+1)+(I+2)+. . .+(I+N).

STEP 2. Next we want to compute K(I) for values of I, from 1 to N. Sum these K's. Print the results.

This could be accomplished using an IF statement.

```
      DIMENSION K (100)
      READ (1,1) N
      ISUM = 0
5     I = 1
10    K (I) = 0
      DO 20 J = 1, N
20    K (I) = K (I)+I+J
      ISUM = K (I)+ISUM
      IF (I−N) 25, 30, 35
25    I = I+1
      GO TO 10
30    WRITE (3,1) ISUM
1     FORMAT (I5)
35    STOP
      END
```

A flow chart follows. (Figure 34.)

As was learned earlier, the combination of an IF statement with a substitution statement in an iteration process was replaced by a DO statement. If we apply this principle to the above problem, that is, if we substitute the DO statement for the IF statement in the iteration process for STEP 2, we get:

```
      DIMENSION K(100)
      READ (1,1) N
      ISUM = 0
5     DO 40 I = 1, N
      K (I) = 0
```

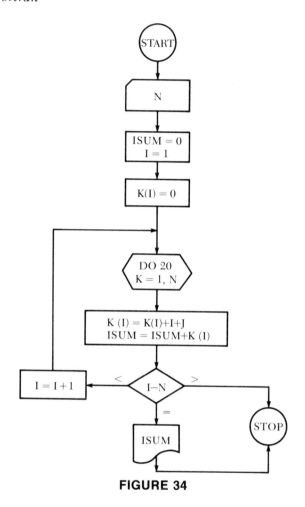

FIGURE 34

```
6    DO 20 J = 1, N
20   K (I) = K (I)+I+J
40   ISUM = ISUM+K(I)
     WRITE (3,1) ISUM
     FORMAT (I5)
     STOP
     END
```

A flow chart follows. (Figure 35.)

   Notice that statement 6 "DO 20 J = 1, N" is contained within the range of statement 5 "DO 40 I = 1, N".

   When the range of a DO loop is contained entirely within the range of another DO loop, we say the DO loops are "nested."

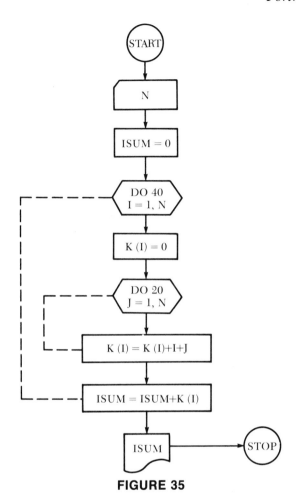

FIGURE 35

Permissible nested DO loops are:

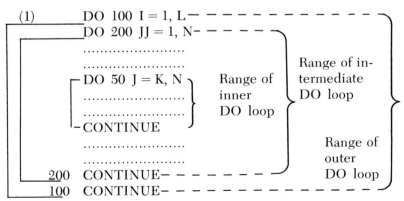

Note that in this case the inner and intermediate DO loops are contained completely within the range of the range of the outer DO loop.

(2)   DO 1000 I = 1, L
            DO 100 J = 1, N
            ....
            ....
    100   CONTINUE
            DO 200 K = 1, M
            ....
            ....
    200   CONTINUE
            DO 300 M = 1, I
    300   CONTINUE
    1000   CONTINUE

In this case several inner DO loops are contained within an outer DO loop.

(3)   DO 100 I = 1, N
            ....
            ....
            DO 100 J = 1, N
            ....
            ....
    100   CONTINUE

The inner and outer DO loops have a common terminus; however, the loops are still nested.

The next combination of DO loops is illegal.

(4)   DO 100 I = 1, M
            DO 500 J = 1, N
            ....
            ....
    100
            _____

            ....
    500   CONTINUE

In the last example, the loops are not nested because the terminus of the second DO loop is outside the range of the first DO loop.

It is important that the controlling index for any DO loop not be modified by an inner DO loop.

(5)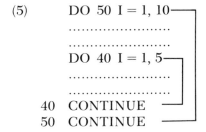
```
        DO 50 I = 1, 10
        .....................
        .....................
        DO 40 I = 1, 5
        .....................
        .....................
 40   CONTINUE
 50   CONTINUE
```

This is not permissible since the inner DO loop changes the value of I which is the controlling index for the outer DO loop.

1.4.9 Implied DO

There are specialized techniques designed for easy input and output of subscripted variables. These techniques are similar to the DO loop and are called *implied* DO loops. This variant of the DO loop appears in the data-list portion of the READ or WRITE statement.

Suppose that 10 numbers $X(1), X(2), X(3), \ldots, X(10)$ are to be read and written.

A program using a DO loop might be:

```
      DIMENSION X(10)
      DO 100 I = 1, 10
      READ (1, 21) X(I)
100   WRITE (3,21) X(I)
21    FORMAT (F8.2)
      STOP
      END
```

To do this in a more efficient way, FORTRAN IV provides special list specification statements.

The general form of the implied DO loop for the list in a READ or WRITE statement is:

(LIST, I = J, K, L)

where LIST is any valid set of variables (subscripted or nonsubscripted). I is any integer variable whose initial value is J. I is incremented by L until I reaches or exceeds K, the terminal value of I. J, K, and L are positive integer variables or constants. When L is omitted, it is understood to have value 1.

Referring to the previous example and using the implied DO loop, the program now might be:

```
      DIMENSION X(10)
      READ (1,21) (X(I), I = 1, 10)
      WRITE (3, 21) (X(I), I = 1, 10)
21    FORMAT (F8.2)
      END
```

The above program reads one item per card and therefore ten cards are read. If the FORMAT statement is rewritten as 21 FORMAT (10F8.2), then only one card is read, with all 10 items transferred with obvious savings of cards.

Note that a combination of READ and WRITE statements as above will be called an *echo check*.

Example 1

READ (1, 50) (X(I), Y(I), I = 1, 50)

This statement accomplishes the same as the alternate:

```
      DO 100 I = 1, 50
100   READ (1, 60) X(I), Y(I)
```

Remark. The alternate form cannot read more than one X and one Y per card. For this reason the FORMAT number is changed.

Example 2

WRITE (3, 45) K, (I, C(I), I = 1, 3)

This statement would write the quantities K, 1, C(1), 2, C(2), 3, C(3) according to FORMAT 45.

Example 3

READ (1, 10) N, (X(I), I = 1, N)

would read first N and then X(1), X(2), . . . , X(N). Note the value N which is read before the X(I)'s is used as the terminus of the implied DO loop.

In arrays of two or more dimensions, "nested implied DO loops" have the form:

((LIST, I = J, K, L), II = JJ, KK, LL)

where LIST is any valid set of subscripted or nonsubscripted variables, I and II are integer variables. J, L, K, JJ, KK, LL are positive integer variables or constants.

In the nested implied DO loops:

(1)   II is set to JJ
(2)   I is set to J

(3)   Data is transferred

(4)   I is incremented by L

(5)   If I ≤ terminal value of K proceed to (3)

If I > K then II is incremented by LL

(6)   If II ≤ terminal value of KK proceed to (2)

If II > KK take the next statement in the program.

Example 4

READ (1, 101) ((M(I, J), J = 1, 7), I = 1, 3)

This statement reads the same data items as the alternate coding

        DO 100 I = 1, 3
        DO 100 J = 1, 7
100   READ (1, 103) M(I, J)

That is, I is set to 1; J is varied from 1 to 7.

I is set to 2; J is varied from 1 to 7.

I is set to 3; J is varied from 1 to 7.

The format used in the READ may cause major differences in the number of data cards used and their punching of M's. FORTRAN IV allows reading of entire arrays by using the array name. For example,

DIMENSION A(25)

READ (1, 100) A

FORMAT (5F5.4)

will read 5 elements of the array per record.

Note the outer implied DO loop "controls" the inner implied DO loop. If the implied DO loops are interchanged to the form

READ (1, 100) ((M(I, J), I = 1, 3), J = 1, 7)

then the 3 × 7 matrix M is read by columns instead of by rows as in the first READ statement.

Example 5

The student council in university X is going to administer a poll to the sophomore class. This poll consists of five questions. Each question has a three-way answer, 1, 2, or 3 corresponding, respectively, to yes, no, or undecided. The answers are to be punched into a card so that question 1 is answered in column 1, question 2 in column 2, etc.

Write a program that will accept as data the answers to the poll. The program should determine the total and percentage in each category. Assume that the last card is artificial and has 9 punched in column one. This is to be used to stop reading and to initiate the output printing. This output should be printed in tabular form as a 5 × 3 matrix.

```
          DIMENSION  M(5, 3), IQ(5), IPER(3)
          DO 1 I = 1, 5
          DO 1 J = 1, 3
     1    M(I,J)  = 0
C         ZERO OUT MATRIX FOR ACCUMULATION
C         PURPOSE
     2        FORMAT (5I1)
          N = 0
C         N IS TO CONTAIN THE TOTAL STUDENT
C         SAMPLE SIZE
     3    READ (1, 2) (IQ(I), I = 1, 5)
C         IQ(1) = ANSWER 1, IQ(2) = ANSWER 2, . . . , IQ(5)
C         = ANSWER 5
          IF (IQ—9) 4, 1000, 4
C         IQ(1) = 9 MEANS LAST CARD IS READ
     4    DO 10 IROW = 1, 5
          ICOL = IQ(IROW)
C         IQ(1) = 1 MEANS RESPONSE TO BE
C         ACCUMULATED IN M(IROW, 1)
C         IQ(2) = 2 MEANS RESPONSE TO BE
C         ACCUMULATED IN M(IROW, 2)
C         IQ(3) = 3 MEANS RESPONSE TO BE
C         ACCUMULATED IN M(IROW, 3) OR
C         EQUIVALENTLY RESPONSE TO BE
C         ACCUMULATED IN M(IROW, IQ(IROW)) OR
C         M(IROW, ICOL).
          M(IROW, ICOL) = M(IROW, ICOL)+1
     10   N = N+1
C         COUNT NUMBER OF STUDENTS
          GO TO 3
C         RESULT IS PRINTED TABULARLY WITH
C         PERCENTAGES IN PARENTHESES
          DO 1010 I = 1,5
          DO 1008 J = 1, 3
          IPER(J) = M(I, J)*100/N
     1008 WRITE (3, 1050) (M(I, J), IPER(J), J = 1, 3)
     1010 CONTINUE
     1050 FORMAT(1H0, 9X, (I4, 3X, 1H(I3, 4H PC )))
          STOP
          END
```

Note the (I4, 3X, 1H(I3, 4H PC)) by being in parentheses is repeated format and is used as many times as is required by the data list. Each usage causes bb17bbb(b77bPC) to be printed.

Exercises

1. Let A be an array of DIMENSION (N,N). Define *TA* by

$$TA = A(1,1) + A(2,2) + \ldots + A(N,N)$$

Write a FORTRAN program to compute *TA*.

2. Let *A* be an array of DIMENSION (*N,N*). The elements of *A* are defined as follows:

$$A(I,J) = I \quad \text{if } I = J.$$
$$A(I,J) = -1 \quad \text{if } I > J.$$
$$A(I,J) = 1 \quad \text{if } I < J.$$

Write a FORTRAN program to output *A* for different values of *N*.

3. An array *A* of DIMENSION (*N,N*) is formed as follows:

$$A(I,J) = 1, \quad \text{for} \quad 1 \leq J \leq N, I = 1.$$
$$A(I,J) = A(I,J-1) + A(I-1,J), \quad I > 1, J > 1.$$

Write a FORTRAN program that would print the array *A* for values of *N* from 1 to 6.

4. Let *A* be an array of DIMENSION (*N,N*). Write a FORTRAN program that would exchange the elements of *A* as follows:

Replace $A(I,J)$ by $A(J,I)$ and conversely.

5. Let $A_1, A_2, \ldots, A_N$ be an array. Compute the value *AN* using the formula

$$AN = A_1^2 + A_2^2 + \ldots + A_N^2.$$

6. Let $A_1, A_2, \ldots, A_N$ and $B_1, B_2, \ldots, B_N$ be arbitrary arrays. Write a FORTRAN program to compute *ASCB* using the formula

$$ASCB = A_1 B_1 + A_2 B_2 + \ldots + A_N B_N.$$

7. Let $A_1, A_2, \ldots, A_N$ be an arbitrary array. Place this array in an array $B_1, B_2, \ldots, B_N$ as follows:

$$B(1) = A(N), \quad B(2) = A(N-1), \ldots, B(N) = A(1).$$

8.   Form an $N \times M$ array A as follows:

$$A(I,J) = \frac{(I+J)}{2} \qquad \text{if } I + J \text{ is even.}$$

$$A(I,J) = \frac{(I+J-1)}{2} \qquad \text{if } I + J \text{ is odd.}$$

9.   Form a set of data cards for example 5 on Implied DO loops. Construct the program, and produce the printed results as described.

10.   Write a program that will have as an input those integers smaller than 100 and multiples of 5.

11.   A card containing three quantities, A, B, and C, is input into a computer. If $A > 0$, then compute the expression

$$X = A + B + C;$$

if $A \leq 0$, then compute

$$X = B + C.$$

1.5   SUBPROGRAMS AND FUNCTIONS

On occasion, a programmer must subdivide a program into "subprograms." Subprograms are programs that can only be used by being "called" from another program. A subprogram may itself be called by another subprogram.

Subprograms allow the division of work into manageable portions, each of which can be written independently of the other programs. Several persons might work to solve a problem through the use of subprograms. In some cases, subprograms will save core storage by allowing multiple sets of almost identical coding to be represented by one subprogram for which the programmer can vary certain parameters.

1.5.1   Subprogram

There are two classes of subprograms, (a) subroutine subprograms and (b) function subprograms. Since subprograms are called from other programs, no subprogram can be used by itself. A subprogram requires a main program or another subprogram to invoke or call it. The program containing the necessary statements to invoke the subroutine is called a *calling program*. In the process of invoking a subprogram, the calling program provides the necessary input data to the subprogram. After the subprogram has been executed, any results are "returned" back to the calling program. Subprograms, in general, must satisfy the same rules or restrictions as programs. Subscripted variables must be dimensioned; naming conventions followed, etc.

The general form of the subroutine subprogram is

SUBROUTINE NAME (LIST)

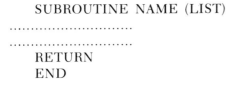

```
        RETURN
        END
```

where NAME is any permissible name and LIST is any set of valid variable names.

Example 1

```
SUBROUTINE AVG (X, Y, Z, ANS)
ANS = (X+Y+Z)/3
RETURN
END
```

Example 2

```
  SUBROUTINE POLY (A, X, VALUE)
  DIMENSION A(3)
C EQU RETURNS VALUE OF 2ND DEGREE
C POLYNOMIAL AT X
  VALUE = A(1)*X**2+A(2)*X+A(3)
  RETURN
  END
```

Example 3

```
  SUBROUTINE EQU (A, B, C, ROOT1, ROOT2)
C EQU COMPUTES ROOT OF SECOND DEGREE
C EQUATION ASSUMING B*B-4.*A*C IS POSITIVE
  ROOT1 = (-B+SQRT (B*B-4.*A*C))/ (2.*A)
  ROOT2 = (-B-SQRT (B*B-4.*A*C))/ (2.*A)
  RETURN
  END
```

Note that all examples contain the statement RETURN.

RETURN must be included in every subprogram. It causes

control to transfer back to the calling program at the next executable statement past the statement which invoked the subprogram.

To invoke or call a subroutine, it is necessary to use the statement CALL.

The general form of the call statement is

CALL NAME (LIST)

where NAME is the name of the subroutine being invoked. LIST is a set of valid variable names with the following properties:

(1) the number of items in the LIST is the same as the number of items in the SUBROUTINE statement.

(2) each item of the list in the CALL statement must be of the same mode and dimension as that item found in the corresponding position of the SUBROUTINE list. The role each variable plays in computation must be identical.

Example 1

Write a program to compute the value of N polynomials of degree 2 for N values of A using the subroutine POLY.

```
C        EACH POLYNOMIAL B(1)*X**2+B(2)*X+B(3) IS TO
C        BE EVALUATED AT EACH A
         DIMENSION B(3)
         READ (1, 1) N
1        FORMAT (I2)
         DO 20 I = 1, N
         READ (1,2) A, B(1), B(2), B(3)
2        FORMAT (4F10.2)
         CALL POLY (B, A, ANS)
20       WRITE (3,4) ANS
40       FORMAT (F15.2)
         END
```

Note. The subroutine POLY is invoked by the statement

CALL POLY (B, Y, ANS)

The following correspondences hold:

Position in Calling Sequence	Program	Subprogram
1	B	A
2	Y	X
3	ANS	VALUE

Further B and A are of the same type, i.e., real subscripted variables. Y and X are both real, as are ANS and VALUE.

Example 2

Write a program to average three sets of three numbers and average the averages.

```
  READ (1, 5) A, B, C
  CALL AVG (A, B, C, AV)
  READ (1, 5) X, Y, Z
  CALL AVG (X, Y, Z, ANS)
  READ (1, 5) T, U, V
  CALL AVG (T, U, V, Q)
  CALL AVG (AV, ANS, Q, TOT)
  WRITE (3, 7) TOT
5 FORMAT (3F10.3)
7 FORMAT (F10.2)
  END
```

Note. This program averages A, B, and C and averages X, Y, and Z; averages T, U, and V getting, respectively, the averages AV, ANS, and Q. Finally, the average of the averages is obtained resulting in TOT.

1.5.2 Functions

The purpose of a function subprogram is to return a single value from the subprogram to the calling program. The general form of a function subprogram is

FUNCTION NAME (LIST)

where NAME is any permissible variable name, and LIST is any set of valid variable names. The value returned through the NAME variable is integer or real according to the first letter of NAME. It is required that the name of the function appear on the left-hand side of a substitution statement.

Example 1–a

```
FUNCTION CIRCLE (RAD)
CIRCLE = 3.14159*RAD*RAD
RETURN
END
```

Functions are called by their name as shown in example 1–b which invokes 1–a.

Example 1–b

```
C        PROGRAM TO COMPUTE THE VOLUME OF A
C        CYLINDER WHOSE RADIUS = R AND HEIGHT = H.
         READ (1, 10) R, H
   10    FORMAT (2F5.2)
C        STATEMENT BELOW CALLS FUNCTION CIRCLE
C        TO FIND AREA OF VASE WHOSE RADIUS IS R
         VOL = CIRCLE (R)°H
         WRITE (3, 100) VOL
  100    FORMAT (11H VOLUME IS   , F10.2)
         END
```

Example 1–c

Write a program to compute the absolute value of a number using a FUNCTION subprogram.

```
         FUNCTION ABSV(X)
         IF (X) 1, 2, 2
   1     ABSV = −X
         GO TO 3
   2     ABSV = X
   3     RETURN
         END


         READ (1, 1) T
   1     FORMAT (F5.2)
         ABV = ABSV(T)
         WRITE (3, 2) T, ABV
   2     FORMAT (2F5.2)
         STOP
         END
```

1.5.3 Equivalence

Arrays use a large amount of core storage. Often the memory of a computer is not sufficient to hold at the same time several arrays as well as the program. If the logical organization of the program is such that once an array is used, it is no longer needed, then the programmer can use this storage for a new array. The easiest way of reusing this storage is with the EQUIVALENCE statement.

The EQUIVALENCE statement has the form:

EQUIVALENCE (LIST)

where LIST is any set of valid subscripted or nonsubscripted variables. The EQUIVALENCE statement will force the compiler to
assign the same storage location to all variables within the same
parentheses.

Example 1

EQUIVALENCE (XY, T, M)

The real variables XY and T share the same location as the integer
variable M. Note EQUIVALENCE does not have to be used with
arrays.

Example 2

DIMENSION X(100), A(100), KAT (100), JACK (50)
EQUIVALENCE (X(1), A(1), KAT (1), JACK (1))

Note the arrays X, A, and KAT use the same 100 words of storage,
while JACK uses only the first 50.

Example 3

DIMENSION X(50), Y(20), Z(30), C(20), DA(20)
EQUIVALENCE (X(1), Y(1)), (X(21), Z(1)), (C(1), DA(1))

The array Z covers the last 30 locations of X.

EQUIVALENCE statements for unsubscripted variables and
for subscripted variables is shown in Examples 1 and 2, respectively. Examples 3–5 indicate more sophisticated uses of the
EQUIVALENCE statement.

Example 4

DIMENSION A(3,4), B(12)
EQUIVALENCE (A(1,1), B(1))

A is two dimensional and occupies 12 locations. If one needs
to use A as if it were a singular dimension variable, introduce B,
a singular dimension vector, and cause B to be identified element
by element with A through the EQUIVALENCE statement. Since
matrices are stored as single strings with the first index varying
most rapidly, A and B look like

$$A_{11} \quad A_{21} \quad A_{31} \quad A_{12} \quad A_{22} \quad A_{32} \quad A_{13} \quad A_{23} \quad A_{33} \quad A_{14} \quad A_{24} \quad A_{34}$$
$$\updownarrow \quad \updownarrow \quad \updownarrow \quad \updownarrow \quad \updownarrow \quad \updownarrow \quad \updownarrow \quad \updownarrow \quad \updownarrow \quad \updownarrow \quad \updownarrow \quad \updownarrow$$
$$B_1 \quad B_2 \quad B_3 \quad B_4 \quad B_5 \quad B_6 \quad B_7 \quad B_8 \quad B_9 \quad B_{10} \quad B_{11} \quad B_{12}$$

The arrows indicate correspondence imposed by identifying the
elements of A with the elements of B.

Example 5

DIMENSION X(8), Y(7), Z(6)
EQUIVALENCE (X(4), Y(2), Z(6))

The relation between X, Y, and Z can be represented by the diagram below.

$$X_1 \quad X_2 \quad X_3 \quad X_4 \quad X_5 \quad X_6 \quad X_7 \quad X_8$$
$$Y_1 \quad Y_2 \quad Y_3 \quad Y_4 \quad Y_5 \quad Y_6 \quad Y_7$$
$$Z_1 \quad Z_2 \quad Z_3 \quad Z_4 \quad Z_5 \quad Z_6$$

Note: In using EQUIVALENCE, one needs to observe that impossible equivalences are not attempted.

Using the above example an additional EQUIVALENCE statement saying

EQUIVALENCE (X(5), Z(6))

is illegal.

If a programmer has written a program using variable TIME, and finds later that he, through mis-keypunching, has also introduced TINE several times, then normally all the error occurrences are re-keypunched. Using

EQUIVALENCE (TIME, TINE)

both spellings of TIME are made names for the same variable, and no other change is required.

Along the same thought, if several programmers are working in different parts of the same program, they can use their own nomenclature for their variables linking them at compilation time through EQUIVALENCE.

Programmer LA uses variables X, Y, and Z, while programmer LD uses S, O, and T. If they have the same meaning then

EQUIVALENCE (X,S), (Y,O), (Z,T)

will make the uses identical.

On occasions it is necessary to use a variable in both integer mode and later in real mode. If so, then

EQUIVALENCE (X,I)

causes X and I to be the names of the same variable. References to X will be handled in real, while I will cause the variable to be treated as integer.

1.5.4 Common

In order that storage can be shared between a calling program and a subprogram, arguments are passes in the LIST portion of the invoking statement. If there are many items in the LIST, the actual writing of these names is tedious. A more sophisticated manner to pass this information is based upon the use of the COMMON statement:

COMMON LIST

where LIST is any set of valid variable names. When a COMMON statement is included in a calling program and in the called subprogram, the variables named in the LIST refer to the same locations. Each variable is located by position within the LIST rather than by its name.

Example 1

```
     COMMON A, B, N, D
     READ (1, 10) A, N
10   FORMAT (F10.2, 14)
     B = A**N
     CALL SUBT
     WRITE (3, 20) D
20   FORMAT (F10.2)
     END



     Subroutine SUBT
     COMMON A, X, M, R
     R = SQRT (A+X**M)
     RETURN
     END
```

Remarks

The variables A, B, N, and D in the "main" program and the variables A, X, M, and R in the subroutine SUBT correspond one to one. That is, A and A, B and X, N and M, and D and R correspond, respectively. The names are arbitrary except for variable type. A good practice is to make the COMMON statements identical, as this insures correspondence as to type, number, and purpose.

Example 2

Another important use of COMMON is to save storage. Suppose that a program uses a matrix A, 10 × 50, and three subprograms also use the same storage defined within their respective subprograms. Rather than storing the same data four times (once in main and three times in subprograms), with the use of COMMON once is sufficient, saving 3 × 10 × 50 locations. We could have the following sequence of statements.

```
COMMON A(10, 50)
.............................
.............................
CALL S1(N,X)
.............................
.............................
CALL S2(N, X, Y)
.............................
.............................
CALL S3
.............................
END


SUBROUTINE S1(N, X)
COMMON A(10, 50)
.............................
.............................
RETURN
END


SUBROUTINE S2(N, X, Y)
COMMON B(10, 50)
.............................
.............................
RETURN
END


SUBROUTINE S3
COMMON C(10, 50)
.............................
.............................
RETURN
END
```

Notice that although storage in COMMON is called A, the variables A, B, and C are all naming the same storage variables since each is 10×50 and each is first in its COMMON list.

Example 3

COMMON is used by allocating from the highest memory location down items as they occur in a COMMON list. Say.

COMMON A, B, X(5), M

are variables in a main program and

COMMON T, U, Y(5), I

are variables in a subprogram S1.

When T is referenced, since T is first, control goes to the highest location for common variables which is the location also called A. Likewise when I is used, since I is the eighth item (Y has five) then the eighth location from the top of memory is used which is the same as M.

Example 4

If a main program has variables A, B, X(10), Y, and I and a subprogram uses B and I only, rather than naming all variables one may use in subprogram

COMMON D, B, DD(11), I

where D and DD are dummy variables (not used other than to keep the relative position within the list). Also names other than B and I could be used, say C and J.

COMMON and EQUIVALENCE may be used together if one keeps in mind that COMMON locates from the top of memory down. One may not extend COMMON upward, only downward. Assume we have the following statements.

DIMENSION X(5)
COMMON A, B(2), N
EQUIVALENCE (B(1), X(1))

The relationship between the storage locations of the distinct variables is:

$$
\begin{array}{ccccc}
A & B_1 & B_2 & N & \\
& \updownarrow & \updownarrow & \updownarrow & \\
X_1 & X_2 & X_3 & X_4 & X_5
\end{array}
$$

which is satisfactory as locations are being used in a downward direction from start of COMMON.

However, it is illegal to attempt to push upward the storage by using a COMMON statement. The following statement will be illegal.

DIMENSION X(5)
COMMON A, B(2), N
EQUIVALENCE (B(1),X(4))

The relationship between storage areas is as follows:

$$
\begin{array}{cccc}
A & B_1 & B_2 & N \\
\updownarrow & \updownarrow & \updownarrow \\
X_1 \quad X_2 & X_3 & X_4 & X_5
\end{array}
$$

This is impossible.

Example 5

COMMON A, B, X(5), M
COMMON T, U, V

is the same as the longer

COMMON A, B, X(5), M, T, U, V

The last remark about COMMON is that because absolute locations are known for each variable (from position in list), data transfer to and from COMMON is very fast. This is not the case with arguments transferred in a subroutine list, as the variable addresses are only transferred and calculations for finding the true effective address of a variable must be made before data transfer can be carried out.

2. FORTRAN IV

This section contains those FORTRAN IV statements which were not included in the previous section and are available in most of the present FORTRAN compilers.

2.1 EXTERNAL LIST

The general form of EXTERNAL statement is:

EXTERNAL LIST

where LIST is any set of permissible function names. The EX-

TERNAL statement allows functions to be used as arguments in subprograms.

Example 1

```
      EXTERNAL RAD1, RAD2
      READ (1, 10) X
10    FORMAT (F10.2)
      IF (X—3.) 50, 50, 100
50    CALL CIR (X, RAD1, ANS)
      GO TO 200
100   CALL CIR (X, RAD2, ANS)
200   WRITE (3, 300) X, ANS
300   FORMAT (4H   X=  , F10.2, 7H   ANS=  , F10.2)
      STOP
      END


      SUBROUTINE CIR(X, RQ, ANSW)
      ANSW = RQ(X)/10.—1.
      RETURN
      END


      FUNCTION RAD1 (X)
      RAD1 = X°X+2
      RETURN
      END


      FUNCTION RAD2 (X)
      RAD2 = X°X°X+1
      RETURN
      END
```

Remarks

This program has two functions, RAD1 and RAD2, which are used as arguments to the subroutine CIR. (See statements 50 and 100). When functions are used as arguments to subprograms, the names must appear in an EXTERNAL statement. When subroutine CIR is invoked, the dummy function name RQ is replaced by either RAD1 or RAD2, calculating either $(x^2 + 2)/10. - 1.$ or $(x^3 + 1)/10. - 1.$ depending on whether $x \leq 3$ or $x > 3$.

Example 2

We desire to construct a subprogram that will construct a table of functional values for two functions, $f(x)$ and $g(x)$, for $a \leqslant x \leqslant b$ in increments $\Delta x = (b - a)/n$. The table will appear

x	$f(x)$	$g(x)$
___	___	___
___	___	___
___	___	___
___	___	___

where the first value of x is a and the last value of x is b. We notice the arguments are a, b, n, f, and g.

```
      SUBPROGRAM TABLE (A, B, N, F, G)
      WRITE (3, 1)
1     FORMAT (25HbbbbbbbXbbbbbF(X)bbbbbG(X))
2     FORMAT (F7.2, 2F9.4)
      DELX = (B−A)/N
      X = A
      N1 = N+1
      DO 10 I = 1, N1
      FX = F(X)
      GX = G(X)
      WRITE (3,2) X, FX, GX
10    X = X+DELX
      RETURN
      END
```

A main program to compute a table for $f(x) = \sin(x)$ and $g(x) = x - \dfrac{x^3}{3!} + \dfrac{x^5}{5!}$ which is an approximation to the $\sin(x)$ might be

```
      EXTERNAL SIN, SINE
      READ (1, 1) A, B, N
1     FORMAT (2F5.2, I5)
      CALL TABLE (A, B, N, SIN, SINE)
      END
```

Let the function $f(x)$ be the library function $SIN(X)$. Let $g(x)$ be the function for which we shall write a subprogram called SINE

```
      FUNCTION SINE(X)
C     6 IS 3 FACTORIAL, 120 IS 5 FACTORIAL
      SINE = X−X**3/6.+X**5/120.
      RETURN
      END
```

If A = 0, B = 1.57079, N = 90 were used as data. This would be a table for SIN(X), SINE(X) from 0 to 90° in increments of 1°. *Angles are used in radians.*

2.2 CHANGING MODE

On occasion the natural name of a variable conflicts with the type of arithmetic to be performed, which is determined by the first character of the name. For instance, simple interest is given by the formula $i = prt$. If this is coded in FORTRAN IV as

I = P*R*T

then, I being integer, P*R*T is truncated to an integer value. If the calculation were in dollars, cents would be lost. This, of course, could be avoided by changing the name I to RI, XI, etc.

FORTRAN IV allows a variable to be declared real or integer as the case might be. The form of the statement which declares the mode of a variable is:

TYPE LIST

where TYPE is integer or real and LIST is a set of variable names. This statement causes the FORTRAN IV compiler to override the natural mode of a variable in the list and instead use the mode found in the type statement.

Example 1

INTEGER TIME, XY, SAM

All variables (TIME, XY, and SAM) are considered as integers in the entire program containing this statement.

Example 2

REAL   INT, RATE, JOY

The variables INT, RATE, and JOY are treated as real. RATE is redundant since it begins with R, but it is not illegal.

Example 3

REAL   INT
DIMENSION INT(10)

causes 10 locations, all real, to be assigned to INT.

2.3 LOGIC

We have seen that in BASIC FORTRAN decisions can be made using the arithmetic IF. FORTRAN IV provides the necessary tools to make decisions based on *logical statements.*

2.3.1 Logical Statement

A logical statement is a statement which can be considered to be *true* or *false.*

2.3.2 Truth Values

We will say that a statement that is true has a truth value .TRUE. Similarly, a statement that is false is said to have a truth value .FALSE.

2.3.3 Logical Constants

The quantities .TRUE. and .FALSE. are called "logical constants."

2.3.4 Logical Variables

Logical variables can be used in FORTRAN IV. These variables can only assume the values .TRUE. or .FALSE..

2.3.5 Declaration Statement

Logical variables must be declared by a "logical type declaration." The form of a logical type declaration is

LOGICAL List

where List is any permissible list of variable names.

Example

LOGICAL CAT, SOFT, X, Z

2.3.6 Input/Output of Logical Variables

To input/output logical variables, a special FORMAT is provided by FORTRAN IV.

The form of a logical FORMAT is

Lw

where w stands for the length of the field.

In input the first letter of the field must be a T if the variable has a truth value .TRUE.. Also the first letter of the field must be F if the variable has a truth value .FALSE.. For example:

```
   LOGICAL TRAY
   READ (1,5) TRAY
5  FORMAT (L5)
```

inputs a logical variable TRAY that has a true value .TRUE..

2.3.7 Logical Operations

Logical statements can be operated on by certain logical operations. These operations are: .AND., .OR., .NOT..

.AND. is called conjunction; .OR. is called disjunction and .NOT. is called negation.

Example

(1) Let A be the statement "Today is Monday," let B be the statement "It is raining." The statement A and B is: "Today is Monday and it is raining." A and B is also written A $\wedge$ B.

(2) Let A be the statement "The book is red," and let B be the statement "May is a beautiful month." The statement A or B is: "The book is red or May is a beautiful month." A or B is also written A $\vee$ B.

(3) Let A be the statement "Peter is ill." The statement not A is: "not Peter is ill." Not A is also written $\sim$A.

2.3.8 Logic Tables

The operations "and," "or," and "not" satisfy the rules given in the following tables.

and	T	F
T	T	F
F	T	F

or	T	F
T	T	T
F	T	F

not T = F

not F = T

where T and F stand for truth values .TRUE. and .FALSE., respectively.

Example

(1) (T $\wedge$ F) $\vee$ T has a truth value .TRUE..
(2) (T $\vee$ F) $\vee$ F has a truth value .TRUE..
(3) (F $\wedge$ T) $\vee$ F has a truth value .FALSE..

2.3.9 Relational Operators

The relational operators with their mathematical meanings are:

Operator	*Meaning*	*Math. Symbol*
.EQ.	Equal to	$=$
.NE.	Not equal to	$\neq$
.GT.	Greater than	$>$
.GE.	Greater than or equal to	$\geq$
.LT.	Less than	$<$
.LE.	Less than or equal to	$\leq$

Observe that the relational operators must be *preceded and followed by a period.*

Relational operators can only be used with arithmetic expressions which are of integer or real type.

Example

(*a*)   If X = 5.3 and Y = 6.4, we have X .GE. Y is a valid expression and has a truth value .FALSE..

(*b*)   Let CAT be a logical variable.

X .LE. CAT

is an invalid expression since CAT has been defined to be a logical variable.

2.3.10 Logical Substitution Statement

The substitution statement for logical expressions has the form

A = B

where A is a logical variable and B is any logical statement. The variable A is assigned the truth value of the statement B.

Example

Let A be a logical variable and let X = 5.65 and Y = 7.8. The statement

A = X .GE. Y

assigns to A the value .FALSE..

The statement

A = X .LT. Y

assigns to A the value .TRUE..

In order that expressions containing arithmetic and logical operations be meaningful, an order of preference between operations is assumed. We have the following hierarchy:

$**, *, /, +, -$	Arithmetic operations
.EQ., .NE., .GT., .GE., .LT., .LE.	Relational operators
.NOT., .AND., .OR.	Logical operations

where arithmetic operations are first and logical operations last. The reader is encouraged to use parentheses in case of doubt.

Example

The statement

ASK .LE. ROW .OR. LINE .GT. SAT

is executed in the way the parentheses are used

(ASK .LE. ROW) .OR. (LINE .GT. SAT)

Example

$A - B + C$ .LE. $A*B*X - 4$

is interpreted as

$(A - B + C)$ .LE. $(A*B*X - 4)$

2.3.11   Logical IF

The logical IF uses logical statements for transfer of control instead of arithmetic statements.

The general form of the logical IF is:

IF (exp) N

where exp. is any valid logic expression and N is any valid FORTRAN statement.

The logical IF works as follows:

(1)   Exp is evaluated.
(2)   Control is true to statement N if the truth value of exp is .TRUE.
(3)   Otherwise control is transferred to the statement following the logical IF.

Example

Let $X = 5.4$ and $Y = 3.2$. The statement

   IF(X .GE. Y) GO TO 20
2   $Z = X - Y$

transfers control to statement 2 since X .GE. Y has a true value .FALSE.

Example

A survey is to be done to find out how many people in a city smoke, read the local paper, and watch television. The results should be given as follows:

(1) Count how many people smoke while reading the paper.
(2) How many people read the paper but do not smoke at the same time.
(3) How many people smoke while watching television.
(4) How many people do not smoke while watching television.
(5) How many people smoke.
(6) How many people read the local paper.
(7) How many people watch television.

A program to compute this could be:

```
      LOGICAL SMOKE, TELEV, PAPER
      INTEGER SAP, SAT, SNP, SNT, P, T, S, NETHER
   20 PAS = 0
      TAS = 0
      NETHER = 0
      PNS = 0
      TNS = 0
      P = 0
      T = 0
      S = 0
      READ (1,30) SMOKE, TELEV, PAPER
      IF (PAPER) P = P+1
      GO TO 1
    1 IF (SMOKE) S = S+1
      GO TO 2
    2 IF (TELEV) T = T+1
      GO TO 3
    3 NETHER = NETHER+1
    4 IF (PAPER .AND. SMOKE) PAS = PAS+1
      GO TO 5
    5 IF (TELEV .AND. SMOKE) TAS = TAS+1
      GO TO 6
    6 IF (PAPER .AND. .NOT. SMOKE) PNS = PNS+1
      GO TO 7
```

```
7   IF (TELEV .AND. .NOT. SMOKE) TNS = TNS+1
    GO TO 8
8   WRITE (1,10) P, S, T, PAS, TAS, TNS, PNS, NETHER
30  FORMAT (3L1)
10  FORMAT (8I5)
    STOP
    END
```

Exercises

1. Write a FORTRAN IV program to construct a truth table for the following statement.

(*a*)   .NOT.(P.OR.Q)
(*b*)   P .AND. (.NOT.P)
(*c*)   (P.OR.Q) .OR.(.NOT.P)

2. Three quantities A, B, and C can be taken as the length of the sides of a triangle ABC if the following conditions hold:

(*i*)   Any magnitude is smaller than the sum of the other two.
(*ii*) Any magnitude is greater than the difference of the other two. Write a program that will accept as data A, B, and C and will give as output whether or not a triangle can be constructed with that data. Use the logical IF.

3. The statement "if P then Q denoted by $P \rightarrow Q$" is called a conditional statement. It is defined to be P or Q. Write a FORTRAN program to find the truth value table for the conditional statement. Call this conditional statement COND. To do this use the substitution statement.

COND = .NOT.P.OR.Q

and give to P and Q different true values. The result should be

P	Q	$P \rightarrow Q$
T	T	T
T	F	F
F	T	T
F	F	T

4. Write a program that will compute a truth table for the logical statement

A = P.OR.(.NOT.Q) .AND.(.NOT.P)

5. Write the necessary FORTRAN statements to obtain a truth table for the statement

.NOT.((P.AND.Q).OR.(.NOT.P.AND.(.NOT.Q))

2.4 COMPLEX NUMBERS

The following should be skipped by those readers not familiar with complex numbers.

Recall that a complex number is "an ordered pair (a,b) of real numbers." FORTRAN IV considered two forms of complex quantities, Constants and Variables. The general form of a constant is (x,y) where each x and y are real numbers (see definition above). Variables must be declared in a type declaration statement. The general form of the type declaration statement for complex variables is

COMPLEX List

where List is any collection of variable names.

Although a complex number is a pair, a single variable name is used to identify a complex variable.

Example

COMPLEX Z, VOLT, MART

declares that Z, VOLT and MART are COMPLEX variables.

To store complex constants and variables FORTRAN IV uses two words of memory.

2.4.1 Input, Output of COMPLEX Numbers

The input/output of complex quantities requires two field specifications, one for each component of the complex number. The field specifications are similar to those used in the case of real quantities.

Example

```
      COMPLEX ZET, RAD, PAT
      READ (1,5) ZET, RAD
      PAT = ZET−RAD
      WRITE (3,6) PAT
5     FORMAT (F8.6, F8.6, F4.5, F4.5)
```

6   FORMAT (F6.4)
    STOP
    END

The above program has input complex numbers ZET and RAD with field specification given on statement 5 and the output field specification of PAT is given on statement 6.

FORTRAN IV allows the use of arithmetic operations on complex numbers. Results with different types of numbers are as follows:

+ − * /	Integer	Real	complex
complex	complex	complex	complex

The only restriction on an arithmetic expression is for exponentiation. The exponent must be an integer.

2.5 DOUBLE PRECISION

Using real constants and variables limits the accuracy of a mathematical solution in several ways. The most obvious is a number whose representation is not complete within the capacity of the storage such as 1/3, which in decimal to several places is .3333333. A representation such as this is called *truncation* of 1/3. Since .3333333 is not equal to 1/3, we say that a truncation error has occurred. A second type of error is inherent in all arithmetic calculations. Unless a number is exact, arithmetic operations using that number will be in error. Multiple uses of that number or numbers resulting from calculations using it can have large errors in them. For example, if a number has $.1 \times 10^{-6}$ error in it, simple addition performed 1000 times can cause accumulated errors amounting to $.1 \times 10^{-3}$. If the resultant number is smaller than $.1 \times 10^{-3}$, then the percentage of error is over 100%. In subtraction, if the numbers are approximately equal, nearly all the precision of the result is lost. Similarly, if in division the divisor is nearly zero, huge amounts of error may result.

One way to minimize this error, even though it is not eliminated, is to use double precision arithmetic. In that case, the precision of a number is at least twice as large as previously. This is normally accomplished by linking two variable locations together and using the combined locations for the double precision variable or constant.

For double precision arithmetic FORTRAN IV provides the statement DOUBLE PRECISION. Its general form is

DOUBLE PRECISION list

where list is a set of variables to be treated in double precision fashion.

Example

DOUBLE PRECISION A, X(10), VALUE

Double precision constants are used by writing the constant in exponential form and replacing the E with a D or by using eight or more decimal digits in its representation.

Examples

98765.43210
98765.4D00
−17.324D−3
+17.3D+3
.02347D04

To input or output double precision variables, one must use either Fw.d format specification for use with numbers represented without exponents or Dw.d format for numbers to be represented with exponents.

The form Dw.d indicates exponential form. The entire field is to be w columns wide with d columns to the right of the decimal point. It behaves as Ew.d except that it is used for double precision numbers.

Arithmetic expressions may contain real numbers and double precision numbers. All rules for the hierarchy of operators and parentheses are the same. Any expression involving a double precision constant or variable is automatically evaluated in double precision. By using substitution statements, this double precision may be stored as integer, real, or double precision depending on the type of the variable in which the result is to be stored.

2.6 ASSIGN GO

Besides the GO TO and the computed GO statements, FORTRAN IV uses another transfer of control statement. This is the assign GO TO statement. This statement is used in conjunction with another statement, the ASSIGN statement.

The general form of the assign GO TO is

GO TO N, (M₁, M₂, . . . Nₚ)

where N is the name of an integer variable and M_1, M_2, . . . , M_p are integer constants corresponding to labels of executable statements.

The general form of the ASSIGN statement is:

ASSIGN MM TO N

where MM is an integer constant that is equal to one of M_1, M_2, . . , M_p of the assign GO TO and N is the integer variable name that is used in the assign GO TO.

Example

M = 4
ASSIGN M TO N
GO TO M,(1,3,7,4,8)

In this example control is transferred to the statement having 4 as statement label.

2.7 LABELLED COMMON

In the use of COMMON, from now on referred to as *unlabelled common,* all items in Common start from the top of memory and are stored in sequential order down. That is, the fifth item appearing in a COMMON statement is the fifth item stored in the memory of the computer. When Common lists are long and not all the items in the lists are needed by each subprogram, the process of constructing COMMON lists for each subroutine is tedious and prone to error. The technique of Labelled COMMON gives relief in this situation.

The general form for Labelled Common is

COMMON   /label₁/list₁/label₂/list₂/ . . .

where label is the main of a storage area, and list is a set of variables.

In this book the storage area associated with label "S" shall be called *Block S.*

Example

COMMON   /S/ U, V, W, Z /T/ X, Y

causes variables U, V, W, and Z to be assigned to COMMON in a block called S, while X and Y are assigned to COMMON area labelled T.

Example

COMMON   X(50), N, /A/ Y (5), D, T / / T, V
COMMON   /A/ M, NN

causes variables, X to be an array with dimension 50, N, T, and V to be stored in unlabelled COMMON. Y is an array with dimension 5. D, T, M, and NN are stored, in that order, in COMMON Block A. One sees that the pair of slashes causes items to be placed in unlabelled COMMON as does starting the naming of variables immediately after the word COMMON. Also, observe that the second COMMON card causes a continuation of COMMON Block A.

Example

Given a main program with

COMMON   A, B(3), N /D/ X(2), Y /E/ I, J
Subprogram FIRST
COMMON   X(4), M /D/ H(2), Z
Subprogram Second
COMMON   F /E/ II, JJ

The following storage assignments result for COMMON:

		MAIN	FIRST UNLABELLED	SECOND
Loc.	1	A	X_1	F
	2	B_1	X_2	
	3	B_2	X_3	
	4	B_3	X_4	
	5	N	M	

BLOCK D

		MAIN	FIRST UNLABELLED	SECOND
	6	X_1	H_1	
	7	X_2	H_2	
	8	Y	Z	

BLOCK E

9	I		II
10	J		JJ

where in unlabelled COMMON $A \leftrightarrow X_1$, $B_1 \leftrightarrow X_2$, ... $N \leftrightarrow M$ (Also $X_1 \leftrightarrow F$ hence $A \leftrightarrow F$); in BLOCK D, $X_1 \leftrightarrow H_1$, $X_2 \leftrightarrow H_2$ and $Y \leftrightarrow Z$ and in Block E I $\leftrightarrow$ II and J $\leftrightarrow$ JJ. (The symbol $\leftrightarrow$ means, here, to share the same storage area.)

2.8 DATA STATEMENT

For the purpose of assigning *initial* values to variables (subscripted or unsubscripted), FORTRAN IV uses a DATA statement. The general form of the DATA statement is:

DATA list $/d_1, d_2, \ldots, d_n/$

where list is a set of variables, and $d_1, d_2, \ldots, d_n$ are the values of the corresponding variables in the list part of the statement.

Note. It is possible to have more than one list on a DATA statement. Each list must be used together with a sequence of d values.

Example

DATA A, X, M /3.141,−5.4, 3/

This statement assigns the following values to the variables:

$A = 3.141$, $X = −5.4$, $M = 3$.

Example

LOGIC A
DIMENSION B(20)
DATA A, B(19) /.False., 5.4/

Example

LOGIC BOOL, MORG
DIMENSION X(25), Y(10)
DATA BOOL /.TRUE./, X(18) /.43/, MORG, Y(4) /.FALSE. 3.2/

These statements assign the values:

Bool = .TRUE., X(18) = .43, MORG = .FALSE., Y(4) = 3.2.

Note. A "," is used after "/" to indicate the beginning of a list. If several variables on the list have the same initial value d, then the symbol p*d is used to indicate that p consecutive elements on the list have the initial value d.

Example

DIMENSION C(14), X, Y
DATA C, X, Y /7*2.5, 7*3.1, 2.6, −1.4/

This statement assigns the values:

$C(1) = C(2) = C(3) = \ldots = C(7) = 2.5,$
$C(8) = (9) = \ldots = C(14) = 3.1,$
$X = 2.6, Y = −1.4.$

2.9 GENERALIZED DATA

In order to facilitate the task of writing format specifications, some FORTRAN IV compilers have a *generalized data* specification. This specification may be used to input/output data in any mode, i.e., Integer, Real, Double Precision, Complex, or Logical. The specification used in the transfer of data is the specification of the corresponding variable in the input/output statement.

The general form of the generalized format specification is

Gw.d

where w is an unsigned integer constant denoting the width of the field; d is the number of significant digits.

2.9.1 Input

In the case of real double precision, and complex numbers, the d is used to position the decimal point as implied by the d in D specifications. (See 2.5 Double Precision.) For real variables Gw.d is treated as the Fw.d, Ew.d, or Dw.d specifications would be. For logical and integer variables, the d portion of Gw.d is ignored and is treated as Iw or Lw.

2.9.2 Output

For logical and integer values, the d is disregarded, and w columns are used. For real, double precision, or complex numbers, if $.1 \leq \text{number} \leq 10^d$, the number is printed as if it were Fw.d.

However, if the number is outside the above range, it will be printed using the Ew.d specification.

Comment

When this specification is used the most general of all formats are employed which prove to be the safest and most flexible of specifications.

Example

(*a*)

        READ (1,17) I, A, B,N
        FORMAT (G5, 2G 12.6, G6)

for data card

        bbb17b−314159E+01bb−3.1415bbb−17345
          ↑   ↑   ↑   ↑
        col 1 col 6   col 18   col 30

would cause I = 17, A = −3.14159, B = −3.14150 and N = −17345.

(*b*)   Given N = 50, A = 123456.7 the statements

        WRITE (3,18) N, A, A
        FORMAT (G5.2, G12.6, G12.4)

cause the output

        bbb50b123456.bbbbbbb.1234E+06

The .2 is ignored in 65.2 for N as N is integer and since $.1 < A < 10^6$ is true, but $.1 < A < 10^4$ is false, A is printed first as F like, and A is printed second as E like.

2.10   TAB SPECIFICATION

Some FORTRAN IV compilers have a FORMAT specification producing the same effect as the tab key in a typewriter. This specification is called T − FORMAT. The general form is:

Tw

where w is an unsigned integer used to indicate the position where the transfer of data is to begin.

The T specification can be used in input and output. It must be followed by the format specification of the data to be transferred. On output, print position 1 is used for printer control so Tw starts really in print position w − 1.

Example

WRITE (3,9) I, A
9 Format (T8, I5, T15, F6.2)

for I = −1234 and A = 17.34 causes bbbbbbb−1234bbb17.34 to be

                            ↑   ↑
                          col 8   col 15

output.

The same output would be formed by

WRITE (3,11) A, I
11 FORMAT (T15, F6.2, T8, I5)

as the order of appearance is immaterial when a specific starting column is identified using Tw.

2.11 ALTERNATIVE OF H FORMAT FOR LITERAL DATA

For Titling purposes the H format is very useful. However it does require one to count the number of data columns used. This column count is used in front of the H in the form wH. Instead of the wH where w is the number of columns used for the data, we may use single quotes to surround the data. This alleviates the necessity for counting the columns.

The general form for literal data within quotes is

'literal data'

where literal data may be any alphabetic, numeric, or special character. If it is necessary to use a quote within the data, use two adjacent quotes for each one to be printed.

Example

The following statements

WRITE (3,11)
11 FORMAT ('1 TODAY IS TUESDAY')

will effect a new page to be printed with the message TODAY IS TUESDAY. Next,

WRITE (3,12) NUMB
12 FORMAT ('TODAY''S MEETING NUMBER', I3)

would produce the print-out

single spacing
message: TODAY"S MEETING NUMBER 17

if the stored value of NUMB is 17.

2.12 INFORMATION STORAGE

If a program has excessive input, output, or if a program pro-
duces output which will be used later as input within the same
program, printer paper and punched cards are not convenient
enough for fast modern computer operations.

First, let us consider volumes. Reels containing 2400 feet of
magnetic tape are approximately 11″ in diameter and ½″ in width.
At an information density of 800 characters per inch, 50,000 cards
each containing 80 columns of information can be written on tape.
Much more information, perhaps five times as much, can be placed
on tape with advanced programming techniques. One reel of tape
thus can contain as much information as fifteen drawers of cards.

A second consideration in favor of magnetic tape over punched
cards is speed. To read at maximum machine speed, 50,000 cards
would take nearly one hour, even disregarding operator handling
of this volume of material. Using tape readers, less than thirty
minutes are used even on very slow tapes, and the tapes are handled
under program control, thereby saving operator and machine time.

A final consideration is cost of cards versus tapes. Fifty thousand
cards cost about $50.00; a magnetic tape costs $20.00. More impor-
tantly, as the cards must be punched to contain information, they
cannot be repunched to change their written information. A new
set of cards must be punched to change the values. A tape may be
rewritten, as it is only a matter of erasing magnetically and re-
recording the new information.

In reading or writing magnetic tapes, the programmer uses the
READ statement and the WRITE statement. There are two ways of
recording information magnetically. One may encode FORMATED
information in an external magnetic configuration, as if the device
had columns, decimal points, negative and positive signs of numbers, or other such editing qualities. On the other hand, if the tape
is to be read by the same or similar program, the procedure of
recording may be UNFORMATED where the data is directly
transferred from the computer memory to the tape without editing
and recording, as if the data were in internal computer form.

In internal form there are no negative signs, decimal points,
or other editing symbols, but, rather techniques for encoding these

information characteristics. Corresponding to the FORMATED and UNFORMATED data recording, there are two types each of READ statements and two types each of WRITE statements.

The general form of the FORMATED READ is

READ (i,n) LIST

and the form of the UNFORMATED READ is

READ (i) LIST

where i is the device number, n is the format list, and LIST is the set of variable names to be input.

Suppose that T,X,Y and Z positive numbers have been written on a tape as if

T is in column   1–4   of form ±X.X;
X   5–10   ±XX.XX;
Y   11–16   ±XX.XX;
Z   17–22   ±XX.XX;

Therefore, each tape record is 24 characters long (about .03″ long). Assume further that tape is on device number seven.

A sequence of a program to read this might be

```
      READ (7,101) T,X,Y,Z
101   FORMAT(F4.1, 3F6.2)
```

Observe that if the decimal point is omitted in the fields of T,X,Y, and Z that the same information columns allow T to be ±XX X; X,Y, and Z to be each ±XXX XX. This convention of an "implied" decimal point is the same as in FORMAT for punched cards and printed output.

However, if T,X,Y, and Z are on a tape having been recorded in unformated form then

READ (7) T,X,Y,Z

In addition to taking less space on the tape due to the more favorable numeric representation for internally stored numbers, this is much more rapidly read as each record can be input directly to memory without format considerations or other data conversions.

The WRITE statements for tape are similar to the READ statements; obviously, the WRITE statements are used only for output data. Performing the functions of writing on tape, the FORMATED WRITE and UNFORMATED WRITE are the principle tools used in recording masses of data for alter machine processing.

The general form of the FORMATED WRITE is

WRITE (i,n) LIST

and the form of the UNFORMATED WRITE is

WRITE (i) LIST

where

> i is the device number
> n is the format number
> LIST is the set of variable names to be output.

If I and J are of form ±XXX while Z is of form ±0.XXXXXXXE±YY then statements to record them might be:

    WRITE (7,102) I,J,Z
102 FORMAT (2I4,F14.7)

or

    WRITE (7) I,J,Z.

The first case is, of course, the FORMATED WRITE; the second case is the UNFORMATED WRITE.

To signal the end of data, a special message is encoded on the magnetic tape. This message, *end-of-file*, or more simply eof, is used by most processing languages as a signal to terminate data output or input.

To record this eof on magnetic tape use

END FILE n

where n is the device which is output.

As mentioned earlier, most processors can recognize eof. Unfortunately, basic FORTRAN cannot test for eof, and if accidentally read, the program may cancel. Good programming practices suggest using this whenever another person is to use your tape as data input.

An artificial eof before the true eof can be written as a dummy record containing information that only the programmer might recognize, such as 987654 for a data item. Testing for 987654 will be done before each record is processed. When 987654 is sensed, the programmer will know no more data follows. Of course, the artificial data must be chosen with the knowledge that it will never occur in real life.

To make an output tape available for input or for demounting the tape to save, it is convenient for the tape to be rewound to its original position. This is done by the REWIND statement.

The general form of the REWIND is

REWIND n

where n is the device that contains the tape to be rewound.

The REWIND n is also used to make certain that a tape is at its beginning before output starts. If it is already at the beginning, nothing happens. However, if it is not at the start point, the tape is rewound to its initial point. Good programming practice suggests that a tape always be rewound in this manner before output is placed on it.

If in processing, a tape for either output or input purposes one finds that it is desirable to reprocess a record that has just been processed, one may use the BACKSPACE command.

The general form is

BACKSPACE n

where n is the device on which the tape resides.

Suppose that an inventory tape numbered 9 has on it two types of 80 position records, *master records* and *detail records*. Master records contain the part number, the location of a part, quantity on hand, and a part description along with an 8 in column 80 of record. Detail records contain part number, customer number, quantity desired, and a 9 in column 80 of record.

Master Record

Part No.	Location	Quantity	Description		8
1–8	9–15	16–20	21	79	80

Detail Record

Part No.	Customer	Unused	Quantity	Unused		9
1–8	9–16	17–30	31–33	34	74	80

```
      DIMENSION DES(15)


      READ (9,105) ITYPE
      BACKSPACE 9
105   FORMAT (79X,I1)
      IF (ITYPE −8) 90,90,91
 90   READ  (9,106)  NOPART,LOCAT,IQUAN,(DES(I),I+1,15),
      ITYPE GO TO 92
 91   READ (9,107) NOPART, NCUST,NQUAN, ITYPE
```

92 ____

106   FORMAT (I8,°7,I5,14A4,A3,I1)
107   FORMAT (I8,I8, 14X,I3,46X,I1)

In the above program after column 80 is read to decide if type 8 (MASTER) or type 9 (Detail) is to be used, the tape is backspaced making the record again available. This time the complete input list and its appropriate format are used to reread the record assigning its values to the input variables. The reader should observe that errors would occur if the inappropriate format were used. For example, an alphabetic description in MASTER record might have the letter L in position 33. If this record were erroneously read by the detail FORMAT, this L in position 33 would be in the quantity field, causing a severe mistake.

The programmer can allow the program to have available again the m–th record previously read, by giving m multiple BACK-SPACE commands, or by putting a BACKSPACE in a loop to be executed m times. For decision purposes, for iteration control, and for reading several data types, the BACKSPACE is a convenient and sophisticated data processing technique.

Example

The meanings of the abbreviations used below are:

> acc = card account number
> acct = tape account number
> bal = balance
> rate = annual interest rate
> pay = monthly payment
> X_{int} = portion of payment which is interest.

An unformated magnetic tape file on device 9 contains about 10,000 accounts of loan customers. Each record contains the variables acct, pay, bal, and rate. The tape file is ordered in increasing order of account (acct) numbers. Assume that an ordered card file of perhaps 90 to 100 cards is to be processed against the tape file. Each card contains acc in columns 1–5 and pay for one month in columns 6–15. Write a program that will perform the following operations:

If there is a tape record that matches the card, calculate X_{int} = balance × rate/12, amt = payment − X_{int}, and bal = bal − amt. If there is no record matching the card, print "no record" and continue. Assume an 9999 acc as a sentinel for end of cards and also 9999 acct as end of tape. (See the flow chart, Figure 36.)

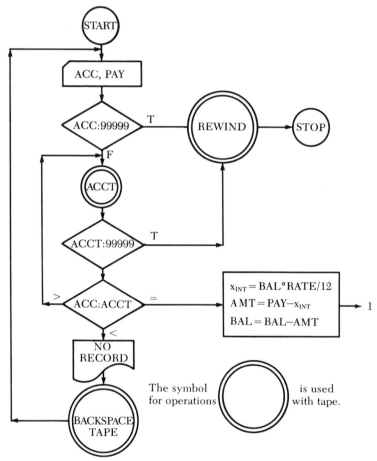

Figure 36

A program to perform the above operations is:

```
  1  READ (1,2) IACC, PAY
  2  FORMAT (I5,F10.2)
     IF (IACC−99999)3; 100, 100
  3  READ (9) ACCT, BAL, RATE
     IF (IACCT−99999)4, 100, 100
100  REWIND 9
     STOP
  4  IF (IACC−IACCT) 6, 5, 3
  5  XINT = BAL°RATE/12.
     AMT = PAY−XINT
```

```
       BAL = BAL—AMT
       GO TO 1
   6   WRITE  (3, 7) IACC
   7   FORMAT (1HO, 15HNO RECORD FOUND, I6)
       BACKSPACE 9
       GO TO 1
       END
```

Statement 5 is a calculation for interest on a monthly basis.

The two IF TESTS for 99999 are looking for the dummy end of file. When it is found on either device the tape is rewound and processing stops.

The IF statement labeled 4 allows the tape to be spaced forward if the desired account has not yet been found. If the numbers disagree processing continues; a new card and new tape record are read. If tape account exceeds card account, no tape account exists. The tape has gone perhaps one record too far, and it is backspaced so that the next card read can be followed by a tape read in looking for equal account numbers.

Chapter IV

THE BEGINNING OF THE END
(WRITING A COMPLETE PROGRAM)

In this chapter we shall discuss what is necessary for solving problems using a computer. Although we shall be using BASIC FORTRAN IV for our source coding, this material is actually independent of the particular language used. We shall see that the total job may be easily broken into smaller and more manageable steps. These will be dealt with individually so as to give ample discussion to this very important task.

Let us assume that we have been given a problem. What shall we do next? We propose that the student visualize the problem in terms of the following:

> Analysis
> Algorithm Construction (Flow chart)
> Programming
> Keypunch
> Testing
> Execution
> Documentation

1. ANALYSIS

From the problem description, the student must first decide if he understands the nature of the problem to be solved including, perhaps, specific required techniques. He must understand the form and data to be used as input and what is expected for output. He also must know if he has to solve a general problem or a particular case of a more general one.

An example of the general case might be to divide two polynomials of any order, while in the specific case divide two polynomials, where the order of the dividend is five. After the problem is recognized and understood, the student might have to do research using notes, his personal library, the university library, and consultation with colleagues and instructors. Although in most cases, research is limited to notes and consultation, it is the student's responsibility to determine the method of solution and the means to implement it.

2. ALGORITHM

Once the analysis is completed, the student must translate this analysis into an algorithm. That is, the technique of solution as implemented on a computer must be constructed. The algorithm will reflect the constraints of input, output, and specific requirements.

In addition, the algorithm must consider the computer's memory quantity, the speed of the processor, and constraints of the system as to duration of run, amount of memory used, quantity of input/output, and peripheral equipment used. Most students will find that it is wise to write a line-by-line statement matching the equivalent flow chart statement.

A flow chart can be built at the general level, which indicates overall logic, or can elaborate some or all of its parts at the "micro" level, which gives a statement-by-statement flow chart from which to code. The programmer will, in cases of extremely complicated logic, be well advised to construct a flow chart.

Sometimes the programmer should segment his algorithm into component parts, input, processing, and output. In some cases, processing will be broken into parts like initialization of variables, writing functional specifications, designing the iteration loops, and setting up program control to handle the logic. If the algorithm is well done, all later steps will benefit.

3. PROGRAMMING

Once the algorithm is designed, then it must be programmed in FORTRAN IV or another source language. In programming there are several good practices to observe. One is to name variables with names suggestive of their meaning, such as RATE, VEL, or INT. When the mode of the variable is wrong, then use as a first letter, systematically, a letter like X to make a quantity real and I to make a variable integer. For example, if INT is to be real, call it XINT, and if R is to be integer, call it IR.

Once the set of variables is named, see that storage is allocated correctly by using DIMENSION statements for arrays and vectors. Then the student must start to program the algorithmic statements in FORTRAN statements. In arithmetic statements, he insures that the signs, operators, and parentheses are as intended. On DO Loops he insures that the loop works correctly on the first, last, and some intermediate iteration values. Further, DO Loops must be constructed *nested*. When coding Control statements such as IF, GO TO, etc., then each statement label must be present somewhere.

Further, each area of the program must be accessible either through sequential flow or transfer through a control statement. On earlier arithmetic IF, care must be exercised to insure that the negative, zero, or positive result of the evaluation of the arithmetic expression sends control to the statement corresponding to the logical test one wishes to make. For example, IF(I−J) 10,11,10 sends control to 11, if I = J, and to 10 if I ≠ J.

When constructing output or input statements, the appropriate variables must be listed in the order required. Corresponding to each variable must be a FORMAT specification suitable for that variable. It is absolutely necessary that real variables be used with Fw.d or Ew.d Formats while integer variables be used only with Iw Formats. Carefulness is the key word; errors result in hasty, sloppy planning and programming.

4. KEYPUNCHING

Although some centers keypunch programmed material for students, this is rare enough that keypunching also must be learned by the student. Some students may use the program card for large keypunching amounts. However, most students use the keypunch without the program card. First, after the keypunch is on, the student presses FEED, next REG. This sequence makes the card available. By observing the column marking in the little window above the card, he can observe what column the keypunch will punch next. Using the keypunch as a typewriter, he types or punches the card from his keypunch unit. All alphabetic keys are lower case; most special characters and numeric characters are upper case. Each is marked on the key. If one must space over several columns, use the space bar as is needed. When the card is finished, press REL and the card is moved to the next station. Repeat above the sequence FEED, REG, punch, and REL. With familiarity, the student can place a switch on AUTOFEED, and after starting, the feeding portion is automatic. If an error is made in punching, FEED and REG a new card immediately at the punch station while the error card is at the READ station.

Duplicate to the column(s) in error by using the DUP key and by simultaneously watching the column indicator. At the point in question, re-keypunch the correct codes. Using these techniques, anyone can produce error free keypunching with only minimal practice.

5. TESTING

In order to test your program, set up the control cards required by your computer operating system, the FORTRAN deck(s) and the data. (See figure below.) Output should be labeled not only for your instructor, but for your testing.

The first execution will probably produce "compilation errors" diagnosed by the compiler. These grammatical errors such as spelling, punctuation, parentheses, and operations misuse may be noted by error lights, coded messages, or as is most common, by descriptive messages. On some computers, these messages are found immediately after each error; on others, they are collected and displayed at the end. Other errors which will be noted at the end of the compilation include logic and control errors. Largely, these are missing statement numbers, unnested DO loops, and control being sent to nonexecutable statements such as a FORMAT statement. The student must correct these errors by reanalyzing the logic and control errors and punching these new corrections as well as re-keypunching the grammatical errors.

Once these are punched and checked for veracity, they are inserted into the FORTRAN deck. These are resubmitted to the

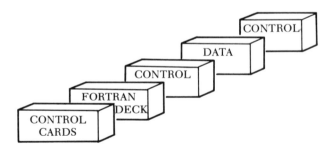

computer. The cycle of submit, find errors, change, is repeated until no compilation errors occur.

At this time, the programmer only knows that his program is consistent with the compiler rules for constructing a program. He does not know if the algorithm programmed is logically correct for his problem. That is, the program still might not produce correct results on execution. Then the program and data are resubmitted to the computer for execution.

When run often, the program has an execution error causing either wrong output results, or the program quits, called "blow up." At this stage, the programmer rechecks his calculation statements; input, output, and associated FORMAT statement; data; and control statements. He may even "desk check" his program by attempting to simulate a computer, line-by-program line. If errors can be found, those are corrected and the program resubmitted.

If all else fails, the programmer may request an output of some or all the memory before, during, or after the failure of the program execution. This bulk output is called a *memory dump* or *post mortem*.

Another good technique, which is less voluminous in output, is to place simple output statements at short intervals through the program. When executed they might print ONE, TWO . . . . This gives the programmer the knowledge of how far the program went before failing and what might be happening between certain of these outputs.

In addition to these writes, he may select to output certain variables before and after loops or sets of complicated programming. A technique of writing each statement number executed and each value being substituted in assignment statements is called *tracing*. Tracing, however, gives huge outputs of paper, is difficult to follow, and is not available on smaller machines. Using the above techniques, the programmer will find his own style of removing compiler and execution errors. This art, called *debugging*, will improve rapidly and dramatically as the programmer writes more challenging problems and larger quantities of programs.

6. EXECUTION

If the program is only to be used several times, this section will not be applicable as the testing process above will include the necessary executions. However, if the program is to be executed

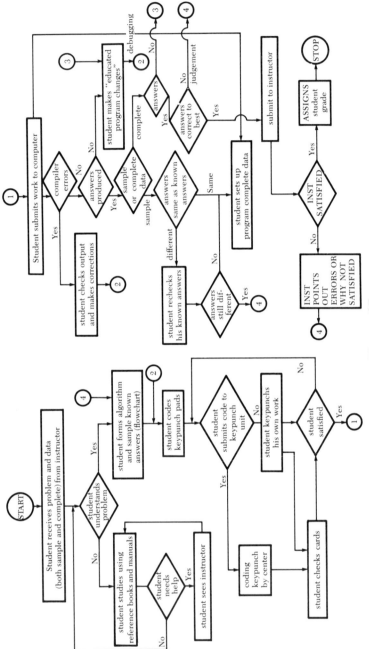

Figure 37

many times, the student will have to make the object program available to the users.

Either the object deck is punched or the object program is catalogued to the computer library. In either case, compilation time is eliminated and only the time needed to load and process the object program is used. This may decrease the execution time of a program by 80% or more. The student should check with his computer center for the actual technique and implementation method to be used.

7. DOCUMENTATION

Again, if the program is used only several times, the documentation is not essential (unless the instructor requires it, as is usual). However, most programs find either expanded usage or change requirements after once used. Nothing is as stale as an old program.

To facilitate program changes and easy use of the program, documentation is necessary. The simplest documentation is a program listing. Next, documentation will include input specification, output description, deck set up, error messages and probable cause, and machine constraints such as memory requirements, length of program execution time, and devices used.

A general flow chart explaining program logic is a good idea, because a flow chart for difficult and logically complex coding is necessary if other reprogramming is ever required. In some cases, the program and its use are explained through discussions, memos, and demonstrations.

Procedures for information flow, data transfer, and their associated control are instituted. The exact amount and types of documentation are either standard within an institution or are evolutionary in growth as custom and demand require. Each student must inquire of his computer center and instructors what is required of him for documentation. The reader is recommended to study carefully the flow-chart shown in Figure 37.

Part II

Chapter V

NUMERICAL ALGORITHMS

This chapter contains a collection of algorithms to solve arith-
metically oriented problems. We use them to illustrate how subroutines are used in a main program. The reader will also appre-
ciate how useful these subroutines are when they can be used in
more than one problem.

1. EUCLID'S ALGORITHM

Write a program that will obtain the greatest common divisor
of two integers.

Analysis

Recall that the greatest common divisor (gcd) of two integers
A and B is a number D such that D divides A, D divides B, and
no integer larger than D divides both A and B. For example,
the gcd of 25 and 30 is 5.

Let A and B be two integers; $A \geq B$. Assume $B \neq 0$. The Euclid's
algorithm proceeds as follows: Divide A by B, obtaining a quotient
Q and a remainder R. This can be expressed as follows:

$$A = BQ + R, \quad 0 \leq R < |B|. \tag{1}$$

If $R = 0$ the algorithm stops. The greatest common divisor is B;
otherwise, we divide B by R, obtaining a quotient Q_1 and a remainder R_1. As before, this can be expressed as follows:

$$B = RQ_1 + R_1, \quad 0 \leq R_1 < R \tag{2}$$

If $R_1 = 0$, the algorithm stops. The greatest common divisor is R.
Otherwise, proceed as before. We obtain

$$R = R_1 Q_2 + R_2, \quad 0 \leq R_2 < R_1 \tag{3}$$

This procedure will stop since we have a decreasing sequence of positive integers B, R_1, R_2, ... R_n eventually one will be zero. The remainder used in obtaining the zero remainder is the greatest common divisor of A and B. Note that Euclid's Algorithm is based on the arithmetic property that if a number divides M and N, it also divides $M + N$.

We are going to use Euclid's Algorithm to illustrate the use of integer division. In the integer division of A by B, the remainder is discarded. For example: If 5 is integer-divided by 4, we get 1 as a quotient. If we divide 6 by 7 we get 0 as a quotient. We shall use integer division to obtain the remainders used in formulas (1), (2), and (3).

We have the following algorithm.

   (1)   Take two integers M and N
   (2)   Set IA = largest of |M| and |N|
   (3)   Set IB = smaller of |M| and |N|
   (4)   If IB = 0, stop since there are not divisors of zero
   (5)   Divide IA by IB getting IQ
   (6)   Obtain IR using IR = IA−IQ°IB
   (7)   Compare IR with 0
   (8)   If IR = 0 proceed to step (10)
   (9)   If IR $\neq$ 0 place IB in IA and IR in IB and proceed to step (5).
 (10)   IB is the highest common factor of M and N.

A computer output of this program is:

```
C                EUCLID'S ALGORITHM
C
C     TO FIND IGCD THE GREATEST COMMON
C     DIVISOR OF TWO INTEGERS M AND N
C
      WRITE (3,6000)
 6000 FORMAT (1H1)
    1 READ (1,11) M,N
      IF(M) 100,9,9
   11 FORMAT (2I6)
    9 IF(M−N) 10,10,20
C
C     MAKE IDD THE LARGER OF M AND N THE
C     DIVIDEND
```

```
C     MAKE IDR THE SMALLER OF M AND N THE
C     DIVISOR
   10 IDD = N
      IDR = M
      GO TO 25
   20 IDD = M
      IDR = N
C
C     IF IR = 0 THEN IGCD IS IDR
```

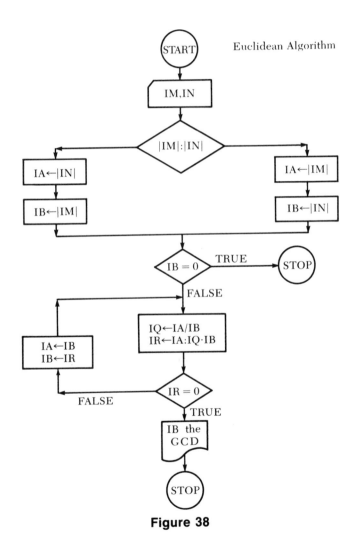

Figure 38

```
C     IF IR IS NOT 0 THEN MOVE DIVISOR TO
C     DIVIDEND
C     MOVE REMAINDER TO DIVISOR AND CALCULATE
C     AGAIN IR
C
C
C     FIND IR THE REMAINDER UPON DIVIDING IDD
C     BY IDR
C
   25  IR = IDD−IDD/IDR*IDR
       IF(IR) 70,80,70
   70  IDD = IDR
       IDR = IR
       GO TO 25
   80  IGCD = IDR
       WRITE(3,90) M,N,IGCD
       GO TO 1
   90  FORMAT(///,'  THE GREATEST COM'
    1  'MON DIVISOR OF ',I4', AND',I4,
    2  '   IS  ',I4)
  100  STOP
       END
```

```
THE GREATEST COMMON DIVISOR OF   100, AND 350 IS   50
THE GREATEST COMMON DIVISOR OF   720, AND 820 IS  20
THE GREATEST COMMON DIVISOR OF  1200, AND 400 IS 400
THE GREATEST COMMON DIVISOR OF    17, AND   17 IS  17
THE GREATEST COMMON DIVISOR OF   170, AND  11 IS    1
```

Exercise

Using the above program, find the greatest common divisor of:

(a) 100 and 350
(b) 720 and 820
(c) 17 and 25

If the greatest common divisor is one, modify the program so it will give the sentence "M AND N ARE RELATIVELY PRIME" (regardless of what M and N might be).

On occasion the digits of a given number must be sorted, one after another, as a string of numbers. The next problem illustrates one algorithm to accomplish this.

2. SELECT THE DIGITS

Given an n digit integer, $N = a_1, a_2, a_3, \ldots a_n$, find a procedure that will write the number N as the sequence $a_1, a_2, a_3, \ldots, a_n$. Example – the integer 537 becomes 5, 3, 7.

Analysis

For efficiency reasons (saving storage), the procedure will select the digits from left to right. Integer division is used in determining the digits. The number 537 has 3 digits. To retrieve the digit 5, integer divide 537 by 10^{3-1} giving a quotient 5 and a remainder 37. Integer divide 37 by 10^{2-1} (since 37 has 2 digits) giving a quotient of 3 and a remainder 7. Thus 537 is decomposed into 5, 3, and 7. This example suggests the following procedure:

(1) Get N and n (n is the number of digits in A)
(2) $I \leftarrow 1$
(3) $R \leftarrow N$
(4) Integer divide R by 10^{n-I} getting a quotient q and a remainder r.
(5) $a_I \leftarrow q$
(6) Compare I with $n - 1$
(7) If I is less than $n - 1$ proceed to step (9)
(8) If I is greater than or equal to $n - 1$ proceed to step (10)
(9) $R \leftarrow r$, $I \leftarrow I + 1$ and proceed to step (4)
(10) $a_n \leftarrow r$ and process stops.

This analysis suggests the flow chart on Figure 39. Next, we write this algorithm as a subroutine called DIGIT. In order to show how this subroutine is used, we have included a main program that calls the subroutine DIGIT.

```
      SUBROUTINE DIGIT(A,L,NUM, LUPPER)
      DIMENSION A(1)
      INTEGER A
C
C     SUBROUTINE DIGIT TAKES AS INPUT THE
C     NUMBER NUM AND AN INTEGER L AND
C     PRODUCE DIGITS STORED IN A(L),A(L+1),A(L+2),
C     ...,A(LUPPER) WHERE LUPPER IS THE LOCATION
C     IN A WHERE DIGITS END THE METHOD USED
C     IS TO TAKE THE HIGHEST POWER OF 10 LESS
C     THAN OR EQUAL TO NUM, DIVIDE NUM BY 10
C     TO THAT POWER, SAVE QUOTIENT DIGIT IN A(L),
```

```
C     SUBTRACT 10 TO THAT POWER TIMES THAT
C     DIGIT FROM NUM AND DIVIDE BY THE NEXT
C     HIGHEST POWER OF 10, CONTINUING TO SAVE
C     THE DIGITS OF REPRESENTATION, ETC.
C
C     NUM = 175
C     HIGHEST POWER USED IS 2 THAT IS 10**2 LESS
C     THAN OR EQUAL TO NUM 175
C     DIVIDING NUM BY 10**2 WE GET FIRST DIGIT 1
C     SUBTRACTING DIGIT 1 TIMES SAME POWER OF
C     10 AS USED BEFORE FROM NUM GIVES
```

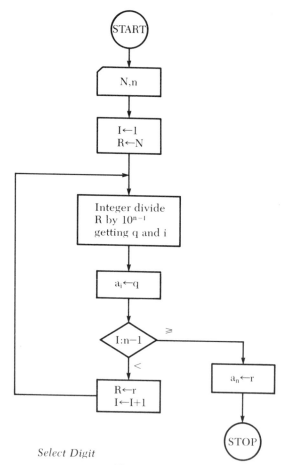

Select Digit

Figure 39

```
C     175-1*10**2 = 75
C     DIVIDING RESULT 75 BY NEXT HIGHEST POWER
C     OF 10 GIVES 75/10**1 = 7, NEXT DIGIT FORMING
C     NUM = 175-1*10**2-7*10**1 = 5/10**0 GIVES LAST
C     DIGIT 5 DIGITS 1,7,5 ARE STORED IN
C     A(L),A(L+1),A(L+2) NOTE LUPPER IS L+2
C
C
         DO 100 K = 2,10
   45    NO = NUM/10**(K-1)
   48    IF (NO) 50,50,100
   50    KDEG = K-2
C
C     KDEG EQUALS HIGHEST POWER SUCH THAT
C     10**KDEG LESS THAN OR EQUAL NUM
         GO TO 60
  100    CONTINUE
C     L IS BEGINNING LOCATION IN A
C     LUPPER IS ENDING LOCATION IN A
C
   60    MM = L
         IF (KDEG) 80,80,90
C
C     ONE DIGIT NUM STORED IN A(L), NOTE LUPPER
C     IS ALSO L
C
   80    A(L) = NUM
         LUPPER = L
         GO TO 250
C
C     FIRST DIGIT IN A(L)
C
   90    A(L) = NUM/10**KDEG
         LUPPER = L+KDEG
         LUPP = LUPPER-1
         DO 200 J = L,LUPP
         M = NUM
C
C     MM+1 IS THE CURRENT DIGIT BEING SELECTED
C     HENCE IS TO BE STORED IN A(MM+1)
C
         DO 150 I = L,MM
```

```
C
C     ONE MUST SUBTRACT FROM NUM ALL DIGITS
C     A(J) TIMES THE APPROPRIATE POWER OF 10
C
  150   M = M−A(I)°10°°(KDEG+L−I)
C
C     LAST DIGIT OR NOT IF SO GO TO 170
C     OTHERWISE GO TO 160
C
        IF(MM+1−LUPPER) 160,170,160
  160   A(MJ+1) = M/10°°(KDEG+L−MM−1)
        GO TO 200
C
C     INCREMENT MM TO FIND NEXT DIGIT A(MM+1)
C
  170   A(MM+1) = M
  200   MM = MM+1
  250   RETURN
        END
C
C         ISOLATE DIGITS
C         TO DEMONSTRATE THE USE OF DIGIT SUB
C         ALGORITHM
C
        DIMENSION I(25)
C
C     FIND THE N TH DIGIT FOR 5 DIFFERENT N
C
        DIMENSION N(5)
        N(1) = 12345
        N(2) = 987123
        N(3) = 6
        N(4) = 987654321
        N(5) = 55556622
        DO 100 J = 1,5
C
C     SUBROUTINE DIGIT SELECTS THE DIGITS N(J)
C     AND PUTS THEM INTO VECTOR I STARTING AT
C     LOCATION 4 AND CONTINUING FOR A LENGTH
C     OF L
C
        CALL DIGIT(I,4,N(J),L)
        WRITE (3,10) (I(K),K = 4,L)
```

```
100   CONTINUE
 10   FORMAT (15I2)
      END
```

3. SOLVING AN ARITHMETIC PROBLEM

Next, we show how the subroutine "DIGIT" can be used to solve an arithmetic problem.

Find a number N such that when 1 is subtracted from its square, a number of four digits is obtained with the first two digits being equal and the last two digits being equal. That is $N^2 - 1 = aabb$.

Analysis

The numbers having this property must be between 32 and 100, since $31^2 - 1 = 960$, $32^2 - 1 = 1023$, and $100^2 - 1 = 9999$. Hence, the algorithm should obtain solutions for all N satisfying $32 \le N \le 100$. To check whether a number $N \le 100$ is a solution, we must:

(1) Square $N = 32$.
(2) Subtract 1 from N^2 obtaining a four-digit number $M = IJKL$.
(3) Use problem 2 to "select" the digits I, J, K, L.
(4) Compare I with J. Two cases occur, $I = J$ or $I \ne J$.
    (*a*) If $I \ne J$ proceed to step (5).
    (*b*) When $I = J$, compare K with L. Two cases occur $K = L$ or $K \ne L$.
        If $K \ne L$ proceed to step (5).
    (*c*) If $K = L$, then $M = IIKK$ and a solution is to be printed.
(5) Increase N by 1. Compare N with 100. If N is greater than 100, problem is ended, otherwise proceed to step (1).

The above analysis suggests the flow chart seen in Figure 40. A program follows that shows how integer statements and equivalence statements can be used.

A computer output of this program is:

```
C     TO FIND N SUCH THAT
C
C     N*N-1 = AABB
C     NOTE SINCE AABB IS FOUR DIGITS LONG
```

```
C      THAT N MUST BE LESS THAN OR EQUAL TO 100.
C      FOR SOME A AND B
       DIMENSION A(4)
       INTEGER A
       EQUIVALENCE (A(1),I),(A(2),J),
     1 (A(3),K),(A(4),L)
       WRITE (3,6000)
 6000  FORMAT (1H1)
       N = 1
    5  IF(N-100) 10,10,1000
   10  M = N*N-1
       CALL DIGIT(A,1,M,LENGTH)
       ISHIFT = 4-LENGTH
C
C      SINCE ALGORITHM NEEDS FOUR DIGITS
C      IN N*N-1 WE SHIFT THE DIGITS
C      ISHIFT = 4-LENGTH TO THE RIGHT AND FILL
C      THE VACATED DIGITS WITH ZERO
C
       DO 15 II = 1,LENGTH
       INEW = II+ISHIFT
   15  A(INEW) = A(II)
       IF (ISHIFT) 18,18,16
   16  DO 17 II = 1,ISHIFT
   17  A(II) = 0
   18  IF(I-J) 25,20,25
   20  IF(K-L) 25,100,25
   25  N = N+1
       GO TO 5
  100  WRITE(3,95) N,M,I,J,K,L
       GO TO 25
   95  FORMAT(/////,I4,I5,//4I2)
 1000  STOP
       END
```

```
   1    0
 0 0 0 0
```

```
  10   99
 0 0 9 9
```

```
34 1155
1 1 5 5


67 4488
4 4 8 8


100 9999
9 9 9 9


      SUBROUTINE DIGIT(A,L,NUM,LUPPER)
      DIMENSION A(1)
      INTEGER A
C
C     SUBROUTINE DIGIT TAKES AS INPUT
C     THE NUMBER NUM AND AN INTEGER L
C     AND PRODUCES DIGITS STORED IN A(L),
C     A(L+1),A(L+2), . . . ,A(LUPPER)
C     WHERE LUPPER IS THE LOCATION IN A
C     WHERE DIGITS END
C     THE METHOD USED TO TAKE THE HIGHEST
C     POWER OF 10 LESS THAN OR EQUAL TO
C     NUM, DIVIDE NUM BY 10 TO THAT POWER,
C     SAVE QUOTIENT DIGIT IN A(L), SUBTRACT
C     10 TO THAT POWER TIMES THAT DIGIT FROM
C     NUM AND DIVIDE BY THE NEXT HIGHEST
C     POWER OF 10, CONTINUING TO SAVE THE
C     DIGITS OF REPRESENTATION,
C     ETC.
C
C     NUM = 175
C     HIGHEST POWER USED IS 2 THAT IS
C     10**2 LESS THAN OR EQUAL TO NUM 175
C     SUBTRACTING DIGIT 1 TIMES SAME POWER
C     OF 10 AS USED BEFORE FROM NUM
C     DIVIDING RESULT 75 BY NEXT HIGHEST
C     POWER OF 10 GIVES 75/10**1 = 7
C     NEXT DIGIT-FORMING NUM = 175–1*10**2–
C     7*10**1 = 5/10**0  GIVES LAST DIGIT 5
C     DIGITS 1,7,5 ARE STORED IN
C     A(L),A(L+1),A(L+2)
C     NOTE LUPPER IS L+2
```

```
        DO 100 K = 2,10
   45   NO = NUM/10**(K−1)
   48   IF (NO) 50,50,100
   50   KDEG = K−2
C
C    KDEG EQUALS HIGHEST POWER SUCH
C    THAT 10**KDEG LESS THAN OR EQUAL
C    NUM
        GO TO 60
  100   CONTINUE
C    L IS BEGINNING LOCATION IN A
C    LUPPER IS ENDING LOCATION IN A
C
   60   MM = L
        IF(KDEG) 80,80,90
C
C    ONE DIGIT NUM STORED IN A(L)
C    NOTE LUPPER IS ALSO L
C
   80   A(L) = NUM
        LUPPER = L
        GO TO 250
C
C    FIRST DIGIT IN A(L)
C
   90   A(L) = NUM/10**KDEG
        LUPPER = L+KDEG
        LUPP = LUPPER−1
        DO 200 J = L,LUPP
        M = NUM
C
C    MM+1 IS THE CURRENT DIGIT BEING
C    SELECTED HENCE IS TO BE STORED IN A(MM+1)
C
        DO 150 I = L,MM
C
C    ONE MUST SUBTRACT FROM NUM ALL DIGITS
C    A(J) TIMES THE APPROPRIATE POWER OF 10
C
  150   M = M−A(I)*10**(KDEG+L−I)
C
06/04/71              DIGIT
C    LAST DIGIT OR NOT IF SO GO TO 170
```

```
C     OTHERWISE GO TO 160
C
      IF(MM+1−LUPPER) 160,170,160
  160 A(MM+1) = M/10**(KDEG+L−MM−1)
      GO TO 200
C
C     INCREMENT MM TO FIND NEXT DIGIT A(MM+1)
C
  170 A(MM+1) = M
  200 MM = MM+1
  250 RETURN
      END
```

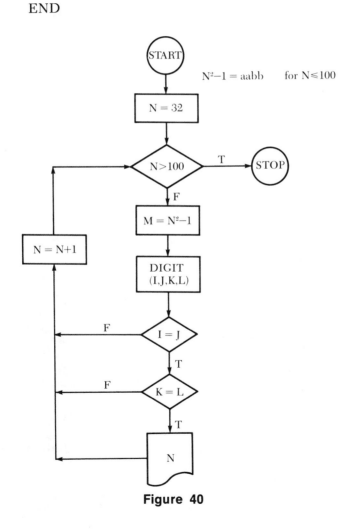

Figure 40

4. FACTORIZATION OF A NUMBER

Given an integer M, we are interested in finding all its prime factors, i.e., we are interested in obtaining a set of integers I, J, $K, \ldots, L$ and integers P, Q, $R, \ldots, S$ such that $M = I^P J^Q K^R \ldots L^S$. Example $- 1620 = 2^2 \cdot 3^4 \cdot 5^1$.

Analysis

Recall that if p is not a factor of M for all p such that $p \leqslant \sqrt{M}$, then M is prime. This follows since if p is a factor of M and $p > \sqrt{M}$ then $M = p \cdot q$ but necessarily $q < \sqrt{M}$ and hence q is not a factor.

To obtain the factor of M we shall use integer division. If integer division of two numbers yields a remainder of zero, the divisor is a factor of the dividend. The remainder, as we have done before, can be obtained by subtracting the quotient times the divisor from the dividend.

Assume that p is the first factor of M, i.e., $M = p \cdot Q$. Every factor of Q is also a factor of M. Therefore, we check to see if p is a divisor of Q. If p is a factor of Q, this yields a new quotient Q_2. This process is continued until we find a Q_i such that p is not a factor of Q_i. At this time we increase p, until either a new factor is found or p exceeds $\sqrt{M}$.

This analysis suggests the following algorithm:

(1)   Set $J = 1$ (J is the index of the factors)
(2)   Set $I = 2$ (Possible first factor)
(3)   Set $MM = M$
(4)   Divide MM by I getting a quotient IQ and remainder IR.
(5)   If I divides MM, proceed to step (6) if not, go to step (10).
(6)   Since I is a factor, save I and increase the exponent count IC by one.
(7)   Compare IQ with one.
(8)   If IQ equals one, then there are no more factors. Process is terminated.
(9)   If IQ is not equal to one, place IQ in MM and proceed to step (4).
(10)   Increase J by one.
(11)   Increase I by one.
(12)   If factors have been found, proceed to step 4.
(13)   If no factors have been found and I exceeds the $\sqrt{M}$ then M is prime and process stops.
(14)   If I does not exceed $\sqrt{M}$, proceed to step (4).

A flow chart for this algorithm is in Figure 41. Next, we in-

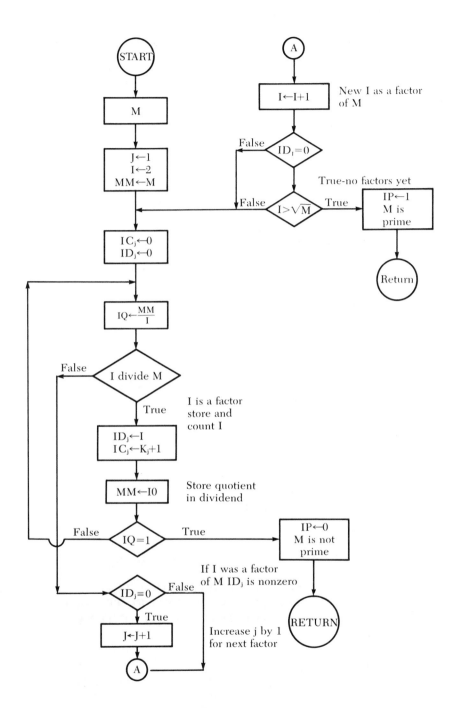

Figure 41

157

cluded a program to find the prime factors, with their corresponding exponents of arbitrary numbers. We have written this algorithm as a subroutine.

```
            SUBROUTINE  FACTOR(M,ID,IC,IP,J)
C
C     M IS TO BE FACTORED INTO PRIMES AND
C     THEIR POWERS
C     PRIMES ARE IN ID
C     POWERS ARE IN IC
C     IF IP = 1 THEN M IS PRIME
C     IF IP = 0 THEN M HAS FACTORS
C
C     J IS NUMBER OF DISTINCT FACTORS
C
            DIMENSION  ID(1),IC(1)
            J = 1
            I = 2
            MM = M
C
C     ZERO OUT IC(J) AND ID(J) FOR NEXT FACTOR
C
      3   IC(J) = 0
            ID(J) = 0
      5   IQ = MM/I
C
C     I IS A FACTOR OF M IF MM−IQ*I = 0
C
            IF(MM−IQ*I)  100,10,100
     10   ID(J) = I
            IC(J) = IC(J)+1
            MM = IQ
C
C     IF THE QUOTIENT IQ BECOMES 1 THEN A
C     FACTOR HAS BEEN FOUND AND FURTHER IT IS
C     NOT POSSIBLE TO CONTINUE TO FIND NEW
C     FACTORS
C
            IF (IQ−1)  5,200,5
C     ID(J) = 0 INDICATES THAT I WAS NOT A DIVISOR
C     AND I SHOULD BE INCREASED BY 1 BUT PLACE
C     HOLDER J LEAVE ALONE
```

```
C
C     WERE THERE ANY FACTORS FOR I ?
C     DIFFERENT FACTOR CHECK TO SEE IF LAST
C     HAD BEEN FOUND IF NOT SAME J IS STILL
C     AVAILABLE
C
  100   IF(ID(J)) 125,130,125
C
C     IF SO THE NEXT IS TO BE STORED IN IC(J+1)
C     AND POWERS IN ID(J+1)
C
  125   J = J+1
  130   I = I+1
        IF(ID(1)) 3,150,3
C
C     IF NO FACTOR HAS BEEN FOUND BY THE
C     TIME I IS GREATER THAN
C     THE SQUARE ROOT OF M THEN M IS PRIME
C
  150   IF(I–SQRT(M)) 3,3,300
  200   IP = 0
        RETURN
  300   IP = 1
        RETURN
        END


C
C     FACTOR
C
        DIMENSION ID(20),IC(20)
    5   READ (1,10) M
        WRITE (3,11) M
   10   FORMAT (I6)
   11   FORMAT ('1',I6)
        CALL FACTOR (M,ID,IC,IP,J)
        IF(IP) 30,30,40
   30   WRITE (3,31) (ID(I),IC(I),I = 1,J)
        GO TO 5
   40   WRITE (3,41) M
        GO TO 5
   31   FORMAT (I3,4X,I3)
   41   FORMAT (I7,' IS PRIME')
        END
```

Exercise

Let $a_1, a_2, \ldots a_n$ be integers. We say that b is a common multiple of $a_1, a_2, \ldots a_n$ if b is divisible by each of $a_1, a_2, \ldots a_n$. The smallest of all the positive common multiples of $a_1, a_2, \ldots a_n$ is called their least common multiple.

The least common multiple of two numbers can be found using the algorithm FACTOR. Write a Fortran program to find the least common factor of $a_1, a_2, \ldots a_n$.

5. FIND THE nTH DIGIT IN THE SEQUENCE

$$1,2,3,4,5,6,7,8,9,10,11,12,13, \ldots \tag{1}$$

obtained by placing the positive numbers one after the other.

Example

The digit that occupies the 12 position is 1. The digit that occupies the 17 position is 3.

Analysis

In trying to obtain an answer to this problem we observe that there are:

9 one-digit numbers which occupy the first nine positions in the sequence (1),
90 two digit numbers occuping the next 180 positions,
900 three digit numbers occupying the next 2700 positions,
..., etc.

This observation suggests the following formula:

$$p = 9 \cdot 1 + 9 \cdot 10 \cdot 2 + 9 \cdot 10^2 \cdot 3 + \ldots + 9 \cdot 10^{m-1} \cdot m,$$

where p is the position of the last digit in the sequence starting at 1 and terminating with 10^{m-1}.

In order to find the position of the nth digit in (1) we proceed as follows:

(1) Find m such that p is the smallest integer with the prop-

erty $p \leqslant n$. This shows that n is among the numbers with m digits.

(2) Subtract

$$p_1 = 9 \cdot 1 + 9 \cdot 10 \cdot 2 + \ldots + 9 \cdot 10^{m-2}(m-1)$$

from n. This gives the position of the nth digit among the numbers with m digits.

(3) Divide $n - p_1$ by m. This way we obtain a quotient q and a remainder r. That is

$$n - p_1 = mq + r.$$

(4) If $r = 0$ then the digit that occupies the nth position is the last digit of the qth m-digit number which is equal to $10^{m-1} + q - 1$.

(5) If $r \neq 0$, then the digit which occupies the nth position is the rth digit in the number $10^{m-1} + q$.

Example 1

Find the digit which occupies 2898th position. We compute the numbers $p = 9 + 180 + 2700 + 9 \cdot 10^3 \cdot 4 + \ldots +$ until $p \leqslant 2898$. This shows that $m = 4$. With this value of m, we obtain

$$p_1 = 9 + 180 + 2700 = 2889,$$

and $d = n - p_1 = 9$. Next we divide 9 by 4, obtaining 2 as quotient and one as remainder. Listing the four-digit numbers, we obtain

$$1000 \quad 1001 \quad 1002 \ldots.$$

one sees that the ninth position is occupied by 1. That is the first digit on the third four-digit number, which is 1002.

Example 2

Find the digit which occupies the 11th position. Compute $p = 9 \cdot 10^{1-1} \cdot 1 + 9 \cdot 10^{2-1} \cdot 2 + \ldots +$ which is the smallest $p \leqslant 11$. Then m is 2, p is 9, and $n - p$, is $11 - 9 = 2$.

2 divided by m gives a quotient of 1 and a remainder of 0. Hence, the 11th digit is last digit of $10^{m-1} + 1 - 1 = 10$ that is a zero. (This can be checked directly from the sequence.)

We have the following flow chart (Figure 42).

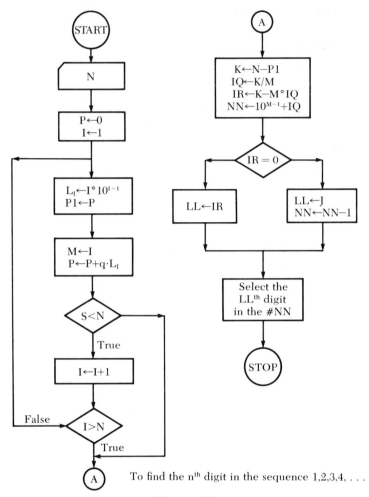

To find the nth digit in the sequence 1,2,3,4, . . .

Figure 42

A computer output of this problem is:

```
C
C      FIND THE NTH DIGIT IN
C      1 2 3 4 5 6 7 8 9 10 11 12 13 14 . . .
C
       DIMENSION  L(10),KD(10)
       INTEGER S,SS
50     S = 0
```

```
        WRITE (3,6000)
  6000  FORMAT (1H1)
        READ(1,1) M
C
C    M = 0 IS USED FOR STOP
C
        IF(M)500,500,2
    1   FORMAT(I7)
    2   WRITE(3,3)M
    3   FORMAT('1',I7)
C    FORM 1 20 300 4000 ETC IN L
C
        DO 100 I = 1,M
        L(I) = I*10**(I-1)
C
C    FORM 9 IN L1 THE # OF 1 DIGIT #S,
C    9 TIMES L(1) = 9*1 = 9 FORM 189 IN L2
C    THE NUMBER OF THREE DIGIT #S IN
C    L3, L3 = 9*L(3)+9*L(2)+L(1) OR L3 =
C    9*300+9*20+9*1 = 2889
C
        SS = S
        S = S+L(I)*9
        J = I
C
C    CONTINUE UNTIL L(N) IS BIGGER OR EQUAL TO
C    M THEN M IS A DIGIT IN THE N DIGIT
C    NUMBERS
C
        IF(S-M) 100,150,150
  100   CONTINUE
C
C    SS IS THE NUMBER OF DIGITS IN
C    THE SEQUENCE 1,2,3, . . . ,FIRST
C    NUMBER WITH I+1 DIGITS
C
C
C    K IS THE AMOUNT OF DIGITS TO BE USED IN
C    THE NUMBERS WITH I+1 DIGITS
C    IT REMAINS TO FIND THE PARTICULAR
C    NUMBER IQ
C
C
```

```
    150  K = M−SS
         IQ = K/J
         IR = K−J*IQ
         N = 10**(J−1)+IQ
         IF(IR) 190,180,190
C
C    FIND IQ THE PARTICULAR NDIGIT NUMBER
C
C
C    N IS THE PARTICULAR NUMBER WE ARE
C    LOOKING FOR AND IS 10 TO THE POWER
C    J−1+IQ IF WE ARE SEEKING J DIGIT NUMBERS
C
C    FIND THE DIGIT L OF THAT NUMBER
C    BY L = J TH DIGIT IF IR = 0 AND J = IR
C    IF IR IS NOT ZERO
C    NOTICE N MUST BE INCREASED ONE IF IR
C    IS NOT ZERO AS INTEGER DIV TAKES PLACE
C    NOTICE N MUST BE DECREASED ONE IF IR
C    IS ZERO AS INTEGER DIV TAKES PLACE
C
    180  LL = J
         N = N−1
         GO TO 200
    190  LL = IR
C
C    WE WANT THE LL TH DIGIT IN N STORED
C    IN KD AND SO WE CALL THE DIGIT
C    ALGORITHM
C
    200  CALL DIGIT(KD,1,N,LUPPER)
         WRITE(3,300) M, KD(LL)
         GO TO 50
    300  FORMAT('0 THE 'I7,' DIGIT OF 1,2, . .9,10,11, . .'
        1 'IS'I4)
    500  STOP
         END


    1000
    THE 1000 DIGIT OF 1,2, . .9,10,11, . . IS 3

1000000
    THE 1000000 DIGIT OF 1,2, . .9,10,11, . . IS 1
```

290
THE 290 DIGIT OF 1,2, . .9,10,11, . . IS 3

```
            SUBROUTINE DIGIT(A,L,NUM,LUPPER)
            DIMENSION A(1)
            INTEGER A
C
C     SUBROUTINE DIGIT TAKES AS INPUT
C     THE NUMBER NUM AND AN INTEGER L
C     AND PRODUCES DIGITS STORED IN A(L),
C     A(L+1),A(L+2), . . .,A(LUPPER)
C     WHERE LUPPER IS THE LOCATION IN A
C     WHERE DIGITS END
C     THE METHOD USED TO TAKE THE HIGHEST
C     POWER OF 10 LESS THAN OR EQUAL TO
C     NUM, DIVIDE NUM BY 10 TO THAT POWER,
C     SAVE QUOTIENT DIGIT IN A(L), SUBTRACT
C     10 TO THAT POWER TIMES THAT DIGIT FROM
C     NUM AND DIVIDE BY THE NEXT HIGHEST
C     POWER OF 10, CONTINUING TO SAVE THE
C     DIGITS OF REPRESENTATION,
C     ETC.
C
C     NUM = 175
C     HIGHEST POWER USED IS 2 THAT IS
C     10**2 LESS THAN OR EQUAL TO NUM 175
C     SUBTRACTING DIGIT 1 TIMES SAME POWER
C     OF 10 AS USED BEFORE FROM NUM
C     DIVIDING RESULT 75 BY NEXT HIGHEST
C     POWER OF 10 GIVES 75/10**1 = 7
C     NEXT DIGIT-FORMING NUM = 175-1*10**2-
C     7*10**1 = 5/10**0 GIVES LAST DIGIT 5
C     DIGITS 1,7,5 ARE STORED IN
C     A(L),A(L+1),A(L+2)
C     NOTE LUPPER IS L+2
C
C
            DO 100 K = 2,10
      45    NO = NUM/10**(K-1)
      48    IF (NO) 50,50,100
      50    KDEG = K-2
C
C     KDEG EQUALS HIGHEST POWER SUCH
```

```
C      THAT 10**KDEG LESSS THAN OR EQUAL
C      NUM
       GO TO 60
  100  CONTINUE
C    L IS BEGINNING LOCATION IN A
C    LUPPER IS ENDING LOCATION IN A
C
   60  MM = L
       IF(KDEG) 80,80,90
C    ONE DIGIT NUM STORED IN A(L)
C    NOTE LUPPER IS ALSO L
C
   80  A(L) = NUM
       LUPPER = L
       GO TO 250
C
C    FIRST DIGIT IN A(L)
C
   90  A(L) = NUM/10**KDEG
       LUPPER = L+KDEG
       LUPP = LUPPER-1
       DO 200 J = L,LUPP
       M = NUM
C
C    MM+1 IS THE CURRENT DIGIT BEING
C    SELECTED HENCE IS TO BE STORED IN
C    A(MM+1)
C
       DO 150 I = L,MM
C
C    ONE MUST SUBTRACT FROM NUM ALL DIGITS
C    A(J) TIMES THE APPROPRIATE POWER OF 10
C
  150  M = M-A(I)*10**(KDEG+L-I)
C
C    LAST DIGIT OR NOT IF SO GO TO 170
C    OTHERWISE GO TO 160
C
       IF(MM+1-LUPPER) 160,170,160
  160  A(MM+1) = M/10**(KDEG+L-MM-1)
       GO TO 200
C
C    INCREMENT MM TO FIND NEXT DIGIT A(MM+1)
```

C
    170 A(MM+1) = M
    200 MM = MM+1
    250 RETURN
         END

6. SQUARING

We observe that the square of 13 is 169 and the square of 31 is 961. Note that if we write 13 in reverse order, we form the number 31 and if we do the same with 169 we get 961. There are other two-digit numbers with this property. Do there exist three-digit numbers with the same property?

Write an algorithm to find numbers with three digits, *abc*, satisfying the conditions,

(1) $(abc)^2 = dfghkl$
(2) $(cba)^2 = lkhgfe$

Analysis

Note that *a* and *c* cannot be zero, as otherwise we would not be finding three-digit numbers. A procedure for obtaining a solution is:

(1) Set *ABC* = 101.
(2) Call SELDI to isolate the digits of *ABC* getting *A*, *B*, and *C*.
(3) Square *ABC*, obtaining *EFGHKL*.
(4) Call DIGIT to isolate the digits of $(ABC)^2$ getting *E*, *F*, *G*, *H*, *K*, and *L*.
(5) Reverse the digits of *ABC*, obtaining *CBA*.
(6) Square *CBA*.
(7) Form the six digit number *LKHGFE*.
(8) Compare $(CBA)^2$ with *LKHGFE*.
(9) If $(CBA)^2$ is not equal to *LKHGFE*, proceed to step (11).
(10) If $(CBA)^2$ equals *LKHGFE*, *ABC* is an answer.
(11) Add 1 to *ABC*.
(12) Compare *ABC* with 999.
(13) If *ABC* is greater than 999, process is terminated.
(14) If *ABC* is less than or equal to 999, call SELDI obtaining *A*, *B*, *C*.
(15) Compare *A* with 0 and *C* with 0.

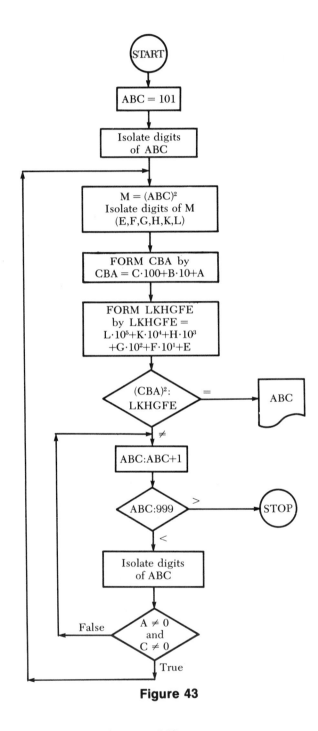

Figure 43

168

(16) If either A or C is zero, proceed to step (11).
(17) If neither A or C is zero, proceed to step (3).

From this we obtain the following flow chart (Figure 43).

Exercise

Using the above procedure and the flow chart in Figure 43, write a FORTRAN program to obtain all the numbers with three digits a, b, and c satisfying the conditions,

(1) $(abc)^2 = efghkl$
(2) $(cba)^2 = lkhgfe$

7. A CRYPTARITHMIC[1] PROBLEM

A student in a certain junior college sent to his father the following message:

$$\begin{array}{r} \text{SEND} \\ \underline{\text{MORE}} \\ \text{MONEY} \end{array}$$

If each of the letters in SEND, MORE, and MONEY represents one of the decimal digits 0, 1, . . . , 9, then write an algorithm to find the values of S, E, N, D, M, O, R, Y that makes the above message true under addition.

Analysis

This problem could be solved by assigning to each letter any one of the digits 0, 1, . . . , 9. In this way one answer could be obtained provided the hypothesis of the problem was satisfied. This certainly would be a long procedure, although very easily carried out on a computer. One can see that the number of possible trials would be $9 \times 8 \times 7 \times 6 \times 5 \times 4 \times 3 \times 2$. In this type of problem

---

[1] The word cryptarithmie appeared for the first time in 1931 in the *Sphinx*, a journal of recreative mathematics that was published from 1931 to 1939. M. Pigeolet, in a conference presented during the First International Congress of Recreative Mathematics (Bruxelles, 1939), stated that the word "Cryptarithmie" was of mysterious origin. However, he added that it was Minos (pen name for S. Vatrignant) who first used it. Minos said, "Les Crytographes, pour dissimuler les sens de leurs phrases, remplacent souvent les lettres par des chiffres. A titre des represailles, nous avons remplace dans nos operations chaque chiffre distinct par une lettre distinct."

one should try to reduce this number of trials by a logical argument. In this particular exercise we argue as follows:

Since two digits add to at most 18, the maximum carry in each column is at most one. This argument shows that M is one. Since a carry must occur in the fourth column, and either a one is carried from the third column or is not, then S must be either eight or nine. The letter O might be either zero or one. The latter is rejected since M is one and this would allow two letters to have the same value. Two possible cases arise from the third column:

(*i*) $E + 0 = N$ and no carry
        $E = N$
(*ii*) $E + 1 + 0 = N$ because of the carry
        $E + 1 = N$ or $E = N - 1$

We reject $E = N$ and we conclude that $E = N - 1$. In summary we have the following:

$M = 1$, $S = 8$ or 9, $0 = o$, $E = N - 1$, $D = 2, \ldots, 9$, $N = 2, \ldots 9$, $R = 2, \ldots, 9$, $Y = 2, \ldots, 9$.

Exercise

The reader, with the help of the above analysis, should write a program in Fortran IV so the values of S, E, N, D, M, O, R, Y might be found.

8. DAY OF WEEK AFTER FEBRUARY 28, 1900 THROUGH 1999

Find the day of the week that corresponds to any date between February 28, 1900 through December 31, 1999.

Analysis

We are assuming a starting date. This is Thursday, March 1, 1900. In order to find the weekday corresponding to March 1, 1901, one year after, we need to correct for the elapse of one year. March 1, 1901, would come one day later than it did the year before, that is, on Friday in 1901 since there are 52 weeks and one day in one year. Next, consider March 1, 1902. It would occur one day later than in 1901 or two days later than in 1900. Proceeding in this way we see that March 1, 19xx, would occur xx days later than it did in

1900. Hence $x = XX$ is a correction for the elapse of years for the same date.

However, we have perhaps not corrected for all the elapsed years. Some years (leap years) contain one extra day in February. These occur in years XX divisible by 4 such as 1904, 1908, 1912, . . . , and 1996. Hence a correction for the passage of leap years must be introduced next. The first leap year occurs in 1904. The extra day is the last day of February. Therefore, one day is added to the calculations necessary for March 1, 1904. Similarly for March 1, 1908, two days are added. In general for 19XX, XX is divided by 4 getting a quotient y' and a remainder r. If r is nonzero, then 19XX is not a leap year. However, leap years have passed since 1900 and a correction for leap years must be added. When $r \neq 0$, this correction for leap year y is y'. If r is zero then 19XX is a leap year. Since the extra day is at the end of February, y' leap years would not have passed until at least the 1st of March, 19XX. Therefore, when $r = 0$, the correction for leap years y is y' if the date is on or after March 1 and $y' - 1$ if before March 1. At this point $x + y$ is the number of weekdays that have transpired between Thursday, March 1, 1900, and weekday, March 1, 19XX.

Example

$$\begin{aligned} \text{March 1, 1908} \qquad x &= 08 \\ \underline{y' = \ 2} \\ x + y &= 10, \ r = 0 \end{aligned}$$

10 days from Thursday is Sunday. Therefore, March 1, 1908, is on Sunday.

Example

$$\begin{aligned} \text{March 1, 1933} \qquad x &= 33 \\ \underline{y' = \ 8} \\ x + y &= 41, \ r = 1 \end{aligned}$$

41 is one day short of 6 weeks hence March 1, 1933, is on Wednesday.

Next, the correction for the passage of months must be considered. April 1, 1900 occurs on Sunday since March has 4 weeks and 3 days (Sunday = Thursday + 3). May 1, 1900 follows 30 days (4 weeks and two days in April); hence it occurs on Tuesday (Thursday + 3 + 2). June 1, 1900 follows 31 days (4 weeks and 3 days in May), so it falls on Friday (Thursday + 3 + 2 + 3 = Thursday + 8

= Thursday + 1). A table for m, the correction for any of the twelve months, follows:

Month	m	Month	m
March	0	September	2
April	3	October	4
May	5	November	0
June	1	December	2
July	3	January	4
August	6	February	0

Example

$$\text{June 1, 1933} \qquad x = 33$$
$$y = 8$$
$$m = 1$$
$$42 = 7 \text{ weeks and 0 days.}$$

Therefore, June 1, 1933, is on Thursday.

Finally, all that remains is to find the correction d for days passing since the last day of the previous month. Suppose the previous month ended on weekday 5. What is the weekday on which the sixth day of this month occurs? This may be computed by adding 5 (last day of the previous month) and 6 (day we are looking for) getting 11. As we start our weekday counting on 0, we must subtract 7, getting 4 as the weekday the sixth day falls on. This example suggests that the correction for the day of the month is just the same as the day, given in the date. Call this correction d.

In order to compute the weekday on which a date occurs, a code is assigned to each day of the week. 1 is Thursday; 2 is Friday; 3 is Saturday; 4 is Sunday; 5 is Monday; 6 is Tuesday; and 0 is Wednesday.

Now putting all the corrections together, one obtains $x + y + m + d$ as the correction for any date in 19XX. If this sum is greater than 7, we divide by 7 (throwing away full weeks) and save the remainder. The remainder, which is the day of the week, corresponds to the code assignments.

A step-by-step procedure follows:

(1)   Get Month $- d - 19XX$
(2)   Set $x \leftarrow XX$
(3)   Divide XX by 4 getting y' as quotient and r as remainder.
(4)   If $r \neq 0$ then set $y \leftarrow y'$ and proceed to step (9).
(5)   If $r = 0$ determine if the date is on or after March 1.

(6) If the date is on or after March 1, then set $y \leftarrow y'$ and proceed to step (8).

(7) If the date is before March 1, then set $y \leftarrow y' - 1$ and proceed to step (8).

(8) Determine m from the table.

(9) Set correction $x + y + m + d$.

(10) Divide correction by 7 saving the remainder R, $0 \leq R \leq 6$.

(11) Day of week is determined by the code.

A flow chart appears in Figure 44.

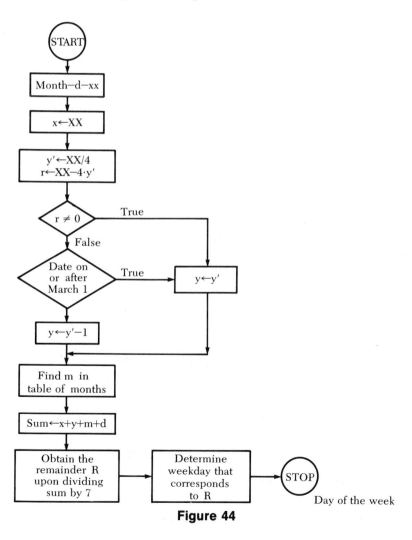

Figure 44

Exercise

Write a Fortran program to find the day of the week that corresponds to any date, between February 28, 1900, through December 31, 1999.

9. THIBAULT PROBLEM

Write a program to find all numbers with the property that each digit except zero appears just once in the number and its square (Thibault).

Analysis

Let $N = a\ b\ c\ d\ \ldots\ e\ f$ be an n-digit number written in base 10. That is,

$$N = a\ 10^{n-1} + b\ 10^{n-2} + \ldots + e\ 10 + f$$
$$= a\ (10^{n-1} - 1) + a + b\ (10^{n-2} - 1) + b + \ldots + e\ (10 - 1) + e + f$$
$$= a\ 99 \ldots 9 + b\ 99 \ldots 9 + \ldots + e\ 9 + e + f$$
$$= K\ 9 + a + b + \ldots + e + f = 9\ K + S$$

where S represents the sum of the digits of N. We have proved the following result:

Any arbitrary number can be written as the sum of two numbers, one containing 9 as a factor and the other as the sum of its digits. N must have 3 digits; its square will contain 6 digits. In this way, N and its square will contain 9 digits.

Let $S_1 = a + b + c$, $S_2 = f + g + h + k + l + m$.
Using the fact just proved we can write

$$N = k_1\ 9 + S_1, \quad N^2 = k_2\ 9 + S_2$$

and

$$N + N^2 = (k_1 + k_2)\ 9 + S_1 + S_2$$

Since N and N^2 contain all the digits from 1 to 9 then

$$S_1 + S_2 = 1 + 2 + \ldots + 9 = 45 = 5 \cdot 9$$

Therefore

$$N + N^2 = (K_1 + K_2 + 5) \cdot 9$$

We have the following procedure:

(1) Set N to 102.
(2) Select 9 locations for counting purposes.

(3) Isolate digits of N, obtaining A_1, A_2, and A_3.
(4) Square N.
(5) Isolate digits of N^2 obtaining A_4, A_5, A_6, A_7, A_8, and A_9.
(6) Place A_1, A_2, . . . , A_9 in their respective locations according to their value. (For instance if $A_3 = 5$, we put a counter in location 5.)
(7) Check locations 1 through 9 to see if any location is empty.
(8) If any one is empty, proceed to step (10).
(9) If none are empty, a solution has been obtained and proceed to step 10.
(10) Increase N by 1.
(11) Compare N with 999.
(12) If N is greater than 999, process is terminated.
(13) If N is less than or equal to 999, proceed to step (2).

Note: If there are nine objects and nine locations where these objects are to be placed and if any location is empty, then some location contains more than one object. In this particular case, there are two digits out of the nine with the same place. (Pigeonhole principle.)

A flow chart for this algorithm is in Figure 45. A computer output to this problem is:

```
C
C      FIND ABCDEFGHI
C      SUCH THAT   ABC*ABC = DEFGHIJ
C      AND EACH ARE DIFFERENT AND NON ZERO
C
       DIMENSION A(9),B(9)
       INTEGER A,B
C
C      N = 123  IS SMALLEST CANDIDATE FOR N
C      SINCE 123 IS SMALLEST 3 DIGIT NUMBER
C      WITH ALL DIGITS DIFFERENT
C
       N = 123
       WRITE (3,6000)
 6000  FORMAT (1H1)
       WRITE (3,46)
   46  FORMAT (20X, 'THE ANSWERS ARE',///
      1 20X,' N        N*N ')
C
C      ISOLATE DIGITS    A(I)   I = 1,2, . . . ,9
```

```
C     BY DIVIDING BY THE APPROPRIATE POWER
C     OF 10 AND THEN SUBTRACTING THIS INTEGER
C     MULTIPLIED BY THE SAME POWER OF 10
C     FROM THE ORIGINAL NUMBER
C     BEFORE CONTINUING THE ISOLATION
C     FOR SUBSEQUENT DIGITS.
C
    1 A(1) = N/100
      A(2) = (N−A(1)*100)/10
      A(3) = N−A(1)*100−A(2)*10
      NN = N*N
      A(4) = NN/100000
      A(5) = (NN−A(4)*100000)/10000
      A(6) = (NN−A(4)*100000−A(5)*10000)/1000
      A(7) = (NN−A(4)*100000−A(5)
    1 *10000−A(6)*1000)/100
      A(8) = (NN−A(4)*100000−A(5)
    1 *10000−A(6)*1000−A(7)
    1 *100)/10
      A(9) = NN−A(4)*100000−A(5)
    1 *10000−A(6)*1000−A(7)
    1 *100−A(8)*10
C
C     ZERO B PLACE HOLDER FOR DIGITS
C
      DO 10 I = 1,9
   10 B(I) = 0
      DO 20 I = 1,9
      L = A(I)
      IF(L) 20,20,18
   18 B(L) = 1
   20 CONTINUE
C
C     IF A(I) = 0 SKIP THAT DIGIT
C     IF A(I) = J PUT 1 IN B(J)
C     ADD UP B(I) I = 1,2, . . . . ,9     IN M
C     DIGITS ARE PRESENT
C     IF SUM OF B'S = 9 THEN ALL 9
C
      M = 0
      DO 30 I = 1,9
   30 M = M+B(I)
      IF(M−9)100,40,100
```

```
 40   WRITE(3,45) (A(L),L = 1,9)
 45   FORMAT(20X,3I1,5X,6I1)
100   N = N+1
C
C     N = 987 IS LARGEST CANDIDATE FOR N
C     WITH ALL DIGITS DIFFERENT
C     SINCE 987 IS LARGEST 3 DIGIT NUMBER
C
      IF(N−987)1,1,200
200   STOP
      END
```

THE ANSWERS ARE

N	N°N
567	321489
854	729316

10. PASCAL'S TRIANGLE

Let n be a positive integer. Expand $(x + y)^n$ where x and y are arbitrary real numbers. The coefficients obtained in the expansion are of the form $\left(\dfrac{n}{m}\right)$ where $m = 0, 1, \ldots, n$.

Analysis

Recall that $\left(\dfrac{n}{m}\right) = \dfrac{n!}{(n-m)!m!}$ where $P! = P\,(P-1)\ldots 2,1$.
These numbers have the following property:

$$\binom{n}{m-1} + \binom{n}{m} = \binom{n+1}{m}$$

Using this recursive relation one gets

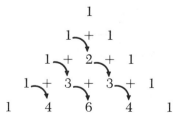

The above arrangement is called the *Pascal Triangle*.

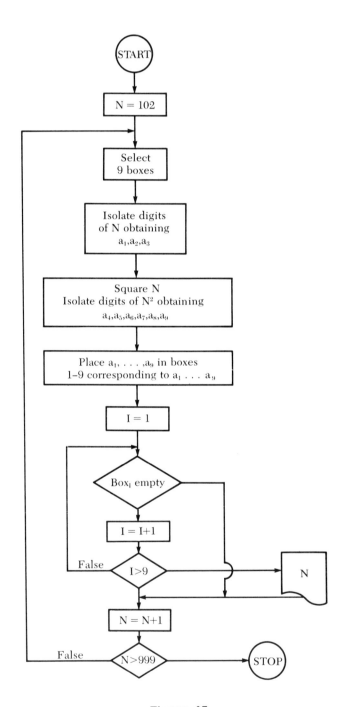

Figure 45

178

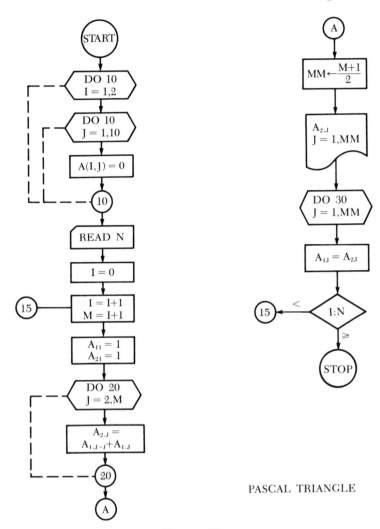

PASCAL TRIANGLE

Figure 46

An algorithm to compute the coefficients up to and including the Nth row follows:

(1) Get N

(2) Set $I \leftarrow 2$, $a_{10} \leftarrow 1$ and $a_{11} \leftarrow 1$

(3) Set $a_{I,0} \leftarrow 1$ and $a_{I,I} \leftarrow 1$

(4) Compare N with I

(5) If $I > N$ proceed to step (12)

(6) If $I \leq N$ proceed to step (7)

(7)   Set $J \leftarrow 1$
(8)   Set $a_{I,J} \leftarrow a_{I-1,J-1} + a_{I-1,J}$
(9)   Compare J with $I - 1$
(10) If $J < I - 1$ then set $J \leftarrow J + 1$ and proceed to step (8)
(11) If $J \geq I - 1$ then set $I \leftarrow I + 1$ and proceed to step (3)
(12) N rows of coefficients have been obtained.

Figure 46 is a flow chart for Pascal's algorithm.

Exercise

Write a FORTRAN program to find the coefficients of the expansion of $(x + y)^n$ for different values of n. The output should be in the following form:

$$1$$

$$1 \quad 2$$

$$1 \quad 3$$

$$1 \quad 4 \quad 6$$

$$1 \quad 5 \quad 10$$

It is not necessary to output more terms since the expansion is symmetric about a certain term that the reader must find.

11. PERMUTATIONS (T. FRENCH'S ALGORITHM)

Given $n > 0$ objects $\{a_1\ a_2\ a_3 \ldots a_n\}$, any arrangement of these objects will be called a *permutation*. For convenience in this section, these objects will be called $1, 2, 3, \ldots, N$. The set $\{1\}$ has 1 permutation 1, the set $\{1, 2\}$ has two permutations, 21 and 12, the set $\{1, 2, 3\}$ has six permutations, 321, 213, 231, 132, 312 and 123. In general, the set $\{1, 2, \ldots, n\}$ has $n!$ permutations.

In tabular form the number of permutations $p(n)$ for the integer n is

n	$p(n)$	n	$p(n)$
1	1	6	$6! = 720$
2	$2! = 2$	7	$7! = 5040$
3	$3! = 6$	8	$8! = 40320$
4	$4! = 24$	9	$9! = 362880$
5	$5! = 120$	10	$10! = 3628800$

A permutation is said to be of order n if it contains n elements. As the table shows there is a tremendous increase in $p(n)$ for small increase in n. The problem in finding the number of permutations is far less difficult than that of enumerating the permutations themselves. Let us attempt to describe an algorithm for enumerating permutations of size n or order n. This algorithm is based on the fact that a permutation of order n is obtained by adding one element to each permutation of order $n - 1$. We shall first illustrate this algorithm by writing all the permutations of order 3. To do this we introduce an index k. The reason for introducing this index will become apparent as the example progresses. We will place the permutations of order 3 into square arrays (Figure 47). The horizontal and vertical lines of each array will be called rows and columns, respectively.

(a)   (b)

Figure 47

At the top of each array there is a permutation of two elements, called p_1 and p_2.

The tables in Figure 47 were constructed as follows:

(i)   Let $k = 1$, $p_1 = 2$, $p_2 = 1$, $I = 1$.

(ii) Compare p_1 with k

If $p_1 \geqslant k$, form $p_1 + 1$ and place the result in the first position of the Ith row.

If $p_1 < k$, place p_1 in the first position of the Ith row.

(iii) Repeat (ii) with p_2 instead of p_1 placing result in second position of Ith row.

(iv) Put k as the last element of the Ith row completing a permutation.

(v)   Increment k and I by one.

(vi) If $k \leqslant 3$ (order of the permutation), go to (ii). Otherwise, go to (vii).

(vii) Set $k = 1$, $I = 1$, $p_1 = 2$, $p_2 = 1$.

(*viii*)   Repeat steps (ii), (iii), (iv), (v), and (vi). When we reach (vii) again all the permutations have been obtained.

Note that to find the permutations of order 3 we have used the two permutations of order two 12 and 21. If we are to obtain the permutation of order four, we shall need the permutations of order three. We shall illustrate the methods of retrieving the permutations of order three as follows:

(*i*)   Form an array N with four rows and four columns. Each position of the array N will be denoted by $N(i, j)$ where i stands for the row and j stands for the column. The value of $N(i, j)$ will be $i - j + 1$ if $i \geqslant j$ and 0 otherwise. As a convention we shall omit these 0's. Thus we obtain

$$\begin{pmatrix} 1 & & & \\ 2 & 1 & & \\ 3 & 2 & 1 & \\ 4 & 3 & 2 & 1 \end{pmatrix}$$

Set $K = N(4, 4) = 1$

Note that the fourth row, 4 3 2 1, is a permutation of order 4.

(*ii*)   Set $k = N(4, 4) + 1 = 2$

(*iii*)   Set $I = 4$ and $J = 1$

(*iv*)   Compare $N(I - 1, J)$ with K
If $N(I - 1, J) \geqslant K$, then $N(I, J) = N(I - 1, J) + 1$
otherwise $N(I, J) = N(I - 1, J)$

(*v*)   Perform (iv) for $j = 2, 33$

(*vi*)   Set $N(I, I) = K$
obtaining

$$\begin{pmatrix} 1 & & & \\ 2 & 1 & & \\ 3 & 2 & 1 & \\ 4 & 3 & 1 & 2 \end{pmatrix}$$

(*vii*)   Increment K by 1 and perform (iii), (iv), (v), and (vi) obtaining

$$\begin{pmatrix} 1 & & & \\ 2 & 1 & & \\ 3 & 2 & 1 & \\ 4 & 2 & 1 & 3 \end{pmatrix}$$

(*viii*) Increment K by 1 and again perform (iii), (iv), (v), and (vi) obtaining

$$
\begin{pmatrix}
1 & & & \\
2 & 1 & & \\
3 & 2 & 1 & \\
3 & 2 & 1 & 4
\end{pmatrix}
$$

(*ix*) Since we have been using the 3rd order permutation 321 to obtain (4 3 2 1), (4 3 1 2), (4 2 1 3), and (3 2 1 4) and as K has reached 4 (the order of the permutation), we need to obtain a new third-order permutation. We shall do this as follows:

(*x*) Set $N\,(4, 4) = 0$, $K = N\,(3, 3) + 1 = 1 + 1 = 2$, $I = 4 - 1 = 3$ perform (iv) for $j = 1, 2$ obtaining

$$
\begin{pmatrix}
1 & & & \\
2 & 1 & & \\
3 & 1 & 2 & \\
3 & 2 & 1 & 0
\end{pmatrix}
$$

Notice that we have obtained a new third order permutation 312.

(*xi*) Set $K = N\,(4, 4) + 1 = 1$, $I = I + 1 = 4$

(*xii*) Repeat (iii) through (vi) obtaining

$$
\begin{pmatrix}
1 & & & \\
2 & 1 & & \\
3 & 1 & 2 & \\
4 & 2 & 3 & 1
\end{pmatrix}
$$

(*xiii*) Incrementing K by 1 and repeating (iii) through (vi) we obtain

$$
\begin{pmatrix}
1 & & & \\
2 & 1 & & \\
3 & 1 & 2 & \\
4 & 1 & 3 & 2
\end{pmatrix}
$$

(*xiv*) Similarly incrementing K by 1 twice more we obtain

$$\begin{pmatrix} 1 & & & \\ 2 & 1 & & \\ 3 & 1 & 2 & \\ 4 & 1 & 2 & 3 \end{pmatrix} \quad \text{and} \quad \begin{pmatrix} 1 & & & \\ 2 & 1 & & \\ 3 & 1 & 2 & \\ 3 & 1 & 2 & 4 \end{pmatrix}$$

(xv)   Proceeding as in (x), (xi), (xii), (xiii), and (xiv) we obtain

```
1               1               1                   1
2 1             2 1             2 1                 2 1
2 1 3      ,    2 1 3      ,    2 1 3       and     2 1 3
3 2 4 1         3 1 4 2         2 1 4 3             2 1 3 4
```

To obtain more permutations of order 4 a new third
order permutation is needed. Next, since the third order
permutation just used ends in 3 (its order), a new permutation of order 2 is needed in order that we may find
a new third order permutation.

(xvi)   Replacing $N(3, 3)$ by 0, I by 2, $K = N(I, I) + 1 + 2$ and
performing (iv) for $J = 1$ we obtain

$$\begin{pmatrix} 1 & & & \\ 1 & 2 & & \\ 2 & 1 & 0 & \\ 2 & 1 & 3 & 0 \end{pmatrix}$$

Next increase I by 1, obtaining $I = 3$. With $K = N(I, I)$
$+ 1 = 0 + 1 = 1$ we obtain a new third order permutation
2 3 1 and N becomes:

$$\begin{pmatrix} 1 & & & \\ 1 & 2 & & \\ 2 & 3 & 1 & \\ 2 & 1 & 3 & 0 \end{pmatrix}$$

Proceeding as before we get

```
1                 1                 1                    1
1  2              1  2              1  2                 1  2
2  3  1     ,     2  3  1     ,     2  3  1      and     2  3  1
3  4  2  1        3  4  1  2        2  4  1  3           2  3  1  4
```

(*xvii*)   Continuing we obtain

```
1                 1                 1                    1
1  2              1  2              1  2                 1  2
1  3  2     ,     1  3  2     ,     1  3  2      and     1  3  2
2  4  3  1        1  4  3  2        1  4  2  3           1  3  2  4
```

and

```
1                 1                 1                    1
1  2              1  2              1  2                 1  2
1  2  3     ,     1  2  3     ,     1  2  3      and     1  2  3
2  3  4  1        1  3  4  2        1  2  4  3           1  2  3  4
```

The algorithm ends when the order is the natural order for all permutations of order 4.

This is algorithmically detected by the diagonal elements each equalling the row number. Therefore if more permutations did exist (they don't), one would now form a new permutation of row 2. But since it has a 2 in row 2 in its position on the diagonal, a new permutation depends on a new permutation of row 1, which is impossible. An algorithm to obtain the permutations of order n is given here. It is divided in two parts, A and B.

Part A.   Form n row matrix N such that row I contains the numbers

$I, I - 1, I - 2, \ldots, 1$. This done using $N(I,J) = I - J + 1$

Step   (1)   Set $I \leftarrow 1$
     (2)   Set $J \leftarrow 1$
     (3) $N(I,J) = I - J + 1$
     (4) $J \leftarrow J + 1$
     (5)   Compare J with I
            if $I \leq N$ go to 2
            if $J > I$ add 1 to I

    (6)   compare I with N
    (7)   if I≤N go to 2
    (8)   if I>N go to Part B

Part B

    (1)   Set L←N
    (2)   Set K←N(L,L)+1
    (3)   Compare K with L
    (4)   If K≤L GO TO 6
    (5)   If K>L GO TO 24
    (6)   Set IMAX←L−1
    (7)   Set I←1
    (8)   Compare N(IMAX,I) with K
    (9)   If N(IMAX,I)<K GO TO 11
    (10) If N(IMAX,I)≥K GO TO 13
    (11) Set N(L,I)←N(IMAX,I)
    (12) GO TO 14
    (13) Set N(L,I)←N(IMAX,I)+1
    (14) Set I←I+1
    (15) Compare I with IMAX
    (16) If I≤IMAX GO TO 8
    (17) If I>IMAX GO TO 18
    (18) N(L,L)←K
    (19) Compare L with N
    (20) If L<N GO TO 24
    (21) If L≥N GO TO 32
    (22) L←L+1
    (23) GO TO 2
    (24) Set N(L,L)←0
    (25) Set L←L−1
    (26) Compare L with 2
    (27) If L<2 GO TO 29
    (28) If L≥2 GO TO 2
    (29) Write "no more permutations available"
    (30) N(1,1)←−1
    (31) STOP
    (32) Set J←1
    (33) Write N(N,J)
    (34) Set J←J+1
    (35) Compare J with N
    (36) If J≤N GO TO 33
    (37) If J>N GO TO 1

Figure 48(a) is a flow chart to generate the array

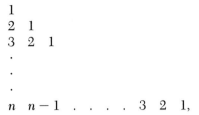

$$
\begin{array}{llll}
1 & & & \\
2 & 1 & & \\
3 & 2 & 1 & \\
\cdot & & & \\
\cdot & & & \\
\cdot & & & \\
n & n-1 & \cdot\ \cdot\ \cdot\ \cdot & 3\ \ 2\ \ 1,
\end{array}
$$

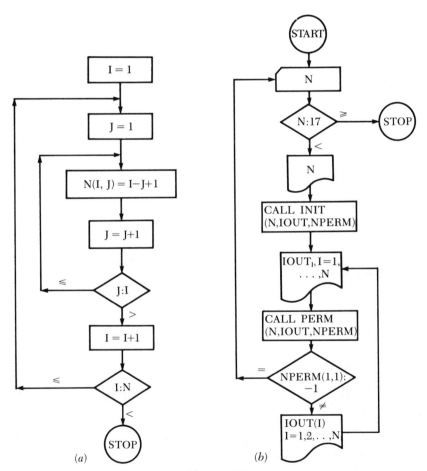

(a)   (b)

Figure 48

Figure 48(b) is a flow chart for an algorithm to generate the permutations. Figure 49 is a flow chart to use the permutation algorithm as a subroutine.

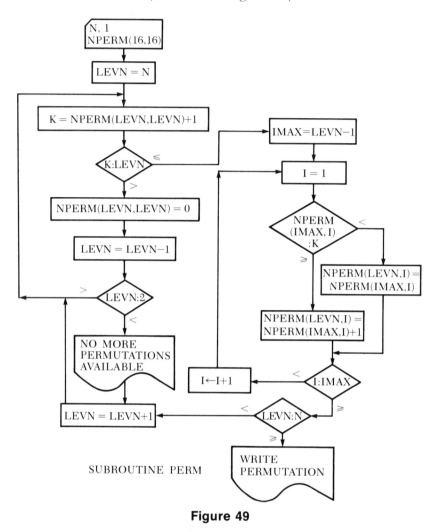

Figure 49

The following is a program to implement the permutation algorithm.

```
      COMMON N,IOUT(16),NPERM(16,16)
      WRITE (3,6000)
6000  FORMAT(1H1)
   3  READ (1,2) N
C     IF N GREATER THAN 16 GO TO 100 AND STOP
      IF(N-17) 4,100,100
   4  WRITE (3,1)N
```

```
        CALL INITP
C                        1
C     BUILD             2  1
C       INITIAL         3  2  1
C         MATRIX        4  3  2  1
C           ETC         5  4  3  2  1
C
        WRITE (3,10) (IOUT(I),I = 1,N)
     5  CALL PERM
C    BUILD A PERMUTATION
C
        IF (NPERM(1,1)+1) 15, 3,15
C
C    WHEN SUBROUTINE PERM COMPUTES
C    NPERM(1,1) = -1, THERE ARE NO
C    MORE PERMUTATIONS POSSIBLE
C
    15  WRITE (3,10) (IOUT(I),I = 1,N)
C
C    WRITE A PERMUTATION
        GO TO 5
   100  STOP
     1  FORMAT ('0','N = ', I2)
     2  FORMAT(I2)
    10  FORMAT (' ',16I5)
        END


N = 3
     3  2  1
     3  1  2
     2  1  3
     2  3  1
     1  3  2
     1  2  3
  NO MORE PERMUTATIONS AVAILABLE
N = 4
     4  3  2  1
     4  3  1  2
     4  2  1  3
     3  2  1  4
     4  2  3  1
     4  1  3  2
```

```
4  1  2  3
3  1  2  4
3  2  4  1
3  1  4  2
2  1  4  3
2  1  3  4
3  4  2  1
3  4  1  2
2  4  1  3
2  3  1  4
2  4  3  1
1  4  3  2
1  4  2  3
1  3  2  4
2  3  4  1
1  3  4  2
1  2  4  3
1  2  3  4
```

NO MORE PERMUTATIONS AVAILABLE


```
        SUBROUTINE PERM
        COMMON N, IOUT(16), NPERM(16,16)
C    LEVL = ORDER OF PERMUTATION
        LEVN = N
C    K = VARIABLE FROM 1 TO LEVL+1
C    INCREASE K BY 1
     1  K = NPERM(LEVN,LEVN)+1
C    WHEN K EXCEEDS LEVL GET A
C    NEW PREVIOUS PERMUTATION
        IF(K−LEVN) 2,2,7
     2  IMAX = LEVN−1
        DO 5 I = 1,IMAX
C    COMPARE PREVIOUS ROW ENTRY TO K
        IF(NPERM(IMAX,I)−K) 3,4,4
C    IF PREVIOUS ENTRY LESS THAN K
C    WRITE DOWN ENTRY
     3  NPERM(LEVN,I) = NPERM(IMAX,I)
        GO TO 5
C    IF PREVIOUS ENTRY GREATER
C    OR EQUAL TO K WRITE DOWN
C    ENTRY PLUS 1
     4  NPERM(LEVN,I) = NPERM(IMAX,I)+1
     5  CONTINUE
```

```
C     WRITE DOWN K
      NPERM(LEVN,LEVN) = K
      IF(LEVN−N) 6,9,9
C     IF ORDER LESS THAN N INCREASE
C     ORDER OF PERMUTATION LEVL
   6  LEVN = LEVN+1
      GO TO 1
C     NO MORE PERMUTATIONS CAN
C     BE GENERATED FROM THE PREVIOUS
C     PERMUTATION ROW
   7  NPERM(LEVN,LEVN) = 0
C     DECREASE LEVL SO AS TO
C     COMPUTE A NEW PERMUTATION
C     OF ORDER LEVL−1
      LEVN = LEVN−1
      IF(LEVN−2) 8,1,1
C     WHEN LEVL REACHES 1 NO MORE
C     PERMUTATIONS AVAILABLE
   8  WRITE(3,99)
      NPERM(1,1) = −1
      RETURN
   9  DO 10 J = 1,N
  10  IOUT(J) = NPERM(N,J)
      RETURN
  99  FORMAT(3X, 'NO MORE PERMUTATIONS'
     1' AVAILABLE')
      END



      SUBROUTINE INITP
      COMMON MAX,LINE(16),IRRAY(16,16)
C     BUILD MAX ROWS
C     CONTAING IN THE I,J POSITION I−J+1
C     THAT IS A TABLE
C           1
C           2    1
C           3    2     1
C           4    3     2      1
C           .    .     .      .
C           .    .     .      .
C          MAX  MAX−1 MAX−2 . . . . . . 2  1
      DO 11 J = 1,MAX
      DO 11 K = 1,J
```

```
11  IRRAY(J,K) = J−K+1
    DO 12 L = 1,MAX
12  LINE(L) = IRRAY(MAX,L)
    RETURN
    END
```

Exercises

1.   Draw a flow chart and write an algorithm to find a number M such that $M^2 = aabb$. Write a FORTRAN program that would find the value (or values) of M.

2.   Draw a flow chart and write an algorithm to find a prime number $N = abcd$ such that $abcd = (b + d)^2$. Write a FORTRAN program to find N.

3.   Draw a flow chart and write an algorithm to find a number N such that if $N^3 = xyzw$ then $N = x + y + z + w$. Write a FORTRAN program to find N.

4.   Write a FORTRAN program to find a number $N = xyz$ such that $n = xy + xz + yz + yx + zx + zy$.

5.   Write a program to find a number $N = ab$ such that if $N^2 = xyzw$ then $x + y = z + w = ba$.

6.   Find a number of four digits $N = abcd$ such that ab and cd are factors of N.

7.   Find $T, W, O, N, E, F, U, R, S, V$, so that the cryptarithmie TWO + ONE + FOUR = SEVEN will be meaningful.

8.   Modify the program output for obtaining permutations so it can be used as a subroutine that will return a permutation to a main calling program. To accomplish this, assume that the permutations are arranged in order of numerical magnitude.

9.   Let E be a variable defined using the expression

$$E = 2 + \frac{1}{2!} + \frac{1}{3!} + \frac{1}{4!} + \ldots + \frac{1}{n!}$$

where $N! = N(N − 1)(N − 2) \ldots (N − N + 1)$.

Write a FORTRAN program to compute E for different values of N. Use the subroutine DIGIT to find the digits of E.

Chapter VI

POLYNOMIALS

We are taking a naive approach to polynomials. In what follows x means any arbitrary real (complex) number. We shall denote polynomials by $f(x)$, that is

$$f(x) = a_0 x^n + a_1 x^{n-1} + \ldots + a_n \qquad (1)$$

where $a_0, a_1, \ldots, a_n, x$ are real (complex) numbers, n is an integer which is called the degree of the polynomial.

It is obvious that polynomials are functions of the real (complex) variable x, since for every x, $f(x)$ yields a unique real (complex) number. It is assumed that the reader is familiar with the usual operations with polynomials. We are going to write algorithms to compute:

(a) Algebraic sum of polynomials
(b) Multiplications of polynomials
(c) Division of polynomials
(d) Highest common factor of two polynomials

1. ADDITION-SUBTRACTION

Let $A(X)$ and $B(X)$ be polynomials of degree n and m, respectively. Write a program to compute the algebraic sum of $A(X)$ and $B(X)$.

Analysis

Recall that the algebraic sum of two polynomials is obtained by algebraically adding the coefficients of the same powers of X.

For example, given

$A(X) = X^3 + 3X^2 + 2$ and $B(X) = X^4 + 3X^2 + X - 1$, we form
$A(X) + B(X) = X^3 + 3X^2 + 2 + X^4 + 3X^2 + X - 1$
$= X^4 + X^3 + 6X^2 + X + 1.$

This example illustrates how convenient it would be if both polynomials were of the same degree. If this were the case, a simple arithmetic statement would suffice to obtain the algebraic sum of

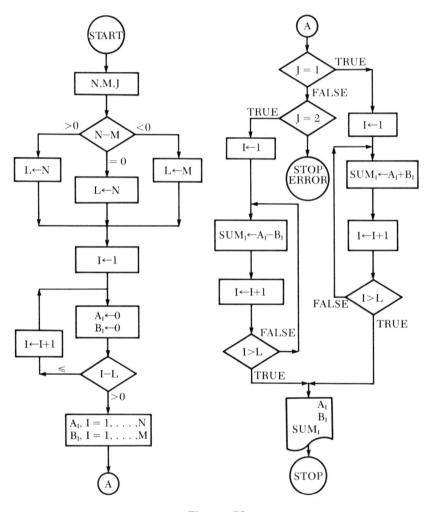

Figure 50

$A(X)$ and $B(X)$. Next, note that each power of X determines a coefficient. That is, we might write a polynomial as follows:

$$A(X) = A(N + 1)X^N + A(N)X^{N-1} + \ldots + A(2)X + A(1)$$

This suggests a procedure to READ and WRITE polynomials. *READ and WRITE polynomials as if there were arrays with the assumption that the value of $A(I)$ is the coefficient of X^{I-1}.*

Since algebraic sums means either to add or to subtract, we would like the program to have a built-in "device" which would allow it to add or to subtract as the case might be. This can be accomplished by using a COMPUTED GO TO statement, which would switch control either to a branch of the program, addition, or to an alternative branch of the program, subtraction.

The above analysis of the problem suggests the flow chart in Figure 50.

Exercise

Write a Fortran program to compute the algebraic sum of two polynomials $A(x)$ and $B(x)$. Set the necessary restrictions so this program can be used as a subroutine. Test this subroutine with a main program.

2. MULTIPLICATION

Write a program to compute the product of two polynomials.

Analysis

Let $A(X)$ and $B(X)$ be polynomials of degree N and M, respectively. Using the distributive law of multiplication, one can compute the product $A(X) \cdot B(X)$.

To illustrate this procedure we use an example.

Let $A(X) = X^3 + 3X^2 + 2X + 1$ and $B(X) = X^2 + 2X + 2$. Then

$$A(X) \cdot B(X) = (X^3 + 3X^2 + 2X + 1) \cdot (X^2 + 2X + 2) = (X^3 \cdot X^2 + 3X^2 \cdot X^2 + 2X \cdot X^2 + 1 \cdot X^2) + (X^3 \cdot 2X + 3X^2 \cdot 2X + 2X \cdot 2X + 1 \cdot 2X) + (X^3 \cdot 2 + 3X^2 \cdot 2 + 2X \cdot 2 + 1 \cdot 2).$$

Next, one groups similar terms obtaining

$A(X) \cdot B(X) = X^3 \cdot X^2 + (2X^3 \cdot X + 3X^2 \cdot X^2) + (2X^3 + 6X^2 \cdot X + 2X \cdot X^2) + (6X^2 + 4X \cdot X + X^2) + (4X + 2X) + 2.$

$A(X) \cdot B(X) = X^5 + 5X^4 + 10X^3 + 11X^2 + 6X + 2.$

Observe that the degree of $A(X) \cdot B(X)$ is $3 + 2 = 5$. Note that each set of parentheses contains terms of the same degree. Also note that every term in each set of parentheses contains one term from $A(X)$ and one term from $B(X)$. In each set of parentheses although the degree of the terms used from $A(X)$ is diminishing, the degree of those terms used from $B(X)$ is increasing in such a way as to keep the power within the parentheses constant.

Assume that

$$A(X) = A(N + 1)X^N + A(N)X^{N-1} + \ldots + A(2)X + A(1)$$

$$B(X) = B(M + 1)X^M + B(M)X^{M-1} + \ldots + B(2)X + B(1)$$

then

$A(X) \cdot B(X) = A(N + 1) \cdot B(M + 1)X^{N+M} + (A(N + 1) \cdot B(M) + A(N) \cdot B(M + 1))X^{N+M-1} + (A(N + 1) \cdot B(M - 1) + A(N) \cdot B(M) + A(N - 1) \cdot B(M + 1))X^{N+M-2} + \ldots + A(1) \cdot B(1). \ (^*)$

The previous analysis suggests the following algorithm.

(1) Compute the number of terms in the product which is $N + M + 1$.

(2) Set $I = 0$ (for counting purposes).

(3) Add 1 to I.

(4) Compare I with $N + 1$.

(5) If $I > N + 1$ then proceed to step (13).

(6) If $I \leq N + 1$ set $J = 0$ (also for counting purposes).

(7) Add 1 to J.

(8) Compare J with $M + 1$.

(9) If $J > M + 1$ proceed to step (3).

(10) If $J \leq M + 1$ compute $A_I \cdot B_J$.
      (This is a term within the parenthesis of $(^*)$ corresponding to X^{I+J-1}.)

(11) Accumulate $A_I B_J$ in C_{I+J-1} (Coefficient of X^{I+J-1} in the product.)

(12) Proceed to step (7).

(13) Write answer C_I for $I = 1, \ldots, N + M + 1$.

The flow chart shown in Figure 51 illustrates this algorithm.

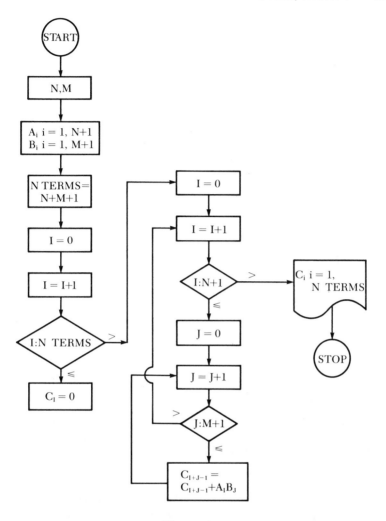

Figure 51

Next we write a subroutine to compute the product of two polynomials $A(X)$ and $B(X)$.

```
        SUBROUTINE POLYM(A,B,C,N1,M1,NSUM)
C       SUBPROGRAM TO MULTIPLY TWO POLYNOMIALS
C
C       COEFFICIENTS ARE IN INCREASING ORDER
C       THAT IS A(1)*X**N+A(2)*X**(N-1)+. . .A(N)*X+A(N)
```

```
C
        DIMENSION A(1),B(1),C(1)
C
C       THE COEFFICIENT OF X(M+1-I) AND X(N+1-J) IN
C       C IS C(K) WHERE
C       K = I+J-1 AND IS SIGMA(A(I)°B(J) FOR ALL I AND J
C       SUCH THAT
C       I+J-2 ADDS TO K)AND IS STORED IN C(K) AND IS THE
C       COEFFICIENT IN
C       THE PRODUCT OF X(M+N-2-(I+J)) TERM.
C
        NSUM = N1+M1-1
        DO 20 I = 1,NSUM
   20   C(I) = 0.0
        DO 100 I = 1,N1
        DO 100 J = 1,M1
        K = I+J-1
  100   C(K) = C(K)+A(I)°B(J)
        RETURN
        END
```

Exercise

Using the subroutine POLYM(A,B,C,N1,M1,NSUM) write a program to compute the product of the two polynomials $A(X) = X^3 + 5X^2 + 6X + 3$ and $B(X) = X^7 + 8X^6 + 3X^2 + 5X + 1$.

3. DIVISION OF POLYNOMIALS

Let $A(x) = a_1x^m + a_2x^{m-1} + \ldots + a_m$ and $B(x) = b_1x^n + b_2x^{n-1} + \ldots + b_n$ be polynomials of degree m and n, respectively.

Write a program to compute the quotient $C(x)$ and remainder $R(x)$ for a given $A(x)$ and $B(x)$.

Analysis

It is known from algebra that $A(x)$, $B(x)$, $C(x)$ and $R(x)$ are related by the equation $A(x) = B(x) \cdot C(x) + R(x)$. This equality implies that the degree of $C(x)$ is $m - n$ and the degree of $R(x)$ is $n - 1$.

Equating the coefficients of the same powers of x on both sides of $A(x) = B(x) \cdot C(x) + R(x)$ (after substituting $A(x)$, $B(x)$, $C(x)$, and $R(x)$ by the polynomials representing them), we have the following relations.

$$c_1 = a_1$$
$$c_2 = (a_2 - c_1 b_2)/b_1$$
.
.
.

$$c_i = (a_i - \sum_{j=1}^{i-1} c_j b_{i-j+1})/b_1 \quad \text{for all values of } i \text{ such that } 2 \leqslant i \leqslant m - n + 1$$

$$c_{m-n+1} = (a_{m-n+1} - \sum_{j=1}^{m-n} c_j b_{m-n-2-j})/b_1$$

The above relation develops the quotient, the coefficients of the remainder follow.

$$c_{m-n+2} = a_{m-n+2} - \sum_{j=1}^{m-n+1} c_j b_{m-n+3-j}$$

.
.
.

$$c_i = a_i - \sum_{j=1}^{m-n+1} c_j b_{i-j+1} \quad \text{for all values of } i \text{ such that } m - n + 2 \leqslant i \leqslant m + 1$$

.
.
.

$$c_{m+1} = a_{m+1} - \sum_{j=1}^{m-n+1} c_j b_{m+2-j}$$

where $b_k = 0$ for all values of k such that $n + 2 \leqslant k \leqslant m + 1$. Note that the degree of the quotient is $m - n$ and the degree of the remainder is $m - 1$.

Example

Let $A(x) = x^5 + 2x^4 + 3x^3 - x^2 - x + 1$ and $B(x) = x^3 - 1$.
Let $C(x) = c_1 x^2 + c_2 x + c_3$ and $R(x) = c_4 x^2 + c_5 x + c_6$.
$A(x)$, $B(x)$, $C(x)$, $R(x)$ are related in the following manner:

$$x^5 + 2x^4 + 3x^3 - x^2 - x + 1 =$$
$$(x^3 - 1) \cdot (c_1 x^2 + c_2 x + c_3) + (c_4 x^2 + c_5 x + c_6)$$

Equating the same powers of x on both sides of the equation we get:

$$1 = c_1 \qquad \text{(coefficient of } x^5)$$
$$2 = c_2 \qquad \text{(coefficient of } x^4)$$
$$3 = c_3 \qquad \text{(coefficient of } x^3)$$
$$-1 = -c_1 + c_4 \quad \text{(coefficient of } x^2)$$
$$-1 = -c_2 + c_5 \quad \text{(coefficient of } x)$$
$$1 = -c_3 + c_6 \quad \text{(coefficient of } x^0)$$

The above relations give $c_1 = 1$, $c_2 = 2$, $c_3 = 3$, $c_4 = 0, -1+1=0, c_5 = c_2 - 1 = 2 - 1 = 1$, and $c_6 = c_3 + 1 = 3 + 1 = 4$.

A procedure to obtain the quotient and remainder follows:

(1) Get M, N, $A(x)$, and $B(x)$
(2) Set $B(k)$ equal to zero for values of k such that $N + 2 \leqslant k \leqslant M + 1$
(3) $c_1 \leftarrow A_1/B_1$
(4) $I \leftarrow 2$ (for counting the coefficients)
(5) $C_I \leftarrow A_I$ (for accumulative purposes)
(6) $J \leftarrow 1$ (to develop the individual C_I's)
(7) $C_I \leftarrow C_I - C_J \cdot B_{I-J+1}$
(8) Add 1 to J
(9) Compare J with $I - 1$
(10) If J is greater than $I - 1$ proceed to step (12).
(11) If J is less than or equal to $I - 1$ proceed to step (7).
(12) $C_I \leftarrow C_I/B_1$
(13) Add 1 to I
(14) Compare I with $M - N + 1$
(15) If I greater than $M - N + 1$ proceed to step (17).
(16) If I is less than or equal to $M - N + 1$ proceed to step (5).
(17) Quotient has been obtained in $C_1, C_2, \ldots, C_{M-N+1}$, proceed to step (18).
(18) $L \leftarrow M - N + 2$ (for counting the subscripts of the remainder)
(19) $C_L \leftarrow A_L$
(20) $JJ \leftarrow 1$ (to develop the individual C_L's)
(21) $C_L \leftarrow C_L - C_{JJ} \cdot B_{L-JJ+1}$
(22) Add 1 to JJ
(23) Compare JJ with $M - N + 1$
(24) If JJ is greater than $M - N + 1$, then proceed to step (26).
(25) If JJ is less than or equal to $M - N + 1$ then proceed to step (21).
(26) Add 1 to L
(27) Compare L with $M + 1$
(28) If L is greater than $M + 1$ then process is finished, that is, the remainder has been obtained in

$$C_{m-n+2}, C_{m-n+3}, \ldots, C_{m+1}.$$

(29)   If L is less than or equal to $M + 1$ then proceed to step (19).

Figure 52 shows a flow chart for this algorithm. Next we present a program to obtain the division of two polynomials $A(X)$ and $B(X)$.

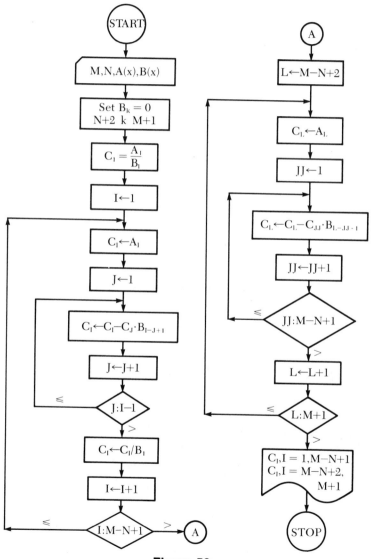

Figure 52

```
          DIMENSION A(10),B(10),C(19)
C    DIVISION OF TWO POLYNOMIALS A(X) AND B(X)
C    OF DEGREE M AND N RESPECTIVELY
C    READ DEGREES FIRST
C    READ THE POLYNOMIALS NEXT IN
C    DESCENDING ORDER OF COEFFICIENTS
C    THAT IS A = A(1)*X**M+A(2)*X**(M-1)+. . .
C    A(M-1)*X+A(M)
          WRITE (3,6000)
   6000 FORMAT(1H1)
          READ (1,11) M,N
     11 FORMAT(I2,I2)
          N1 = N+1
          M1 = M+1
          READ (1,12) (A(I),I = 1,M1)
          READ (1,12) (B(I),I = 1,N1)
     12 FORMAT(10F5.1)
C    CALL POLYD WHICH DIVIDES A(X) BY B(X)
C    GETTING
C    QUOTIENT IN C(1), . . . ,C(MN1)
C    AND A REMAINDER OF LENGTH M+1-MN1
C    STORED IN C(MN1+1), . . . ,C(M+1)
C
          CALL POLYD(A,B,C,M,N,MN1)
C
C    WRITE A(X),B(X),QUOTIENT OF A(X) AND B(X),
C    AND THE REMAINDER UPON DIVISION
C
          WRITE(3,13) (A(I),I = 1, M1)
          WRITE(3,14) (B(I),I = 1,N1)
          WRITE(3,15) (C(I), I = 1,MN1)
          MN2 = MN1+1
          WRITE(3,16) (C(I),I = MN2,M1)
          STOP
     13 FORMAT(' DIVIDEND ',10F5.1)
     14 FORMAT(' DIVISOR ',10F5.1)
     15 FORMAT(' QUOTIENT ',10F5.1)
     16 FORMAT(' REMAINDER ',10F5.1)
          END
```

DIVIDEND	1.0	4.0	9.0	9.0
DIVISOR	1.0	2.0	4.0	

```
QUOTIENT      1.0  2.0
REMAINDER     1.0  1.0


      SUBROUTINE POLYD(A,B,C,M,N,MN1)
      DIMENSION A(1),B(1),C(1)
C
C     COEFFICIENTS ARE IN INCREASING ORDER
C     THAT IS A = A(I) *X**M+A(2)*X(M-1)+. . .
C     A(M-1)*X+A(M)
C     IF C(X) IS THE QUOTIENT OF A(X) BY B(X)
C     AND R(X) IS THE REMAINDER, THEN SINCE
C     THEY ARE RELATED BY THE EQUATION
C     A(X) = B(X) *C(X)+R(X) IT FOLLOWS THAT
C     C(X) IS OF DEGREE M-N, AND
C     R(X) IS OF DEGREE N-1.
C
      N2 = N+2
      M1 = M+1
C
C     EQUATING THE COEFFICIENTS OF THE
C     SAME POWER OF X ON BOTH SIDES OF
C     A(X) = B(X)*C(X)+R(X) WE GET THE
C     FOLLOWING RELATIONS
C     FOR C(X) THE QUOTIENT WE GET
C     C(1) = A(1)/B(1)
C     C(2) = (A(2)-C(1)*B(2))/B(1)
C     C(3) = (A(1)-C(1)*B(3)-C(2)*B(2))/B(1)
C       .
C       .
C     C(I) = (A(I)-SIGMA(C(J)*B(I-J+1)
C     FOR J = 1, . .(I-1))/B(1) FOR I SUCH
C     2LE I LE M-N+1)
C     C(M-N+1) = (A(M-N+1-SIGMA(C(J)*B(M-N-2-J)
C     FOR ALL J FROM I, . . .M-N))/B(1)
C
C     CALCULATE QUOTIENT
C
      DO 10 I = N2,M1
   10 B(I) = 0.
      C(1) = A(1)/B(1)
      MN1 = M-N+1
      DO 100 I = 2,MN1
```

```
        C(I) = A(I)
        I1 = I−1
        DO 90 J = 1,I1
        IJ1 = I−J+1
   90   C(I) = C(I)−C(J)*B(IJ1)
  100   C(I) = C(I)/B(1)
        MN2 = M−N+2
C    THE ABOVE DEVELOPS THE QUOTIENT,
C    THE COEFFICIENTS OF THE REMAINDER
C    FOLLOW
C    LET US PLACE THE REMAINDER IN C(X)
C    FROM M−N+2, . . . ,TO M+1
C    IN THE FOLLOWING EXPRESSION SIGMA
C    RUNS FROM J = 1, . . . ,TO M−N+1
C    C(M−N+2) = A(M−N+2)−SIGMA(C(J)*B(M−N+3−J))
C    .
C    .
C    C(I) = A(I)−SIGMA(C(J)*B(I−J+1) FOR
C    ALL I SUCH THAT M−N+2 LE I LE M+1)
C    .
C    .
C    C(M+1) = A(M+1)−SIGMA(C(J)*B(M+2−J)
C    WHERE B(K) = 0 FOR ALL K SUCH THAT
C    N+2 LE K LE M+1)
C    CALCULATE REMAINDER
C
        DO 200 I = MN2,M1
        C(I) = A(I)
        DO 190 J = 1,MN1
        IJ1 = I−J+1
  190   C(I) = C(I)−C(J)*B(IJ1)
  200   CONTINUE
        RETURN
        END
```

4. VALUE OF A POLYNOMIAL AT x

Write a program to compute the value of a polynomial $f(x)$ at $x = b$.

Analysis (Synthetic Division)

Let $f(x)$ be a polynomial of degree n. On dividing $f(x)$ by a binomial $x - b$, we obtain a quotient $f_1(x)$ of degree $n - 1$ and a constant R as remainder. We can express this symbolically as follows:

$$f(x) = (x - b)f_1(x) + R. \tag{1}$$

If we substitute the value $x = b$ on (1), we get

$$f(b) = R.$$

We have proved the following result.

The value of a polynomial $f(x)$ at $x = b$ is the remainder obtained on dividing $f(x)$ by $x - b$.

If the value of $f(x)$ at $x = b$ happens to be zero, we say that b is a zero of the polynomial or that b is a root of the equation $f(x) = 0$.

Using the previous result, we obtain the following condition:

A polynomial $f(x)$ of degree n has a zero at $x = b$ if and only if the remainder obtained on dividing $f(x)$ by $x - b$ is zero.

Using the first result an algorithm can be written that computes the value of a polynomial $f(x)$ at $x = b$. It can be obtained as follows:

Let $f(x) = a_0x^n + a_1x^{n-1} + a_2x^{n-2} + \ldots + a_{n-1}x + a_n$ be a polynomial of nth degree. Let $f_1(x) = c_0x^{n-1} + c_1x^{n-2} + \ldots + c_{n-1}$ be the quotient and c_n the remainder obtained on dividing $f(x)$ by $x - b$. We can express this symbolically by the following identity:

$$a_0x^n + a_1x^{n-1} + a_2x^{n-2} + \ldots + a_{n-1}x + a_n =$$
$$(x - b)(c_0x^{n-1} + \ldots + c_{n-2}x + c_{n-1}) + c_n \tag{2}$$

Identifying coefficients of the same power of x in (2) we obtain

$$a_0 = c_0, a_1 = c_1 - bc_0, \ldots, a_i = c_i - bc_{i-1}, \ldots, a_n = c_n - bc_{n-1} \tag{3}$$

Using the above relations, we can compute $c_0, c_1, c_3, \ldots c_{n-1}, c_n$ by the following formulas:

$$c_1 = a_0, c_1 = a_1 + bc_0, \ldots, c_i = a_i + bc_{i-1}, \ldots, c_n = a_n + bc_{n-1}. \tag{4}$$

Computing the coefficients c_i in the above fashion is what constitutes the so-called *synthetic division* or *Horner's Algorithm*. The coefficients c_i can be obtained in an orderly way if we proceed as follows.

(a) Place all coefficients $a_0, a_1, \ldots, a_n$ in order in the first row, writing a zero wherever the coefficient of some power of x is missing.

(b) Write down a_0 in the first place on the third row. Denote this number by c_0, i.e., $c_0 = a_0$.

(c) Multiply $c_0 = a_0$ by b and place the result in the second row under a_1.

(d) Place the sum $a_1 + a_0b$ in the second place in the third row. This sum becomes c_1.

(e) Multiply c_1 by b and place it under a_2.

(f) Place the sum $c_1b + a_2$ in the third row. Denote it by c_2.

Continue in this way until there are no more a_i left. The last coefficient obtained in the third row is the remainder. The preceding sums are the coefficients of the quotient.

We illustrate this with an example.

Example

Divide $x^4 + 4x^3 - 2x + 8$ by $x - 2$ using Horner's Algorithm.

	1	4	0	-2	8
2		2	12	24	44
	1	6	12	22	52

The quotient is $x^3 + 6x^2 + 12x + 22$ and the remainder is 52. We have the following procedure:

(1) Get the polynomial $A(x)$ whose coefficients are $A_0, A_1, \ldots, A_n$ written in descending order.

(2) Get b, the value at which the polynomial $A(x)$ is to be evaluated.

(3) Set $V = A_0$ (To initialize the value V of the polynomial).

(4) Set $I = 1$ (For counting purposes).

(5) Set $V = V + A_I \cdot b$.

(6) Compare I with N.

(7) If $I < n$ then set $I = I + 1$ and proceed to step 5.

(8) If $I \geqslant n$ then V is the value of $A(x)$ at b.

A flow chart for this algorithm is seen in Figure 53. Next, we will write a subroutine to implement Horner's Algorithm.

```
      SUBROUTINE POLYV(A,N,D,C,R)
C     SUBROUTINE FOR SYNTHETIC DIVISION OR
C     HORNERS ALGORITHM
C     POLYNOMIAL STORED IN A, A = A(1)*X**N+A(2)
C     *X**(N-1)+...+A(N)*X+A(N+1)
      REDUCED POLYNOMIAL IN C REMAINDER IN R
C
C     POLYNOMIAL STORED IN A, A = A(1)*X**+A(2)
C     *X**(N-1)+...+A(N)*X+A(N+1)
C
```

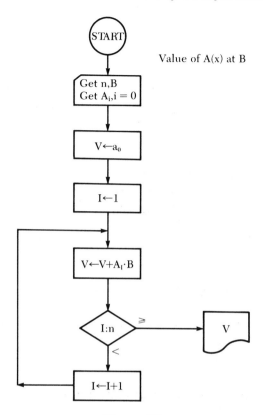

Value of A(x) at B

Figure 53

```
C      GIVEN POLYNOMIAL X**3+2*X**2−1*X+3 FIND
C      REDUCED POLYNOMIAL AND VALUE
C      AT X = 3
C      1    2    −1    3    I    3
C           3    15    42    I
C      -----------------
C      1    5    14    45
C      HENCE REDUCED POLYNOMIAL IS X**2+5*X+14
C      AND F(3) IS 45
C
       DIMENSION A(1),C(1)
       C(1) = A(1)
       M = N+1
       DO 10 I = 2,M
   10  C(I) = A(I)+D*C(I−1)
```

R = C(M)
RETURN
END

Exercise

Check the above subroutine using the polynomial

$$8X^7 - 3X^5 + 2X^4 + X^2 + X + 4$$

for the following values of X, $-3, -2, -1, 1, 2$. Save the values so obtained in a vector array V and compare the sign of each consecutive pair. If the sign is negative write a statement that says "Polynomial has a root between a and b," whatever the values of a and b might be. Otherwise do not print out anything.

5. GREATEST COMMON FACTOR OF TWO POLYNOMIALS

Let $A(x)$ and $B(x)$ be two polynomials of degree M and N, respectively. Write a program to find the greatest common factor of the polynomials $A(x)$ and $B(x)$.

Analysis (Euclid's Algorithm for Polynomials)

Recall that the greatest common factor (gcf) of two polynomials $A(x)$ and $B(x)$ is a polynomial $D(x)$ such that $D(x)$ is a factor of $A(x)$, a factor of $B(x)$, and no factor of higher degree is a factor of both $A(x)$ and $B(x)$.

Example

If $A(x) = (x^2 - 1)(x + 3)^2(x^2 + 2x - 3)$ and $B(x) = (x - 1)(x + 3)$ $(x^2 + 2x + 5)$ then the greatest common factor of $A(x)$ and $B(x)$ is $(x - 1)(x + 3)$.

The procedure to obtain the greatest common factor of two polynomials is based on the following property of algebra.

If $D(x)$ is a factor of $F(x)$ and $G(x)$, then $D(x)$ is also a factor of $F(x) + G(x)$.

Using this property for polynomials one obtains a procedure similar to the Euclid's Algorithm.

The Euclid's Algorithm for polynomials follows:

Assume that the degree M of $A(x)$ is greater than or equal to the degree N of $B(x)$. Divide $A(x)$ by $B(x)$ obtaining a quotient $Q(x)$ and a remainder $R(x)$. This can be expressed as follows:

(1) $A(x) = B(x) \cdot Q(x) + R(x)$ (the degree of $R(x)$ is less than the degree of $B(x)$).

If the degree of $R(x) = 0$, the algorithm stops with the greatest common factor of $A(x)$ and $B(x)$ being $B(x)$. Otherwise we divide $B(x)$ by $R(x)$ obtaining a quotient $Q_1(x)$ and a remainder $R_1(x)$. As before this can be expressed as follows:

(2) $B(x) = R(x) \cdot Q_1(x) + R_1(x)$ (the degree of $R_1(x)$ is less than the degree of $R(x)$).

If $R_1(x) = 0$, the algorithm stops; the gcf is $R(x)$. Otherwise we divide $R(x)$ by $R_1(x)$.

This procedure will eventually stop since we obtain a sequence of polynomials $B(x)$, $R(x)$, $R_1(x)$, . . . whose degrees form a decreasing sequence of non-negative integers. Eventually some degree will be zero. The polynomial last used as a divisor is the greatest common factor.

This can be summarized as follows:

(1) Get M, $A(x)$, N, and $B(x)$ ($M \geq N$).
(2) Set DIVIDEND $(x) \leftarrow A(x)$.
(3) Set DIVISOR $(x) \leftarrow B(x)$.
(4) Divide DIVIDEND (x) by DIVISOR (x) obtaining $Q(x)$ and $R(x)$.
(5) Compare degree of $R(x)$ with zero.
(6) If degree of $R(x)$ is zero proceed to step 8.
(7) If degree of $R(x)$ is not zero, then
$$\text{set DIVIDEND } (x) \leftarrow \text{DIVISOR } (x)$$
$$\text{set DIVISOR } (x) \leftarrow R(x)$$
proceed to step (4).
(8) The greatest common factor has been obtained and its value is the polynomial DIVISOR (x).

A flow chart for this algorithm is seen in Figure 54. The program follows.

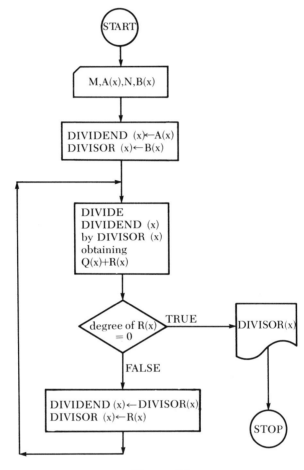

Figure 54

```
      SUBROUTINE POLYD(A,B,C,M,N,MN1)
      DIMENSION A(1),B(1),C(1)
C
C     COEFFICIENTS ARE IN INCREASING ORDER
C     THAT IS A = A(I)*X**M+A(2)*X(M−1)+. . .
C     A(M−1)*X+A(M)
C     IF C(X) IS THE QUOTIENT OF A(X) BY B(X)
C     AND R(X) IS THE REMAINDER, THEN SINCE
C     THEY ARE RELATED BY THE EQUATION
C     A(X) = B(X)*C(X)+R(X) IT FOLLOWS THAT
```

```
C       C(X) IS OF DEGREE M−N, AND
C       R(X) IS OF DEGREE N−1
C
        N2 = N+2
        M1 = M+1
C
C       EQUATING THE COEFFICIENTS OF THE
C       SAME POWER OF X ON BOTH SIDES OF
C       A(X) = B(X)*C(X)+R(X) WE GET THE
C       FOLLOWING RELATIONS
C       FOR C(X) THE QUOTIENT WE GET
C       C(1) = A(1)/B(1)
C       C(2) = (A(2)−C(1)*B(2))/B(1)
C       C(3) = (A(1)−C(1)*B(3)−C(2)*B(2))/B(1)
C       .
C       .
C       C(I) = (A(I)−SIGMA(C(J)*B(I−J+1))
C       FOR J = 1, . .(I−1))/B(1) FOR I SUCH
C       2LE I LE M−N+1)
C       C(M−N+1) = (A(M−N+1)−SIGMA(C(J)*B(M−N−2−J)
C       FOR ALL J FROM I, . . .M−N))/B(1)
C
C       CALCULATE QUOTIENT
C
        DO 10 I = N2,M1
   10   B(I) = 0.
        C(1) = A(1)/B(1)
        MN1 = M−N+1
        DO 100 I = 2,MN1
        C(I) = A(I)
        I1 = I−1
        DO 90 J = 1,I1
        IJ1 = I−J+1
   90   C(I) = C(I)−C(J)*B(IJ1)
  100   C(I) = C(I)/B(1)
        MN2 = M−N+2
C       THE ABOVE DEVELOPS THE QUOTIENT,
C       THE COEFFICIENTS OF THE REMAINDER
C       FOLLOW
C       LET US PLACE THE REMAINDER IN C(X)
C       FROM M−N+2, . . .,TO M+1
C       IN THE FOLLOWING EXPRESSION SIGMA
C       RUNS FROM J = 1, . . . , TO M−N+1
```

```
C      C(M−N+2) = A(M−N+2)−SIGMA(C(J)*B(M−N+3−J)
C      .
C      .
C      C(I) = A(I)−SIGMA(C(J)*B(I−J+1) FOR
C      ALL I SUCH THAT M−N+2 LE I LE M+1
C      .
C      .
C      C(M+1) = A(M+1)−SIGMA(C(J)*B(M+2−J)
C      WHERE B(K) = 0 FOR ALL K SUCH THAT
C      N+2 LE K LE M+1)
C      CALCULATE REMAINDER
C
       DO 200 I = MN2,M1
       C(I) = A(I)
       DO 190 J = 1,MN1
       IJ1 = I−J+1
 190   C(I) = C(I)− C(J)*B(IJ1)
 200   CONTINUE
       RETURN
       END


C      HIGHEST COMMON FACTOR OF TWO
C      POLYNOMIALS
       DIMENSION A(10),B(10),C(10)
  11   READ (1,1) M,N
C
C      A IS APOLYNOMIAL OF DEGREE M
C      COEFFICIENTS ARE IN INCREASING ORDER
C      B IS A POLYNOMIAL OF DEGREE N
C
 400   M1 = M+1
       N1 = N+1
       WRITE (3,6000)
6000   FORMAT(1H1)
       READ (1,4) (A(I),I = 1,M1)
       READ (1,4) (B(I),I = 1,N1)
   5   CALL POLYD(A,B,C,M,N,LL)
C
C      DIVIDE POLYNOMIAL A(X) BY B(X)
C      GETTING A QUOTIENT AND REMAINDER
C      BOTH IN C(X) WHERE THE QUOTIENT
C      IS IN C(1),C(2), . . . ,C(LL) AND
```

```
C     THE REMAINDER IS IN C(LL+1),
C     C(LL+2), . . . ,C(M+1)
C     LL IS THE NUMBER OF TERMS IN QUOTIENT
C     M+1-LL IS THE NUMBER OF TERMS IN THE
C     REMAINDER
C
      M1 = M+1
      MNZ = LL+1
      DO 10 I = MNZ,M1
C
C     IF ALL THE TERMS C(I) IN REMAINDER
C     ARE ZERO THEN WE ARE THROUGH AND
C     THE LAST DIVISOR IS THE GREATEST
C     COMMON FACTOR, THEREFORE IF ANY OF
C     THE C(I) IS DIFFERENT FROM ZERO
C     WE MUST REPLACE A(X) AND B(X)
C     WITH B(X) AND R(X) RESPECTIVELY.
C
      IF (C(I)) 15,10,15
   15 II = I
      IF(M1-II) 20,45,20
C
C     IF ALL TERMS IN REMAINDER ARE ZERO
C     BUT THE LAST TERM WHICH IS C(M+1) IS
C     NOT 0
C     THEN THE POLYNOMIALS HAVE ONLY A
C     COMMON FACTOR OF DEGREE ZERO
C     HENCE THE TWO POLYNOMIALS ARE
C     PRIME TO EACH OTHER.
C
   10 CONTINUE
      N1 = N+1
C
C     WRITE THE GREATEST COMMON FACTOR
C     B(1),B(2), . . . ,B(N+1)
C
      WRITE(3,300) (B(I),I = 1,N1)
  300 FORMAT(//,'0 GREATEST COMMON'
     1 ' FACTOR IS ',10F9.2)
      GO TO 11
   20 CONTINUE
C
C     MOVE B(X) TO A(X) AND
```

```
C     MOVE THE REMAINDER C(LL+1),
C     C(LL+2), . . . ,C(M+1) TO B(X)
C
      DO 25 I = 1,N
   25 A(I) = B(I)
      L = M+1−II+1
      DO 30 I = 1,L
      IK = II+I−1
   30 B(I) = C(IK)
C
C     ADJUST M AND N FOR THE NEW
C     DEGREES OF A AND B RESPECTIVELY
C
      M = N
      N = L−1
      GO TO 5
   45 WRITE (3,301)
  301 FORMAT ('0 PRIME POLYNOMIALS')
      GO TO 11
    1 FORMAT (I2,I2)
    4 FORMAT(10F5.0)
  500 STOP
      END
```

Exercise

Modify the above main program to compute the highest common factor of two polynomials in such a way that the original polynomial B will be saved. The print out of the highest common factor should have the following message:

THE HIGHEST COMMON FACTOR OF
A .... and B .... is

when the .... must be substituted by the coefficients of A and B, respectively.

Chapter VII

SOLUTION OF EQUATIONS AND PLOTTING

In this chapter some algorithms used to find the rational roots of algebraic equations are introduced. This chapter also contains Sturm's method for separating the roots of an algebraic equation. We also include a plotting algorithm and iteration algorithm. The chapter concludes with a method to approximate the roots of an algebraic equation.

1. RATIONAL ROOTS OF ALGEBRAIC EQUATIONS

Let $f(x) = a_0 x^n + a_1 x^{n-1} + \ldots + a_{n-1} x + a_n$ be a polynomial of degree n, with $a_i (i = 0, 1, \ldots n)$ real or complex numbers. The expression $f(x) = 0$ is called an algebraic equation of degree n.

Recall that a real or complex number α is said to be a root of $f(x) = 0$ if the value of $f(x)$ at $x = \alpha$ is zero.

We quote, without proof, a very important result known as the Fundamental Theorem of Algebra:

Any algebraic equation has at least one root.

We use this result to prove the following result, which plays an important role in the solution of algebraic equations.

An algebraic equation $f(x) = 0$ of degree n has n roots. Assume that $x = \alpha_1$ is a root of $f(x) = 0$. We can represent $f(x)$ as follows:

$$f(x) = (x - \alpha_1) f_1(x)$$

where $f_1(x)$ is a polynomial of degree $n - 1$. Using the *Fundamental Theorem of Algebra*, $f_1(x)$ has at least one root, say α_2. Hence, $f_1(x)$ can be represented as

$$f_1(x) = (x - \alpha_2) f_2(x)$$

215

where $f_2(x)$ is a polynomial of degree $n - 2$. We can continue this procedure until we finally get a constant A. We can write

$$f(x) = (x - \alpha_1)(x - \alpha_2) \ldots (x - \alpha_n)A.$$

where $\alpha_1, \alpha_2, \ldots \alpha_n$, A are real or complex numbers and the α_i's are not necessarily different. This shows that $f(x) = 0$ has n roots.

1.1

Assume that $x = \alpha$, α an integer, is a root of the algebraic equation

$$f(x) = a_0 x^n + a_1 x^{n-1} + \ldots + a_{n-1} x + a_n = 0.$$

Then we must have

$$f(\alpha) = a_0 \alpha^n + a_1 \alpha^{n-1} + \ldots + a_{n-1} \alpha + a_n = 0.$$

From the above expression, we obtain

$$a_n = -(a_0 \alpha^n + a_1 \alpha^{n-1} + \ldots + a_{n-1} \alpha).$$

a_n can also be expressed in the form

$$a_n = -(a_0 \alpha^{n-1} + a_1 \alpha^{n-2} + \ldots + a_{n-1}) \alpha = B\alpha.$$

This shows that α is a divisor of a_n. We have obtained the following result.

"In order that an integer α be a root of an algebraic equation $a_0 x^n + \ldots + a_n = 0$, it must be a divisor of the coefficient a_n."

1.2

Assume that $\alpha = \dfrac{p}{q}$ where $\dfrac{p}{q}$ is reduced to lowest terms is a root of the algebraic equation $a_0 x^n + \ldots + a_{n-1} x + a_n = 0$.
We must have

$$a_0 \frac{p^n}{q^n} + a_1 \frac{p^{n-1}}{q^{n-1}} + \ldots + a_{n-1} \frac{p}{q} + a_n = 0.$$

This can be written as follows:

$$a_0 p^n + a_1 p^{n-1} q + \ldots + a_{n-1} p q^{n-1} + a_n q^n = 0.$$

We can compute $a_0 p^n$ from the above expression in the form

$$a_0 p^n = -(a_1 p^{n-1} q + \ldots + a_{n-1} p q^{n-1} + a_n q^n) = -(a_1 p^{n-1} + \ldots + a_{n-1} p q^{n-2} + a_n q^{n-1})q.$$

Next, p and q are relatively prime; hence, q must be a divisor of a_0. Combining this result with the previous result, we have:

In order that $\frac{p}{q}$ (reduced to its lower terms) be a root of $a_0 x^n + a_1 x^{n-1} + \ldots + a_{n-1} x + a_n = 0$, p must be a divisor of a_n and q must be a divisor of a_0.

1.3

Assume that $x = \alpha$ is a root of the nth degree equation $f(x) = a_0 x^n + a_1 x^{n-1} + \ldots + a_{n-1} x + a_n = 0$. We know that we can write $f(x)$ as follows:

$$f(x) = (x - \alpha) f_1(x),$$

where $f_1(x)$ is the quotient obtained on dividing $f(x)$ by $(x - \alpha)$. If we give to x the value 1 we obtain:

$$f(1) = (1 - \alpha) f_1(1) = -(\alpha - 1) f_1(1).$$

Similarly, if x takes the value -1 we obtain:

$$f(-1) = (-1 - \alpha) f_1(-1) = -(1 + \alpha) f_1(-1).$$

We have obtained the following result.

In order that an integer α might be a root of $f(x) = a_0 x^n + \ldots + a_{n-1} x + a_n = 0$ it must satisfy the following conditions:

(1) $\alpha - 1$ must be a divisor of $f(1)$
(2) $\alpha + 1$ must be a divisor of $f(-1)$

We shall use the notation $p = \overset{.}{q}$ to indicate that p and q are integers and that q is a divisor of p, i.e., there exists an integer $k \neq 0$ such that $p = kq$.

1.4

It is often very convenient to know if an algebraic equation does not have integral roots. This can be found applying the following test.

Let $f(x) = 0$ be an algebraic equation. If any of the numbers $f(-1)$, $f(0)$, or $f(1)$ is not a multiple of 3, then $f(x) = 0$ has no integral roots. To show this let us assume that $x = \alpha$ is a root of $f(x)$, then

$$f(x) = (x - \alpha) f_1(x)$$

where $f_1(x)$ is a polynomial of $n - 1$ degree; substitute x by -1, 0, 1, in the above expression and we get $f(-1) = \overline{(1 + \alpha)}' f(0) = \overline{\alpha}'$ $f(1) = \overline{(\alpha - 1)}$. The numbers $\alpha - 1$, α, $\alpha + 1$ are consecutive; hence, one must be a multiple of 3.

1.5

The process of obtaining all the integral roots of an algebraic equation may be very tedious. This process can be shortened if one knows an upper bound of the values of these roots, i.e., a number that is bigger than any of the roots. An upper bound for the positive roots is found by using the *Laguerre-Thibault method.*

L will be an upper bound for the algebraic equation $f(x) = 0$, if all the coefficients and the remainder obtained on dividing $f(x)$, by $x - L$ are non-negative. (Laguerre-Thibault).

This method can be justified as follows:

Let $f(x) = 0$ be an nth degree equation then

$$f(x) = (x - L)(c_0 x^{n-2} + \ldots + c_{n-1}) + f(L),$$

where $f(L) \geqslant 0$ and $c_i \geqslant 0$, $i = 0, 1, \ldots, (n - 1)$.

Let $x > L$. Then $f(x) > 0$. Hence $f(x)$ cannot be zero and L is an upper bound for the roots of $f(x) = 0$.

1.6

We are now in a position to write an algorithm to find the integral roots of a polynomial. We shall proceed in two steps.

Step 1.   We shall find an algorithm to find an upper bound for the positive roots of a polynomial.

Analysis.   There is a procedure to obtain an upper bound suggested by the previous result and the Horner's algorithm. Recall that the coefficients $c_0, c_1, \ldots, c_n$ obtained on dividing a polynomial $f(x) = a_0 x^n + \ldots + a_n$ by $x - \alpha$ satisfy the following recurrence relation:

$$c_0 = a_0, \ldots c_i = \alpha c_{i-1} + a_i, i = 1, \ldots, n.$$

This relation could be written in the following form:

$$c_0 = a_0, \ c_1 = a_0 \alpha + a_1, \ c_2 = (a_0 \alpha + a_1)\alpha + a_2 = a_0 \alpha^2 + a_1 \alpha + a_2 \ldots,$$
$$c_n = a_0 \alpha^n + a_1 \alpha^{n-1} + \ldots + \alpha_n. \tag{4}$$

Consider the following sequence of polynomials,

$$f_0(x) = a_0, \quad f_1(x) = xf_0(x) + a_1 = a_0 x + a_1,$$
$$f_2(x) = xf_1(x) + a_2 = a_0 x^2 + a_1 x + a_2, \ldots, f_n(x) = xf_{n-1}(x) + a_n = a_0 x^n + a_1 x^{n-1} + \ldots + a_n. \tag{5}$$

Using the polynomials in (5), we find that

$$c_0 = f_0(\alpha), \quad c_1 = f_1(\alpha), \ldots, c_n = f_n(\alpha)$$

Note that

$$f_i(x) = a_0 x^i + a_1 x^{i-1} + \ldots + a_i = (x - \alpha)[f_0(\alpha)x^{i-1} + f_1(\alpha)x^{i-2} + \ldots + f_{i-1}(\alpha)] + f_i(\alpha).$$

These polynomials $f_i(x)$ have the following properties

(i) If for some $\alpha > 0$, $f_1(\alpha) \geq 0$, $f_2(\alpha) \geq 0, \ldots, f_{n-1}(\alpha) \geq 0$ and $f_n(\alpha) > 0$ then α is an upper bound of the roots of $f(x) = 0$.

(ii) If for some $a > 0$ the number, $f_1(\alpha), f_2(\alpha), \ldots, f_i(\alpha)$ $(i \leq n)$ are non-negative then for $\beta > \alpha$, $f_1(\beta) > 0$, $f_2(\beta) > 0, \ldots,$ $f_i(\beta) > 0$ $(i \leq n)$.

We are now in a position to state a procedure to find an upper bound of the positive roots of an nth degree algebraic equation.

(1) Start with a positive number α which makes $f_1(\alpha)$ positive. This should not be difficult since $f_1(\alpha) = \alpha a_0 + a_1$ must be positive.

(2) Compute $f_2(\alpha), f_3(\alpha) \ldots f_n(\alpha)$.

(3) Stop at the first $i \leq n$ such that $f_i(\alpha) < 0$

(4) Increase the value of α, say β, until $f_i(\beta)$ becomes positive, then $f_1(\beta), f_2(\beta), \ldots, f_i(\beta)$ are positive.

(5) Compute $f_{i+1}(\beta), f_{i+2}(\beta), \ldots, f_n(\beta)$.

(6) Stop at the first value of i which makes $f_i(\beta) < 0$.

(7) Proceed as in (4).

In this way we will finally find a value γ such that $f_1(\gamma), f_2(\gamma), \ldots, f_n(\gamma)$ are positive. It could happen that $f_n(\gamma) = 0$. In which case we have also found a root. The remaining roots will be smaller than γ.

A flow chart to show this algorithm is in Figure 55. Next, we write a subroutine, UPBND(A,N,UP), to compute the upper bound of an algebraic equation.

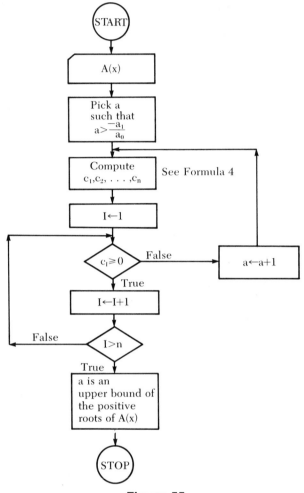

Figure 55

SUBROUTINE UPBND(A,N,UP)
```
C
C     SUBROUTINE TO FIND UPPER BOUND OF ROOTS
C     OF POLYNOMIAL
C     POLYNOMIAL STORED IN A, A = A(1)*X**N+A(2)
C     *X**(N−1)+ . . . +A(N)*X+A(N+1)
C
```

```
      DIMENSION A(20)
      DIMENSION C(20)
      M = N+1
C
C     USE AS STARTING VALUE FOR X A2/A1
C
      I = ABS(A(2)/A(1))
      X = I
C
C     USING HORNERS ALGORITHM TO EVALUATE
C     FUNCTION AT X
C
    5 CALL POLYV(A,N,X,C,R)
      DO 10 I = 1,M
C
C     IF ALL COEFFICIENTS C(I) ARE POSITIVE THEN
C     GO TO 10
C     UNTIL YOU HAVE CHECKED THEM ALL AT
C     WHICH TIME YOU HAVE AN UPPER
C     BOUND X OR UP
C
      IF(C(I))15,15,10
   10 CONTINUE
      UP = X
      RETURN
C
C     IF ANY C(I) IS NEGATIVE OR ZERO GET A NEW
C     CANDIDATE FOR UPPER BOUND
C     BY GOING TO 15 AND ADDING 1 TO X FOR
C     NEW VALUE
   15 X = X+1.
      GO TO 5
      END
```

Exercise

Test the above subroutine with a main program calling UPBND(A,N,UP) using the equation $x^5 - 3x^4 + 6x^3 - 2x + 5 = 0$.

Step 2. Once we have an upper bound for the positive integer roots we proceed to find an algorithm to find them as follows:

Analysis. We assume that the coefficient of x^n is one. This is no loss of generality since it is always possible to find a suitable change of variable which will make this coefficient one. Using the previous remarks we have the following algorithm.

(1)   Get $A(x)$ where $A(x) = x^n + a_1 x^{n-1} + \ldots + a_n$.

(2)   Compute $A(1)$, $A(-1)$, $A(0)$.

(3)   If $A(1)$ or $A(-1)$ or $A(0)$ is divisible by 3, proceed to step (5).

(4)   If none of $A(1)$ or $A(-1)$ or $A(0)$ is divisible by 3, $A(x)$ has no rational roots.

(5)   Compute L, the upper bound of the positive roots of $A(x)$.

(6)   Compute all the divisors, d, of a_n that are less than or equal to L.

(7)   Let dd be a divisor not previously picked.

(8)   Compute $dd + 1$ and $dd - 1$.

(9)   If $dd + 1$ divides $A(-1)$ or $dd - 1$ divides $A(1)$, then go to step (11).

(10) If either $dd + 1$ does not divide $A(-1)$ or $dd - 1$ does not divide $A(1)$, then go to step (14).

(11) Compute $A(dd)$.

(12) If $A(dd)$ is zero, dd is a root of $A(x)$; proceed to step (14).

(13) If $A(dd)$ is non zero, dd is not a root of $A(x)$; proceed to step (14).

(14) If there are any divisors d that have not been used as a dd, proceed to step (7).

(15) If all d's have been used as dd's stop as the algorithm has exhausted possibilities for roots.

Integer Roots (continued)

Example

$$A(x) = x^3 - 3x^2 - 4x - 12$$
$$A(1) = -18$$
$$A(0) = -12$$
$$A(-1) = -12$$

The equation $A(x) = 0$ might have integer roots since at least one of $A(1)$, $A(0)$, $A(-1)$ is divisible by 3.

Try 6 as an upper bound; one gets

	1	3	−4	−12
6		6	54	300
	1	9	50	288

Therefore, 6 is an upper bound since all the coefficients are non-negative and the remainder is positive. Next, we determine all the divisors of 12 that are smaller than 6. They are 1, 2, 3, and 4. Using synthetic division, we find that $x = 2$ is the only positive root.

In order to find the negative roots of any equation, one may substitute $-x$ for x in the equation $A(x) = 0$, obtaining $A(-x) = 0$. The positive roots of $A(-x)$ will be the negative roots of the original equation $A(x) = 0$.

To illustrate this technique, we use $A(x) = x^3 + x^2 - 14x - 24 = 0$. $A(-x)$ becomes $A(-x) = x^3 - x^2 - 14x + 24 = 0$. The reader should check that 2 and 3 are roots of $A(-x)$. Then -2 and -3 are the negative roots of $A(x) = 0$.

We use an example to show a method to reduce the coefficient of x^n to 1.

Let $A(x) = 3x^4 + 2x^3 + 4x + 1 = 0$.

Substitute $x = \dfrac{y}{3}$ obtaining

$$3(y/3)^4 + 2(y/3)^3 + 4(y/3) + 1 = 0$$

Multiplying through by 3^3 one gets

$$y^4 + 2y^3 + 36y + 27 = 0.$$

A flow chart is seen in Figure 56.

Exercise

Write a program that will find all the integer roots of an algebraic equation of the form

$$A_0 x^n + A_1 x^{n-1} + \ldots + A_n = 0 \tag{1}$$

Use the subroutine UPBND(A,N,UP) to find upper bounds for positive roots. [By putting instead of x, $-x$ in (1) and instead of x, $\dfrac{1}{x}$, one can find lower bounds for the roots of (1).] Note that the algorithm given in the text assumes that $A_0 = 1$. Do the necessary changes in your program so the equation will be transformed in $x^n + B_1 x^{n-1} + \ldots + B_n = 0$. (See the flow chart in Figure 56.)

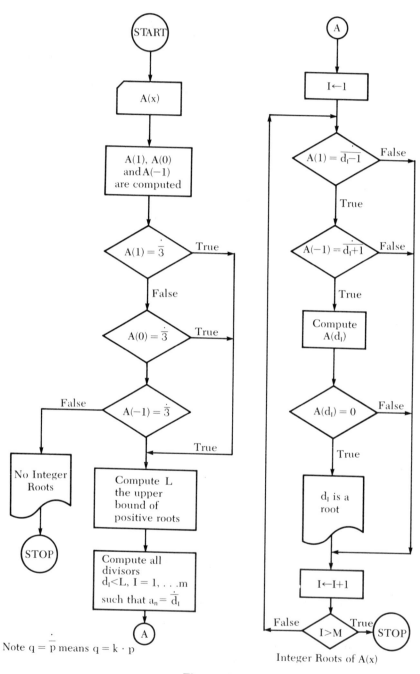

Note $q = \overline{p}$ means $q = k \cdot p$

Integer Roots of A(x)

Figure 56

2. SEPARATING THE ROOTS IN AN ALGEBRAIC EQUATION

The roots of an algebraic equation are said to be separated whenever a set of intervals (a_i, b_i) are obtained such that no interval contains more than one root.

We are now going to introduce here a method discovered by Sturm.

Sturm's Method

Analysis. Sturm's method assumes that the algebraic equation has no repeated roots (multiple roots).

Although calculus is not a prerequisite to read this book, we have to introduce a formal definition of derivative of a polynomial. Let $f(x) = a_0x^n + a_1x^{n-1} + \ldots + a_{n-1}x + a_n$ be a polynomial of degree n. The $n-1$ degree polynomial $f'(x) = d_0x^{n-1} + d_{n-1}x^{n-2} + \ldots + d_{n-2}x + d_{n-1}$ obtained using the formulas

$$d_i = (n-i)a_i, \quad 0 \leqslant i \leqslant n-1$$

is called the derivative of the polynomial $f(x)$.

$f'(x)$ can be written as follows:

$$f'(x) = na_nx^{n-1} + (n-1)a_{n-1}x^{n-2} + \ldots + 2a_{n-2}x + a_{n-1}.$$

For example, the derivative of $x^3 + 3x^2 - x + 5$ is $3x^2 + 6x + 1$.

We introduce now a few more definitions, the so-called *Sturm auxiliary functions* and *Sturm's Functions*. This terminology is attributed to F. Cajori.

Let $f(x) = 0$ be an algebraic equation without multiple roots. Let $f'(x)$ be the derivative of $f(x)$. Divide $f(x)$ by $f'(x)$. Change the sign of the remainder. Proceed as in the process of finding the highest common factor of $f(x)$ and $f'(x)$ changing every time the sign of the remainder before it is used as a divisor. Continue this procedure until a constant is obtained as a remainder. Change the sign of that remainder also. Let the different remainders with their sign changed be denoted by $f_2(x), f_3(x), \ldots, f_n(x)$.

These polynomials $f_i(x)$ $(i = 2, \ldots n)$ are called *Sturm's auxiliary functions*. The functions $f(x), f'(x), f_2(x), \ldots, f_n(x)$ are called *Sturm's Function*.

Let $f(x), f'(x), f_2(x), \ldots, f_n(x)$ be a sequence of Sturm's functions corresponding to an algebraic equation $f(x) = 0$. Compute the values of this sequence at $x = a$. That is, form the sequence $f(a), f'(a), \ldots, f_n(a)$. Two consecutive terms have the same or opposite sign. (The case in which both are zero is ruled out by the property of Sturm's functions quoted below.) If the two consecutive terms have the same sign, we say a *permanence* has occurred. If they have different signs we say a *variation* has occurred.

Example

Assume the values taken by the Sturm's function of a certain algebraic equation are -6, 3, 2, -1, 6. We find that this sequence presents three variations and one permanence.

Sturm's functions have the following properties:

(a) Two consecutive auxiliary functions cannot vanish for the same value of x.

(b) When any auxiliary function vanishes, the two adjacent functions have opposite signs.

(c) When x, in passing from the value a to the value b, passes through a value which makes an auxiliary function vanish, Sturm's functions neither gain nor lose variations in sign.

(d) When x, passing from the value a to the value b, assumes a value which is a root of the equation $f(x) = 0$, then Sturm's functions lose one variation in sign. Using properties (a), (b), (c), and (d), it is possible to prove the following.

Sturm's Theorem

The number of roots of the algebraic equation $f(x) = 0$ that are located in an interval (a,b) is equal to the number of variations lost in passing from the sequence, $f(a), f'(a), f_1(a), \ldots, f_n(x)$ to the sequence $f(b), f'(b), f_1(b), \ldots, f_n(b)$.

Example

Compute the Sturm functions for the equation $f(x) = x^4 + 3x^3 + 3x^2 + 3x + 2$. Note that $f'(x) = 4x^3 + 9x^2 + 6x + 3$.

Multiply $f(x)$ by 4 and divide by $f'(x)$

$$
\begin{array}{r}
x + 3 \\ \hline
\end{array}
$$

$$
4x^3 + 9x^2 + 6x + 3 \,\big)\; 4x^4 + 12x^3 + 12x^2 + 12x + 8
$$

$$
\underline{4x^4 + 9x^3 + 6x^2 + 3x}
$$

$$
3x^3 + 6x^2 + 9x + 8
$$

Multiply by 4

$$
12x^3 + 24x^2 + 36x + 32
$$

$$
\underline{12x^3 + 27x^2 + 18x + 9}
$$

$$
-3x^2 + 18x + 23
$$

$$
f_1(x) = -(-3x^2 + 18x + 23) = 3x^2 - 18x - 23.
$$

Since the quotient is to be disregarded, the partial remainders can be multiplied by appropriate constants to facilitate the division.

$$3 \cdot f'(x) = 12x^3 + 27x^2 + 18x + 9$$

dividing by $f_1(x)$ we get

$$
\begin{array}{r}
4x + \quad 33 \\
3x^2 - 18x - 23 \quad \overline{)12x^3 + 27x^2 + \quad 18x + \quad 9} \\
\underline{12x^3 - 72x^2 - \quad 92x} \\
99x^2 + 110x + \quad 9 \\
\underline{99x^2 - 594x - 759} \\
704x + 768 = 64(11x + 12)
\end{array}
$$

$f_2(x) = -11x - 12$

To divide $f_1(x)$ by $f_2(x)$ we multiply $f_1(x)$ by 11

$$
\begin{array}{r}
- \quad 3x + \quad 234 \\
-11x - 12 \quad \overline{)33x^2 - 198x - \quad 253} \\
\underline{33x^2 + \quad 36x} \\
-234x - \quad 253 \\
\text{multiply by 11} \quad -2574x - 2783 \\
\underline{-2574x - 2808} \\
25
\end{array}
$$

hence $f_3(x) = -25$.

To summarize, the Sturm functions are

$$f(x) = x^4 + 3x^3 + 3x^2 + 3x + 2$$
$$f'(x) = 4x^3 - 9x^2 + 6x + 3$$
$$f_1(x) = 3x^2 - 18x - 23$$
$$f_2(x) = -11x - 12$$
$$f_3(x) = -25$$

The sign of the value of the Sturm functions for $x = -3$, $x = 0$, and $x = 3$ are

x	-3	0	3
f	$+$	$+$	$+$
f'	$-$	$+$	$+$
f_1	$+$	$-$	$-$
f_2	$+$	$-$	$-$
f_3	$-$	$-$	$-$

If $V(x)$ is the number of variations at x then $V(-3) = 3$, $V(0) = 1$, $V(3) = 1$. The number of variations lost between $x = -3$ and $x = 0$ is $3 - 1 = 2$. Hence, there are two roots in the interval $(-3,0)$. Similarly, there are no roots in the interval $(0, +3)$.

A FORTRAN flow chart is seen in Figure 57, Figure 58; A FORTRAN program follows. This program uses a subroutine DPOLY(A,N,DA) which is used to compute the derivative of a polynomial.

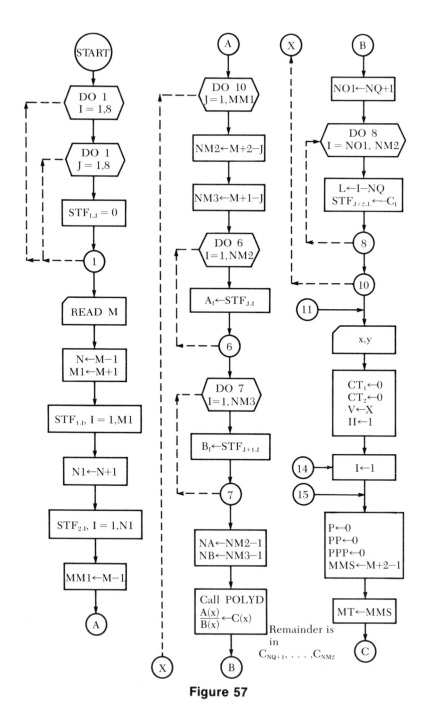

Figure 57

228

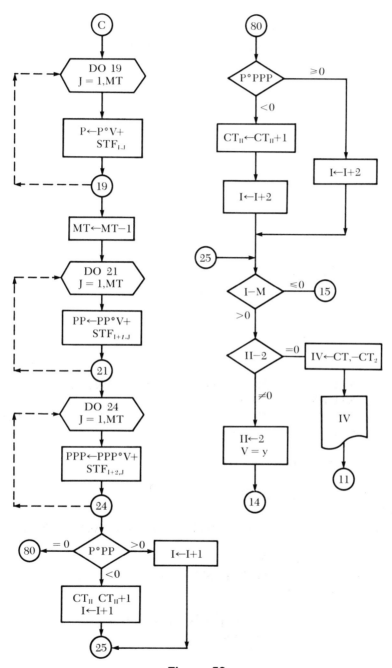

Figure 58

229

```
C
C     STURM'S METHOD FOR SEPARATING
C     THE ROOTS OF AN EQUATION
C     PROGRAM ASSUMES THAT THE EQUATION HAS
C     ONLY SIMPLE ROOTS
C
      DIMENSION STF (8,8),C(9),A(8),B(8)
      DIMENSION CT(2)
      INTEGER CT
      DO 1 I = 1,8
      DO 1 J = 1,8
    1 STF(I,J) = 0.0
    2 FORMAT(I2)
C
C     M IS THE DEGREE OF F(X)
C     N IS THE DEGREE OF THE DERIVATIVE OF F(X)
C     M1 IS THE NUMBER OF TERMS IN F(X)
C     N1 IS THE NUMBER OF TERMS IN 'DERIVATIVE
C     OF F(X)'
C
      READ(1,2) M
      N = M−1
      M1 = M+1
C
C     STF(1,I) IS THE FUNCTION OF X AND IS FIRST
C     STURM FUNCTION
C     STF(2,I) IS 'DERIVATIVE OF F(X)' AND IS SECOND
C     STURM FUNCTION
C
      READ (1,3) (STF(1,I),I = 1,M1)
      N1 = N+1
    3 FORMAT(8F5.0)
C
C     DERIV D(I) = (N−I) °STF(1,I) FOR I = 0,1, . . .,N−1
C
      DO 4 I = 1,M
    4 STF(2,I) = (M−I+1)°STF(1,I)
      MM1 = M−1
C
C     LOOP DOWN TO 10 FINDS STURM FUNCTIONS
C     OF DEGREE N−2,N−3, . . . ,3,2,1
C
      DO 10 J = 1,MM1
      NM2 = M+2−J
```

```
      NM3 = M+1−J
C
C     PREPARES STF(J,I) FOR DIVISION BY STF(J+1,I)
C     TO GENERATE STF(J+2,I) THAT IS STURM
C     FUNCTION J IS DIVIDED BY
C     STURM FUNCTION J+1 GETTING STURM
C     FUNCTION J+2 TERMINATING WHEN
C     J+2 IS DEGREE 0
C     PUT ST(J,I) IN A,STF(J+1) IN B, AND STF(J+2) IN C
C
      DO 6 I = 1,NM2
    6 A(I) = STF(J,I)
      DO 7 I = 1,NM3
    7 B(I) = STF(J+1,I)
      NA = NM2−1
      NB = NM3−1
      CALL POLYD(A,B,C,NA,NB,NQ)
      NQ1 = NQ+1
      DO 8 I = NQ1,NM2
      L = I−NQ
    8 STF(J+2,L) = −C(I)
   10 CONTINUE
C
C     X AND Y ARE ENDPOINTS OF INTERVAL FOR
C     WHICH WE ARE SEEKING HOW
C     MANY ROOTS ARE IN THAT INTERVAL
C
   11 READ(1,3) X,Y
C
C     CT(2) ARE COUNTERS FOR PERMANENCE AND
C     VARIATION
C
      CT(1) = 0.0
      CT(2) = 0.0
      V = X
      II = 1
   14 I = 1
C
C     P, PP, AND PPP ARE POLYNOMIAL EVALUATIONS
C     AT V = X FOR STURM FUNCTIONS
C     J,J+1, AND J+2
C
   15 P = 0.0
      PP = 0.0
```

```
            PPP = 0.0
            MMS = M+2−I
            MT = MMS
            DO 19 J = 1,MT
     19     P = P°V+STF(I,J)
            MT = MT−1
            DO 21 J = 1,MT
     21     PP = PP°V+STF(I+1,J)
            DO 24 J = 1,MT
     24     PPP = PPP°V+STF(I+2,J)
C
C     IF P°PP IS NEGATIVE THEN P AND PP ARE
C     DIFFERENT SIGNS SO
C     COUNT SIGN CHANGE
C
            IF (P°PP) 100,80,23
    100     CT(II) = CT(II)+1
            I = I+1
            GO TO 25
     23     I = I+1
            GO TO 25
C
C     IF P°PP = 0 CHECK P°PPP
C     IF P°PPP IS NEGATIVE THEY ARE OF DIFFERENT
C     SIGNS SO COUNT IN CT
C
     80     IF(P°PPP) 90,94,94
C
C     CT(II) IS VARIATION AT V = X
C
     90     CT(II) = CT(II)+1
            I = I+2
            GO TO 25
     94     I = I+2
     25     IF(I−M) 15,15,900
    900     IF(II−2) 950,1000,950
C
C     CHANGE II TO 2 SO WORKING WITH CT(2)
C     CHANGE V TO Y
C
    950     II = 2
            V = Y
            GO TO 14
```

```
C
C     IV IS THE DIFFERENCE IN CT HENCE IS TOTAL
C     DIFFERENCE OF VARIATION
C     AND IS THE NUMBER OF ROOTS BETWEEN X
C     AND Y FOR THE FUNCTION F(X)
C
 1000  IV = CT(1)−CT(2)
       WRITE(3,95) X,Y,IV
       WRITE (3,96)
       GO TO 11
   95  FORMAT(' THE NUMBER OF ROOTS BETWEEN',
      1 2F10.3,' ARE', I3)
   96  FORMAT(1H0)
   20  FORMAT(8F15.0)
       END


       SUBROUTINE DPOLY(A,N,DA)
       DIMENSION DA(1),A(1)
C
C     POLYNOMIAL STORED IN A,  A = A(1)*X**N+A(2)
C     *X**(N−1)+. . .+A(N)*X+A(N+1)
C     FIND DERIVATIVE OF POLYNOMIAL IN A,
C     STORE IN DA
C
C     DERIVATIVE OF TERM AT A(I) IS A(I)*(N−I+1)*X**
C     (N−I+1) FOR
C     I BETWEEN 1 AND N
C
       DO 10 I = 1,N
   10  DA(I) = (N−I+1)*A(I)
       RETURN
       END
```

Exercise

Find the number of roots of the equation $x^4 + 3x^2 + 3x + 5 = 0$ between 0 and 1 using the Sturm's method.

3. PLOTTING

In describing how one variable is related to another variable it is often convenient to use a plot of one variable against the other. We would like to construct a plot of y against x on an output device, i.e., the printer. Although it is impossible to construct a continuous line with the printer, it is possible to suggest this line by spacing the points close enough together. In constructing the plot one needs to have given the function $y = f(x)$, the beginning and ending values of x, a and b, and the size of the increment Δx to use in moving from a to b. Once this is known, by evaluating $y = f(x)$ for all values of x between a and b, it is possible to find the maximum y and the minimum y (for any x). Using this maximum and this minimum, one can scale and translate the y's so as to fit on one line of the printer. The value of y can be represented by printing a symbol like * in the appropriate position of the print line.

Let NO represent the number of print positions. Let C represent the vector of print positions. Let BLNK stand for "blank symbol" and AST stand for *. We have the following algorithm for the plotting of $y = Y(x)$:

(1)   Set X←A, BIG←Y(X), SMALL←Y(X)

(2)   SET N←1 + (B−A)/ΔX

(3)   Set I←1.

(4)   Compute Y(X)

(5)   Compare Y(X) with SMALL
         IF Y(X)<SMALL then SMALL←Y(X)

(6)   Compare Y(X) with BIG
         IF Y(X)>BIG then BIG←Y(X)

(7)   Set X←X+ΔX and I←I+1

(8)   Compare I with N
         If I≤N then go to step (4)
         If I>N then go to step (9)

(9)   Compute DEL, DEL = NO/(BIG−SMALL)

(10) X←A, I←1

(11) Set J←1

(12) C(J)←BLNK, J←J+1

(13) Compare J with NO
         If J ≤ NO go to step (12)
         If J > NO then go to step (14)

(14) Compute K, K = [ABS(SMALL)+Y(X)]*DEL+1

(15) C(K)←AST

(16) Print X, Y(X), C(K) for K = 1,100

(17) X←X+ΔX, I←I+1

(18) Compare I with N
         If I≤N, go to (11)
         If I>N stop

Figure 59 has a flow chart for this algorithm. Next, we present an example in which the above algorithm is used to plot the graph of $F = SIN(X)+SIN(XA)+SIN(XB)+SIN(XC)$.

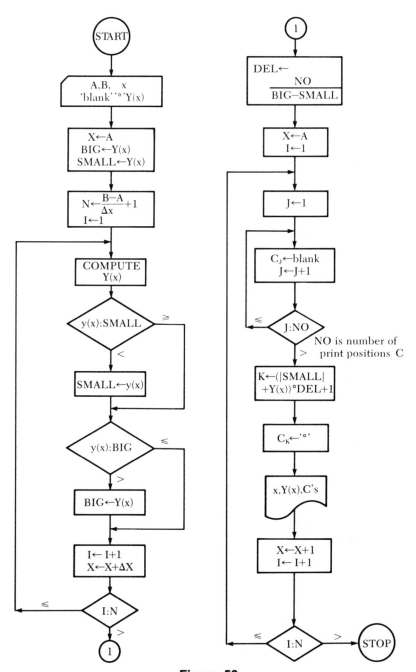

Figure 59

```
C    GRAPH OF F(X)
     DIMENSION C(100)
 1   FORMAT(1X,F5.1,F10.1,100A1)
 2   FORMAT(A1,A1)
33   FORMAT('1')
     WRITE(3,33)
     READ (1,2) BLANK,AST
     SMALL = 100000.
     BIG = −100000.
     A = 0.0
     B = 4.0
     H = .1
     X = A
     DO 10 I = 1,41
     XA = 2.*X
     XB = 3.*X
     XC = 4.*X
     F = SIN(X) +SIN(XA)+SIN(XB)+SIN(XC)
     IF(F−SMALL) 3,5,5
 3   SMALL = F
 5   IF (F−BIG) 10,10,6
 6   BIG = F
10   X = X+H
     DEL = 99./(BIG−SMALL)
     X = A
     DO 100 I = 1,81
     DO 90 J = 1,100
90   C(J) = BLANK
     XA = 2.*X
     XB = 3.*X
     XC = 4.*X
     F = SIN(X)+SIN(XA)+SIN(XB)+SIN(XC)
     K = (ABS(SMALL)+F)*DEL
     K = K+1
     C(K) = AST
     WRITE (3,1) X,F, (C(L),L = 1,100)
100  X = X+H
     END
```

Exercise

Use the above algorithm to plot the graph of $y = x^3 + 3x^2 - 2x - 1$. Choose values of x from 0 to 10.

4. ITERATION

One of the most valuable properties of a computer is its capability for repeating an operation an almost unlimited number of times. In the next algorithm, called *Iteration*, we are going to take advantage of this property.

Assume that we have a collection of numbers $A_1, A_2, \ldots, A_n$, and we know that "initially" $A_1 = 1$, $A_2 = 2$ and that A_i, A_{i+1}, A_{i+2} are related by

$$A_{i+2} = 2A_{i+1} + 3A_i$$

Giving different values to i we obtain:

$$A_3 = 2 \cdot 2 + 3 = 7, \quad A_4 = 20, \quad A_4 = 61, \ldots,$$

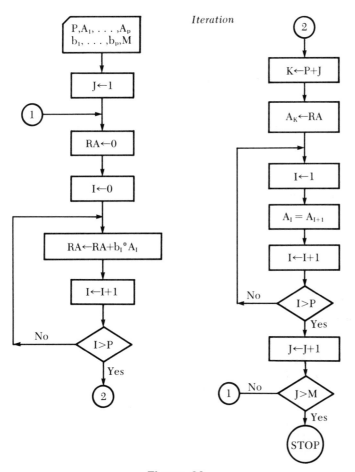

Figure 60

This problem can be "generalized," as follows: Let $A_1, A_2, \ldots,$ $A_n \ldots,$ be a collection of numbers. Assume that the first p numbers $A_1, A_2, \ldots, A_p$ are known. A_{p+1} is computed using the expression:

$$A_{p+1} = b_1 A_1 + b_2 A_2 + \ldots + b_p A_p$$

Similarly

$$A_{p+2} = b_1 A_2 + b_2 A_3 + \ldots + b_p A_{p+1}$$

In this fashion we can compute the value of any number provided we know the previous p values. Figure 60 contains a flow chart for this algorithm. Note that if $A_1 = A_2 = 1 = b_1 = b_2$ and $A_{i+2} = A_i + A_{i+1}$ we generate the *Fibonacci numbers*, 1,1,2,3,5,8, ...

The flow chart in Figure 60 shows the necessary steps to compute M values of A once the values of $A_1, A_2, \ldots A_p, b_1, b_2, \ldots b_p$ are known.

Exercises

In the algorithms that follow, write the necessary FORTRAN program to implement them.

1.   Construct a number E performing the following steps:

   (*i*)   Set E←1
   (*ii*) Set I←1
   (*iii*) SE←E
   (*iv*) E←E+1/I!
   (*v*)   DIF←|E−SE|
   (*vi*) If DIF$\leq 10^{-5}$ STOP. E has been computed.
           Otherwise
               I←I+1
           and return to step (*ii*)

2.   We want to construct a number, LOG 2 using the following algorithm;

   (*i*)   Set LOG 2←1
   (*ii*) Set I←2
   (*iii*) SLOG 2←LOG 2
   (*iv*) IF I is even Set LOG 2←LOG 2−1/I
           Otherwise   Set LOG 2←LOG 2+1/I
   (*v*)   DIF←|LOG 2−SLOG 2|
   (*vi*) IF DIF$\leq 10^{-3}$, STOP. LOG 2 has been computed.
           Otherwise,
               I←I+1
   (*vii*) Return to step (*iv*).

3.   Compute a number called SIN as follows:

(*i*)   Set SIN←1/2
(*ii*)   Set X←1/2
(*iii*)   Set FACT←1
(*iv*)   Set I←1
(*v*)   Set X←X · (1/2)²
(*vi*)   FACT←−FACT·(1/2I)(1/2I+1)
(*vii*)   SIN←SIN+X·FACT
(*viii*)   IF |X·FACT|←10⁻⁵ STOP. SIN has been computed. Otherwise,
     I←I+1
(*ix*)   Go to step (*v*)

4.   Write a FORTRAN program that would accept as data

(1)   XZERO
(2)   XONE
(3)   DELX
(4)   A

The program will be used to compute values of y as follows:

(*a*)   y←A, x←XZERO
(*b*)   x←x+DELX
(*c*)   DELY←x°y°DELX
(*d*)   y←y+DELY
(*e*)   Go to step (*a*)

These steps are continued until the value of x is greater than or equal to XONE. Output should be in tabular form, showing which value of y corresponds to the value of x used in step (*d*).

5.   Once a root of an algebraic equation has been separated, i.e., once an interval (a,b) has been found containing one root and such that $f(a) f(b) < 0$, we would like to know a little more about the value of the root. This is done by obtaining an approximated value of x, say α, such that $|f(\alpha)| < \epsilon$ where ϵ gives a measure of the error made in taking α to be the true value of the root of $f(x)$ between a and b.

We can write an algorithm to approximate a root x by an α such that $a < \alpha < b$ and $|f(\alpha)| < \epsilon$ as follows:

Step 0.   Assume that f(a)f(b)<0, and ε>0.
Step 1.   Set x←a, y←b.
Step 2.   Set m←(x+y)/2.
Step 3.   Compute f(m)

Step 4. Compare f(m) with ϵ.
If $|f(m)|<\epsilon$ STOP as m is the approximate value
of the root.
If $|f(m)|\geq\epsilon$ Go to step 5.
Step 5. Set PROD←f(m)·f(x)
Step 6. Compare PROD with 0
If PROD<0 Go to step 7.
If PROD>0 Go to step 9.
If PROD=0 STOP as m is an approximated
value of the root.
Step 7. Set y←(x+y)/2.
Step 8. Go to Step 2.
Step 9. Set x←(x+y)/2
Step 10. Go to step 2.

6.   Use Sturm's algorithm to separate the roots of the equation

$$7x^5 + 5.47x^3 + 3.33x^2 + 1.72x - 0.15 = 0.$$

Find first an upper bound for the roots, showing that this upper bound is smaller than .4. Obtain the smaller positive root with two decimals.

Chapter VIII

SYSTEMS OF NUMERATION

In this chapter systems of numeration are discussed. Section 1 presents algorithms to find the equivalent representation of a number using different forms of representation. This is an application of the previous chapter. In section 2 we study the binary system, a particular system of numeration.

1. SYSTEMS OF NUMERATION

The natural numbers were created for counting the objects in a collection. It would be an impossible task to try to represent each natural number using different symbols. Hence special notations were invented for representing the natural numbers. Each notation is called a *system of numeration.*

The most common systems of numeration in the past were the Roman and the decimal. We shall discuss here other systems of numeration based on the same principle as the decimal system.

It seems that the decimal system was invented in India, about 600 B.C. and imported to Europe by the Arabs during the Middle Ages. In the decimal system a number plays an important role. This number is ten. We count by forming groups of ten. There are, in the decimal system, ten digits, 0, 1, 2, 3, 4, 5, 6, 7, 8, and 9. The basic principle in which the decimal system operates is that each digit on a number represents a value that depends on its relative position. That is, the same digit represents different values depending on its location within the number. For example, consider the number 343. There are two 3's and one 4. However, the number on the far left represents a value of three hundred.

Let us look closely at an arbitrary number, such as 2,835, represented in the decimal system. We read this as two thousand eight hundred and thirty (three, ten) five. We can represent all this as follows:

$$2{,}835 = 2 \cdot 10^3 + 8 \cdot 10^2 + 3 \cdot 10 + 5.$$

We observe that we have introduced *powers* of ten. We could also represent an arbitrary number N by a polynomial in which the *base* would be an arbitrary number, that is, we could have

$$N = a_0 r^n + a_1 r^{n-1} + \ldots + a_{n-1} r + a_n \tag{1}$$

where $a_0, a_1, \ldots, a_n$ would be *digits* used in a specific system of numeration.

It seems natural, therefore, to call a system of numeration by the name of the number whose powers are used to compute the polynomial (1).

Assume that m is a decimal representation of an arbitrary natural number. How can one obtain the representation that corresponds to m on any given base n? That is, how can one find $a_0, a_1, \ldots, a_h$ such that

$$m = a_h n^h + a_{h-1} n^{h-1} + \ldots + a_1 n + a_0 \tag{2}$$

and $a_i < n$ for $i = 0, 1, \ldots, h$?

In trying to answer this question we observe that (2) can be written as follows:

$$m = (a_h n^{h-1} + a_{h-1} n^{h-2} + \ldots + a_1)n + a_0 = An + a_0. \tag{3}$$

This shows how we can obtain a_0:

Divide m by n and take a_0 equal to the remainder obtained in this division. Next we write:

$$\frac{m - a_0}{n} = A = (a_h n^{h-2} + \ldots + a_2)n + a_1$$

and a_1 is computed dividing $\dfrac{m - a_0}{n}$ by n and taking the remainder as the value of a_1.

The rest of the coefficients can be obtained in a similar way.

Example

Represent 247 in base 6. We proceed as follows:

$$\begin{aligned}
247 &= 41 \cdot 6 + 1 \\
41 &= 6 \cdot 6 + 5 \\
6 &= 1 \cdot 6 + 0 \\
1 &= 0 \cdot 6 + 1
\end{aligned}$$

Hence 1051 in base 6 is equivalent to 247 in base 10. This will be abbreviated by writing $1051_6 = 247$. A concise way of performing the above computation is

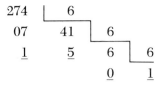

What about the converse of the previous question? That is, how to find the decimal representation of a number N expressed in base n?

This problem can be easily solved if we look at the polynomial representation of N. For example, what is the decimal representation of 764_8? We proceed as follows:

$$764_8 = 7 \cdot 8^2 + 6 \cdot 8 + 4 = 500.$$

Suppose that N is a number in base n. That is

$$N_n = a_0 n^h + a_1 n^{h-1} + \ldots + an + a_0.$$

If we perform the operation in the right hand side we will be finding the value of the polynomial

$$a_0 x^h + a_1 x^{h-1} + \ldots + a_{n-1} x + a_n$$

at $x = n$.

The above discussion can be summarized by the following two algorithms.

(a) Algorithm for converting base b to base 10.
  (1) Obtain the digits $a_i = 1, 2, \ldots, n+1$ and the base b.
  (2) Call the algorithm that evaluates the polynomial $a_1 x^n + a_2 x^{n-1} + \ldots + a_{n+1}$ at $x = b$.

(b) Algorithm for passing from base 10 to base b.
  (1) Obtain integer N written in base 10 and the base b.
  (2) Let $Q \leftarrow N$
  (3) Compare Q with b.
  (4) If $Q < b$, then the number N in base b is Q.
  (5) $I \leftarrow 1$
  (6) Integer divide Q by b getting quotient q and remainder r.
  (7) Let $Q \leftarrow q$ and $d_I \leftarrow r$.
  (8) Compare Q with b.
  (9) If $Q \geqslant b$, then set $I \leftarrow I+1$ and proceed to step 6.
  (10) If $Q < b$ the digits are $Q, d_I, d_{I-1}, \ldots, d_1$.

A flow chart combining algorithms (a) and (b) is in Figure 53.

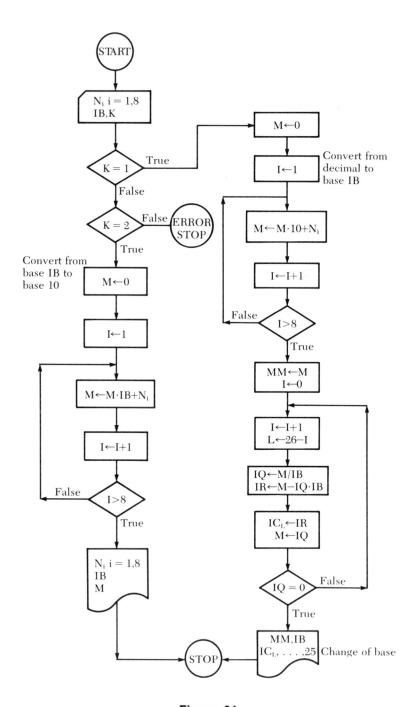

Figure 61

Exercise

Write a FORTRAN program for implementing the algorithm represented in Figure 61.

2. BINARY SYSTEM OF NUMERATION

One of the systems of numeration most frequently used in computer calculations is the *binary system*. This system is an obvious choice for an OFF and ON system (remember the system we considered in Chapter II). We may represent OFF and ON by zero and one, respectively. The binary system having as the only digits 0 and 1 can be used to represent any ON and OFF combination as a number written in the binary system. For example, 10010 represents the state ON OFF OFF ON OFF.

Although we have shown in the previous section how to convert integer decimal numbers into any arbitrary base and conversely, we shall repeat here these procedures to show how simple these procedures are when the binary system is involved.

Suppose we want to represent 47 in the binary system. We proceed as follows:

$$
\begin{array}{ccccccc}
47 & | & 2 \\
07 & & 23 & | & 2 \\
1 & & 03 & & 11 & & 2 \\
& & 1 & & 1 & & 5 & | & 2 \\
& & & & & & 1 & & 2 & | & 2 \\
& & & & & & & & 0 & & 1
\end{array}
$$

and we obtain that $47 = 101111_2$. Conversely, find the decimal value that corresponds to 110111. We arrange the necessary computations as follows:

	1	1	0	1	1	1
2		2	6	12	26	54
	1	3	6	13	27	55

Since 55 is the value of the polynomial

$$1 \cdot x^5 + 1 \cdot x^4 + 0 \cdot x^3 + 1 \cdot x^2 + 1 \cdot x + 1 \cdot x^0$$

when $x = 2$.

Next we shall find out how to convert decimal fractions into binary fractions and conversely.

Let N be an arbitrary decimal fraction smaller than 1. Let $. \, x_{-1} \, x_{-2} \ldots x_{-n}$ be its binary representation. We would like to have a procedure that will produce the digits $x_{-1}, x_{-2}, \ldots, x_{-n}$. To accomplish this we first represent $. \, x_{-1} \, x_{-2} \ldots x_{-n}$ in polynomial form as follows:

$$N = x_{-1} \, 2^{-1} + x_{-2} \, 2^{-2} + \ldots + x_{-n} \, 2^{-n}. \tag{1}$$

Next, we multiply both sides of relation (1) by 2 obtaining

$$2N = x_{-1} + x_{-2} \, 2^{-1} + \ldots + x_{-n} \, 2^{-n-1} \tag{2}$$

(2) shows that x_{-1} is the integer part of $2N$. Similarly we will have

$$(2N - x_{-1}) \, 2 = x_{-2} + \ldots + x_{-n} \, 2^{-n-2} \tag{3}$$

and again x_{-2} would be the integer part of $(2N - x_{-1}) \, 2$. This process will continue until we have obtained the desired precision in the binary representation of N. We shall illustrate this procedure with an example.

Find the binary equivalent of 14.63.

We first find that $14 = 2^3 + 2^2 + 2 + 0$. Next we multiply .63 by 2 getting 1.26, hence $x_{-1} = 1$. Next we multiply .26 by 2 getting .52; therefore $x_{-2} = 0$. Again we multiply .52 by 2 getting 1.04 and $x_{-3} = 1$. We have obtained that $14.64 = 1110.101$. The above computations could be arranged as follows:

$$
\begin{array}{r}
63 \\
2 \\
\hline
1.26 \\
-\ 2 \\
\hline
0.52 \\
-\ 2 \\
\hline
1.04 \\
\hline
\end{array}
$$

To represent a binary fraction it is sufficient to represent it in polynomial form and then find the value of the polynomial. For example

$$1101.101 = 2^3 + 2^2 + 1 + \frac{1}{2} + \frac{1}{2^2} = 8 + 4 + 1 + .5 + .25 = 13.75.$$

Next, we shall proceed to consider the four elemental arithmetic operations, that is, addition, subtraction, multiplication, and division.

(*i*) Addition

The "rules" of addition can be summarized in the following table.

$$
\begin{array}{c|cc}
 & 0 & 1 \\
\hline
0 & 0 & 1 \\
1 & 1 & 10 \\
\end{array}
$$

Example

Add 1011 to 111. We can arrange the computation as it is done in base 10. We have:

$$
\begin{array}{r}
1011 \\
+\ 111 \\
\hline
10010
\end{array}
$$

We have used the addition table in the following manner: We say, $1 + 1 = 10$, therefore we write a 0 and carry a 1; next, $(1 + 1) + 1 = 10 + 1 = 11$, write down 1 and carry 1; next, $1 + 1 = 10$, write down 10. That this result is correct, can be checked by converting all the numbers to base ten and performing the addition in this system obtaining $11 + 7 = 18$. But 18 is equivalent to 10010 in base 2.

(*ii*) Subtraction

To obtain the difference between two numbers we use the same technique that is used to obtain the difference between two numbers in base ten.

Example

Compute $111010 - 11011$. We have

$$
\begin{array}{r}
111010 \\
-\ 11011 \\
\hline
11111
\end{array}
$$

We proceed as follows: Since 1 is greater than 0, we borrow 1 and then we say 1 to 10 is 1, and carry 1; $1 + 1 = 10$, borrowing 1 we have: 10 to 11 is 1, and carry 1; $1 + 0 = 1$, borrowing 1 we have: 1 to 10 is 1, and carry 1; $1 + 1 = 10$, borrowing 1 we have: 1 to 10 is 1 and carry 1; $1 + 1 = 10$, borrowing 1 we have: 1 to 10 is 1 carry 1; 1 to 1 is 0.

Computers, in general, do not perform subtraction as we have described. To perform this operation advantage is taken of the fact that binary numbers are represented as a sequence of ON and OFF stages. Before we proceed with the operation of subtraction, we shall show how integers are represented in a binary computer.

Assume that we have a computer whose word length is nine bits (Figure 62).

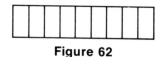

Figure 62

We shall call the bits, from left to right, B_0, B_1, B_2, B_3, B_4, B_5, B_6, B_7, and B_8. The B_0 bit is also called the *sign bit*. There are two different techniques for representing integers, according to whether the numbers are positive or negative.

Assume we want to represent the positive number $48 = 110000_2$. We have represented the number in Figure 63.

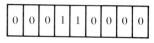

Figure 63

Note that B_0 contains a 0. If the zero at the B_0 bit is omitted, we will assume that the number represented is positive. Negative numbers are stored using the one-complement of this number. Assume we would like to find the one-complement of $48 = 110000_2$. This is obtained by replacing in every bit the zeros by ones and vice versa. That is, the one-complement of 000110000 is 111001111 (Figure 64).

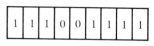

Figure 64

Figure 64 also represents -48.

Observe that a negative number is characterized by having a 1 in the B_0 bit. Now we can subtract two numbers, A and B, by adding to A the one-complement of B.

Example 1

Compute $11011 - 10001$. We proceed as follows: First we compute the one-complement of 10001 (Figure 65).

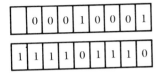

Figure 65

Next we add the one-complement to 11011.

$$00011011$$
$$\underline{11101110}$$
$$00001011$$

Since the first bit B_0 contains a zero, the result is positive. Hence $11011 - 10001 = 1011$.

Example 2

Compute $11101 - 111111$. Note that 111111 is greater than 11101. Hence, we should get a negative result. We have

$$000011101$$
$$\underline{111000000}$$
$$111011101$$

which is the one-complement of the difference. Note that B_0 bit contains a 1. Hence

$$11101 - 111111 = -000100010.$$

(iii) Multiplication

To multiply two binary numbers we shall use the table

	0	1
0	0	0
1	0	1

That is, $0 \times 0 = 0$, $0 \times 1 = 1 \times 0 = 0$, and $1 \times 1 = 1$.

Example

Compute 10101×1011. The multiplication is performed as in the case of the two decimal numbers.

$$
\begin{array}{r}
10101 \\
\underline{1011} \\
10101 \\
10101 \\
\underline{101010} \\
11100111
\end{array}
$$

Check: $10101_2 = 21$, $1011_2 = 11$, $11100111_2 = 231$; $21 \times 11 = 231$.

(iv) Division

Division is performed in a way similar to the method used in the decimal system.

Suppose we want to divide 1010 into 11. We can arrange the computation as follows:

$$
\begin{array}{r}
.010011001100000 \\
1010 \,\overline{)11.00000000} \\
\underline{1010} \\
10000 \\
\underline{1010} \\
1100 \\
\underline{1010} \\
10000 \\
\underline{1010} \\
1100
\end{array}
$$

hence we get

$$
\frac{11}{1010} = .01\overline{0011}
$$

Check

$$
11_2 = 3, \qquad 1010_2 = 10; \qquad \frac{3}{10} = .3
$$

$$
.01\overline{0011} = 0 \cdot \frac{1}{2} + 1 \cdot \frac{1}{2^2} + \left(0 \cdot \frac{1}{2^3} + 0 \cdot \frac{1}{2^4} + 1 \cdot \frac{1}{2^5} + 1 \cdot \frac{1}{2^6}\right) +
$$

$$
\left(0 \cdot \frac{1}{2^7} + 0 \cdot \frac{1}{2^8} + 1 \cdot \frac{1}{2^9} + 1 \cdot \frac{1}{2^{10}}\right) + \ldots + \left(\frac{1}{2^{4k+1}} + \frac{1}{2^{4k+2}}\right) + \ldots =
$$

$$
\frac{1}{2^2} + \sum_{k=1}^{\infty} \left(\frac{1}{2^{4k+1}} + \frac{1}{2^{4k+2}}\right) = \frac{1}{4} + \frac{1}{2} \sum_{k=1}^{\infty} \frac{1}{2^{4k}} + \frac{1}{4} + \sum_{k=1}^{\infty} \frac{1}{2^{4k}} =
$$

$$
\frac{1}{4} + \left(\frac{1}{2} + \frac{1}{4}\right) \sum_{k=1}^{\infty} \frac{1}{2^{4k}}
$$

Recall that in a geometric progression

$$a + a^2 + \ldots + ar^a + \ldots = \frac{a}{1-a}$$

for $|r| < 1$. Hence we have

$$.0\overline{10011} = \frac{1}{4} + \frac{3}{4} \cdot \frac{\frac{1}{2^4}}{1 - \frac{1}{2^4}} = \frac{1}{4} + \frac{3}{4} \cdot \frac{1}{15} = \frac{6}{20} = .3.$$

This example illustrates the fact that a terminating decimal fraction might be converted into a periodic binary fraction.

Exercises

1. Given two numbers A and B on base 12, find $A + B$, $A - B$, $A \cdot B$, and A/B using the subroutine that converts them into numbers on base 10. Perform the above operations on base 10 and convert their result on base 12.

2. Write addition and multiplication tables for numbers written in base 6. Use these tables to compute.

    (a) $314 + 13$,   (b) 235×54.

Chapter IX

SORTING

In this chapter we present some algorithms for arranging the members of a collection on a specified order. This arrangement will be called *sort*. The algorithms are called *sorting algorithms*. There are two main types of sorting algorithms, numerical and alphabetical.

1. NUMERICAL SORTING

We shall consider only numerical sorting. Assume we have a collection of n objects arranged in an arbitrary way, say, A_1, A_2, $\ldots A_n$. We would like to rearrange them in a new collection B_1, B_2, $\ldots B_n$ so that $B_1 \leq B_2 \leq \ldots \leq B_n$.

Analysis

We assume here that we do not have any prior knowledge of sorting techniques. What should we do to rearrange A_1, A_2, $\ldots A_n$ in order of magnitude? The first thing that comes to mind is to compare A_1 with A_2. One of three things can happen. (*a*) $A_1 > A_2$, (*b*) $A_1 < A_2$, (*c*) $A_1 = A_2$.

If $A_1 = A_2$ or $A_1 < A_2$, we shall proceed to compare A_1 with A_3.

The above argument suggests the following procedure. We shall start by placing A_1 on a temporary location Z. Then we compare Z with A_2. In the event that A_2 is smaller than Z, we shall put A_2 on Z. At the end of this step we will have on the temporary location Z the smallest of the two elements A_1 and A_2. The algorithm proceeds in this way until there are no more elements to be compared.

The above argument suggests the following problem. Given a collection of unordered elements $A_1, A_2, \ldots, A_n$, find the smallest element.

We have the following MINA algorithm

(1) *Get N, $A_1, A_2, \ldots, A_N$.*
(2) Set index I to the value 1.
(3) Put A_I into the temporary storage Z.
(4) Add 1 to I.
(5) Is $I > N$? If $I \leqq N$ proceed to step (6). Otherwise, proceed to step (8).
(6) Compare A_I with Z. If $Z = A_I$ proceed to step (4). Otherwise, proceed to step (7).
(7) $T \leftarrow Z, Z \leftarrow A_I; A_I \leftarrow T$ proceed to step (4).
(8) The minimal element is in Z.

Z represents, now, the value of the smallest element in the collection $A_1, \ldots, A_n$. We replace A_1 by this value and get a collection containing $n - 1$ elements to which we apply the previous MINA algorithm. We proceed in this way until there are no more elements to compare. We have the following algorithm.

(1) Get N, $A_1, A_2, \ldots, A_N$.
(2) Set index I to the value 1.
(3) Call MINA.
(4) $A_I \leftarrow Z$.
(5) $I \leftarrow I + 1$.
(6) If $I \geq N$, proceed to step (7); otherwise, proceed to step (3).
(7) The collection has been rearranged.

Figure 66(a) and Figure 66(b) show flow charts for MINA and SORT 1.

In order to illustrate the procedure introduced above, we shall rearrange the set $\{6, 8, 4, 5, 3\}$. First we shall place these numbers in boxes named B_1, B_2, B_3, B_4, and B_5, respectively. Each time that the algorithm MINA is used it will be called a *stage* on the sorting procedure. In the first stage we place number 6 in B_1, that is, we assume that the smallest element is 6. (Note that we do not have any reason to know otherwise.) We proceed to compare B_1 with the rest of the boxes. The number on B_1 swaps places with any one number that is smaller than it. This is illustrated in Figure 67. At the end of the first stage, we have the following situation: B_1 con-

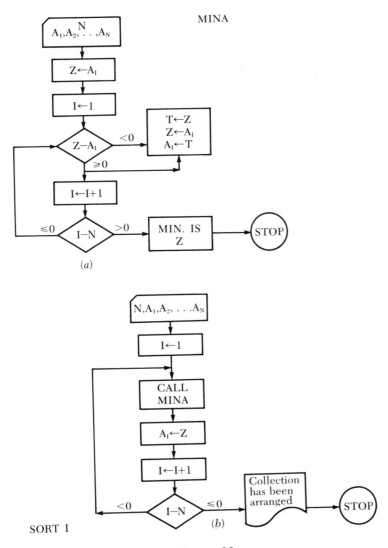

MINA

(a)

SORT I

(b)

Figure 66

tains 3, B_2 contains 8, B_3 contains 6, B_4 contains 5, and B_5 contains 4. The smallest element in the first stage is in B_1. In the second stage, we compare the element place on B_2 with the rest of the boxes, proceeding in the same way as in the first stage. The procedure ends when we reach the fourth stage. At this time we have the rearranged set {3, 4, 5, 6, 8}.

	1	2	3	4
$B_1 \leftarrow 6$	~~6~~ ~~4~~ 3	3	3	3
$B_2 \leftarrow 8$	8	~~8~~ ~~6~~ ~~5~~ 4	4	4
$B_3 \leftarrow 4$	6	8	~~8~~ ~~6~~ 5	5
$B_4 \leftarrow 5$	5	6	8	~~8~~ 6
$B_5 \leftarrow 3$	4	5	6	8

Figure 67

With this example we observe that during the performance of stage 1 we did two exchanges. We first replaced 6 by 4 and then replaced 4 by 3. One can easily see that the number of exchanges would increase if the number of items in the set to be rearranged increases. To save some number of exchanges we proceed as follows:

	1	2	3	4
B_1	6	3	3	3	3
B_2	8	8	4	4	4
B_3	4	4	8	5	5
B_4	5	5	5	8	6
B_5	3	6	6	6	8

We begin by placing an index 1 into an index box. This is telling us that the smallest element is assumed to be in B_1. We proceed to compare B_1 with the rest of the boxes. Instead of 6 swapping positions with the number placed in box 3 (i.e., 4) as we did before, we place an index 3 in the index box (remember to erase the previous index, 1). Next we proceed to compare B_3 with the other boxes, and finally, we see that the content of box B_5 is smaller than the content of box B_3. Hence, we put 5 in the index box. Since there are no more boxes to compare, we swap the content of B_1 with the content of the box with index 5, i.e., the number that is placed in the index box. At the end of this first stage we have the following situation: B_1 contains 3, B_2 contains 8, B_3 contains 4, B_4 contains 5, and B_5 contains 6. The smallest element is in B_1. In the second stage, we compare the element place on B_2 with the rest of the boxes, proceeding in the same way as we did in the first stage. The procedure ends when we reach the fourth stage. A flow chart for this algorithm, SORT II, is seen in Figure 68.

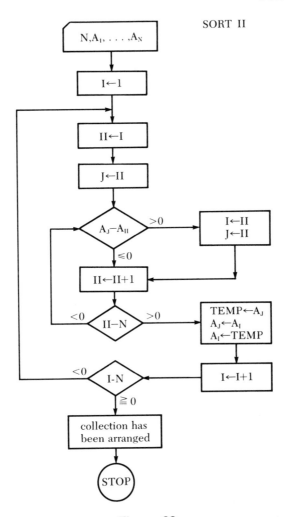

SORT II

Figure 68

2. SORT 3

In the previous two sorting methods, a fixed number was compared with the rest of the elements of the set, performing an exchange whenever a smaller element was found. In this way at the end of each stage we had at the top of the list the smallest element. Now we shall use a method based in a different principle, the technique of comparing consecutive elements by swapping the elements of a pair whenever a change in the natural order is found, saving the index, and sending the smallest element to the top of the list. We shall illustrate this procedure with an example.

Let $a_1 = 5$, $a_2 = 6$, $a_3 = 7$, $a_4 = 8$, $a_5 = 4$, $a_6 = 9$, $a_7 = 3$. We proceed as follows: Compare 5 with 6; 6 with 7; 7 with 8; 8 with 4; 4 is smaller than 8; we save the index of 4, that is 5, and exchange 4 with 8, sending 4 at the top of the list, getting the partial arrangement 4, 5, 6, 7, 8, 9, 3. Next we return to start the comparisons at the element with the index that we saved previously, that is, index 5 and the element is 8. Compare 8 with 9; 9 with 3, 3 is smaller than 9. Save the index 7; exchange 3 with 9 and move 3 to the top of the list obtaining the arrangement 3, 4, 5, 6, 7, 8, 9. Since the index saved is 7, there are no more pairs to compare. The rearrangement has been accomplished. These steps can be seen in Figure 69.

	1	2	3	4
a_1	5	4	4	3
a_2	6	5	5	4
a_3	7	6	6	5
a_4	8	7	7	6
a_5	4°	8°	8	7
a_6	9	9	9	8
a_7	3	3	3°	9

Figure 69

3. SORT 4

In this sorting technique, at the end of each stage the smallest element appears in the first position and the largest element appears in the last position. Next, the second smallest element goes to the second place, and the second largest element goes to the second last place.

Assume we want to sort the elements of the vector A = {8, 5, 10, 11, 3, 9} into ascending order. Assume that the largest is 8. We place this in a box which we call SMALL. Also, we assume that 8 is the largest element and we place it in a box that we call LARGE. Start to compare every element of the vector A with SMALL; whenever we find an element smaller than or equal to SMALL (8) we place it in the SMALL box deleting the element there (in this case 8). Next we save its index in SMALL box and proceed with the next element. If however, we find an element that is larger than that in SMALL box, we then compare it to the contents of LARGE box; if this element happens to be larger than LARGE, then we put it in LARGE box deleting the number that was there, and the index is saved in LARGE box. At the end of this first pass we will put the element that is in the SMALL box in the first position. The element that was in the first position is placed at the position that is indicated by the SMALL index. The element that is placed in the LARGE box replaces the element that occupies the last position in the A vector. The element that was occupying this position goes to the position indicated in the LARGE index. The process continues in the same way with two elements less in the vector A. Figure 70 shows all the steps to sort A to its final form A = {3, 5, 8, 9, 10, 11}. Figure 71 shows a flow chart for this algorithm.

Stages			SMALL box	SMALL index	LARGE box	LARGE index
A_1	8	3	3	8, 5, 3	1, 2, 5	8, 10, 11	1, 3, 4
A_2	5	5°	5	5	2	5, 10	2, 3
A_3	10	10°	8				
A_4	11°	9	9				
A_5	3°	8	10				
A_6	9	11	11				

Figure 70

A computer program and output for this method follows.

```
C     UP AND DOWN SORT
C     START WITH I = 1 AND K = N
C     SMALLEST ELEMENT INTO A(I) AND LARGEST
C     INTO A(K)
C     INCREASE I BY 1 AND DECREASE K BY 1
C     AS LONG AS K-1 IS GREATER THAN 1
          DIMENSION A(100)
          WRITE (3,6000)
 6000     FORMAT (1H1)
    1     READ (1,2) N
C     N = 0 IS USED FOR STOP
          IF (N) 105,105,100
    2     FORMAT(I3)
  100     READ (1,3) (A(I),I = 1,N)
          WRITE (3,21) (A(J),J = 1,N)
```

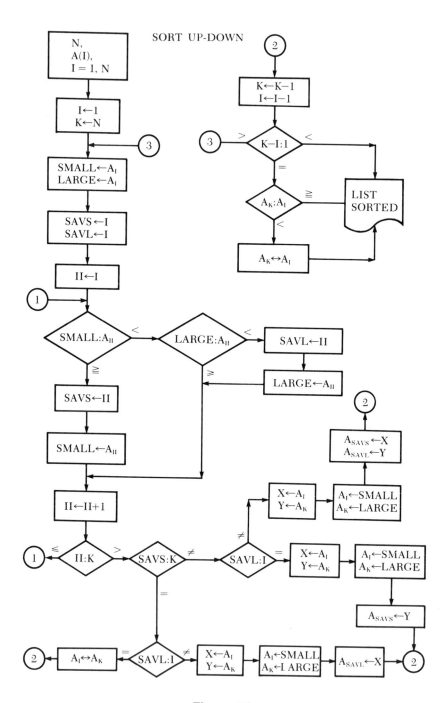

SORT UP-DOWN

Figure 71

```
    3   FORMAT(8F10.0)
   21   FORMAT (14H0UNSORTED LIST,//
    1   (5F10.0))
        I = 1
        K = N
C   SAVE INDEX AND VALUE FOR BOTH BIG AND
C   SMALL FOR A(J)
C   WHERE J VARIES FROM I TO K FOR LATER
C   INTERCHANGING
    4   SMALL = A(I)
        BIG = A(I)
        ISAVS = I
        ISAVL = I
        DO 9 II = I,K
    5   IF (SMALL-A(II)) 7,6,6
    6   ISAVS = II
        SMALL = A(II)
        GO TO 9
    7   IF (BIG-A(II)) 8,9,9
    8   ISAVL = II
        BIG = A(II)
    9   CONTINUE
        IF (ISAVS-K) 10,13,10
   10   IF (ISAVL-I) 12,11,12
   11   Y = A(K)
        A(I) = SMALL
        A(K) = BIG
        A(ISAVS) = Y
        GO TO 16
   12   X = A(I)
        Y = A(K)
        A(I) = SMALL
        A(K) = BIG
        A(ISAVS) = X
        A(ISAVL) = Y
        GO TO 16
   13   IF ( ISAVL-I) 15,14,15
   14   X = A(I)
        A(I) = A(K)
        A(K) = X
        GO TO 16
   15   X = A(I)
        A(I) = SMALL
```

```
         A(K) = BIG
         A(ISAVL) = X
         GO TO 16
   16    K = K−1
         I = I+1
         IF (K−I−1)19,17,4
   17    IF (A(K)−A(I))18,19,19
   18    X = A(K)
         A(K) = A(I)
         A(I) = A(K)
   19    WRITE (3,20) (A(J),J = 1,N)
         WRITE(3,22)
   20    FORMAT (12H0SORTED LIST,//,(5F10.0))
   22    FORMAT(//////)
         GO TO 1
  105    STOP
         END
```

UNSORTED LIST
      8.   5.   10.   11.   9.
      3.
SORTED LIST
      3.   5.   8.   9.   10.
     11.

UNSORTED LIST
     12.   −20.   5.   9.   3.
      9.   5.   1.   −30.
SORTED LIST
    −30.   −20.   1.   3.   5.
      5.   9.   9.   12.

UNSORTED LIST
     15.   14.   13.   12.   11.
     10.   9.   8.   7.   6.
      5.   4.   3.   2.   1.
SORTED LIST
      1.   2.   3.   4.   5.
      6.   7.   8.   9.   10.
     11.   12.   13.   14.   15.

UNSORTED LIST

1.	2.	3.	4.	5.
6.	7.	8.	9.	10.
11.	12.	13.	14.	15.

SORTED LIST

1.	2.	3.	4.	5.
6.	7.	8.	9.	10.
11.	12.	13.	14.	15.

4. DELETE

Next we present an algorithm to delete duplicates from a vector $A_1, A_2, \ldots A_n$ with ordered elements, that is $A_1 \leq A_2 \leq A_3 \leq \ldots \leq A_n$. Also we would like to find the number of times each element was in the original vector. We proceed as follows:

Let J be the location where the next non-duplicated item is to be stored in A. Let K be the number of occurrences of the number stored in A_j. Let B be the vector where the K's are stored, that is, $B_j = K$ indicates that A_j occurs K times. Let S contain the item in A that is to be compared with successive A's until an unequal comparison results. Let M be the number of different items in the vector A.

Starting with J, K and I having initial values of 1 and with $S = A_I$ we compare A_{I+1} with S. If $S = A_{I+1}$, then we add one to K, we add one to I, and proceed to compare S with the next A_I. If $S = A_I$, then we must save K in B_J, set $A_{J+1} \leftarrow A_I$, reset K to 1 and S to A_I, add 1 to I, and proceed to compare A_I with S. When I has proceeded through all the values up to and including N, in order to save the value of K corresponding to the number of occurrences of the last element, we set $B_J \leftarrow K$ and place in M the value of J. We have the following algorithm.

(1) Set $S \leftarrow A_1, J \leftarrow 1, K \leftarrow 1, I \leftarrow 2$

(2) Compare A_I:S
   If $A_I > S$ then go to step (5)
   If $A_I \leq S$ then go to step (3)

(3) Set $K \leftarrow K + 1$

(4) Go to step (6)

(5) Set $B_J \leftarrow K, K \leftarrow 1, J \leftarrow J + 1, S \leftarrow A_I$

(6) Set $I \leftarrow I + 1$, Compare I:N
   If $I > N$ go to step (7)
   If $I \leq N$ go to step (2)

(7) Set $B_j \leftarrow K$, $M \leftarrow J$
(8) Stop. The vector B contains the delete vector.

Figure 72 contains a flow chart for this algorithm.

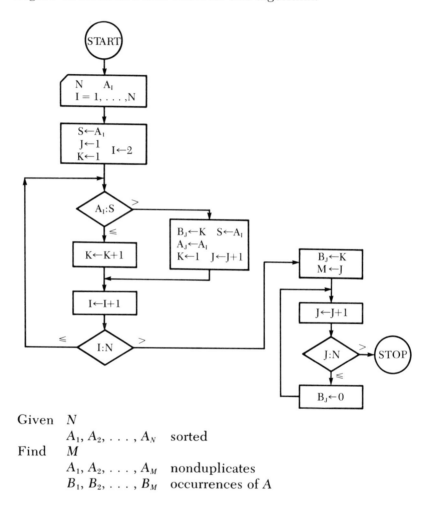

Given   N
         $A_1, A_2, \ldots, A_N$ sorted
Find   M
         $A_1, A_2, \ldots, A_M$ nonduplicates
         $B_1, B_2, \ldots, B_M$ occurrences of A

Figure 72

5. SORT 5. (CLOYD'S SORT)

In the previous sorting techniques we either compared two consecutive numbers or we compared a number versus the rest of the numbers in the set. The procedure that we are going to illustrate gives a point to the largest of the two elements being compared. At the end of all comparisons, the number with the largest number of points is the biggest element in the set. We shall call this sorting method *relative ranking*. We shall illustrate this algorithm with an example.

Suppose that we want the set A

$$17, 25, 13, 14, 2, 18, 17$$

to be sorted in ascending order. We shall construct an array M with 0 and 1 in each place as follows:

The first element of the column A_1 is compared with each element of the row A_j. Each time the comparison $A_i{:}A_j$ is made, we shall place a zero or a one in M_{ij} (the (i, j) element of the array M). A 1 placed in M_{ij} will indicate that $A_i > A_j$ or that $A_i = A_j$ and that $i \leq j$. A 0 placed in M_{ij} indicates that $A_i < A_j$ or that if $A_i = A_j$ that A_i is placed later than A_j in the original set. The sum of the elements in row i is the rank of the element A_i (Figure 73).

For example, the seventh element is 17, the fourth element is 13, etc. We shall place the sorted elements in a new array called B. The device of storing 1 or 0 in the array M takes a very large amount of storage (n^2 places) and we find it unnecessary, since we can add the ones and the zeros for each fixed A_i against all the A_j's and this sum will determine the rank of A_i. An algorithm follows:

(0) Get set A and number of elements n.
(1) Set $i \leftarrow 1$,
(2) Set $j \leftarrow 1, m \leftarrow 0$.
(3) Compare $A_i{:}A_j$
        if $A_i > A_j$ then go to step (5)
        if $A_i < A_j$ then go to step (6)
        if $A_i = A_j$ then go to step (4).
(4) Compare $i{:}j$
        if $i \leq j$ then go to step (5)
        if $i > j$ then go to step (6).
(5) Set $m \leftarrow m + 1$
(6) Set $j \leftarrow j + 1$
(7) Compare $j{:}n$
        if $j \leq n$ then go to step (3)
        if $j > n$ then go to step (8)
(8) Set $B_m \leftarrow A_i$
(9) Set $i \leftarrow i + 1$
(10) Compare $i{:}n$
        if $i \leq n$ then go to step (2)
        if $i > n$ then stop.

A_i/A_j	17	25	13	14	2	1	8	17	RANK
17	1	0	1	1	1	1	1	1	7
25	1	1	1	1	1	1	1	1	8
13	0	0	1	0	1	1	1	0	4
14	0	0	1	1	1	1	1	0	5
2	0	0	0	0	1	1	0	0	2
1	0	0	0	0	0	1	0	0	1
8	0	0	0	0	1	1	1	0	3
17	0	0	1	1	1	1	1	1	6

Figure 73

Next we present a computer output for deleting the elements of an array using Cloyd's sort algorithm.

```
          DIMENSION A(100),L(100)
          DIMENSION C(100)
C     MAIN PROGRAM TO CALL CLOYDS SORT AND
C     THEN COUNT AND DELETE DUPLICATES.
C
C     N = 0 IS USED FOR STOP.
C
C     OBSERVE THAT THE DEVICE NUMBERS
C     HAVE BEEN CHANGED FROM 1 AND 3
C     TO 5 AND 6 TO CONFORM TO WICHITA
C     STATE UNIVERSITY STANDARDS
C
     1 READ (5,101) N
       IF (N) 500,500,2
     2 WRITE (6,6000)
  6000 FORMAT (1H1)
       READ (5,102) (A(I),I = 1,N)
       WRITE (6,106) N
       WRITE (6,104) (A(I),I = 1,N)
       CALL CSORT (A,C,N)
       CALL DELETE (C,N,L,M)
       WRITE (6,103) (C(I),L(I),I = 1,M)
   101 FORMAT (I3)
   102 FORMAT (16F5.0)
   103 FORMAT (F10.2,I10)
   104 FORMAT ('0',4F7.2)
```

```
106  FORMAT ('1','THIS IS THE ORIGINAL'/
   1 ' UNSORTED DATA WITH',I3,' ITEMS'/
   2 ' SORTED AND COMPRESSED LIST AND'/
   3 ' FREQUENCY FOLLOWS')
     GO TO 1
500  CALL EXIT
     END



     SUBROUTINE  DELETE(A,N,L,M)
C    THIS ROUTINE USES THE STORAGE SPACE
C    OF THE VECTOR INPUT A,
```

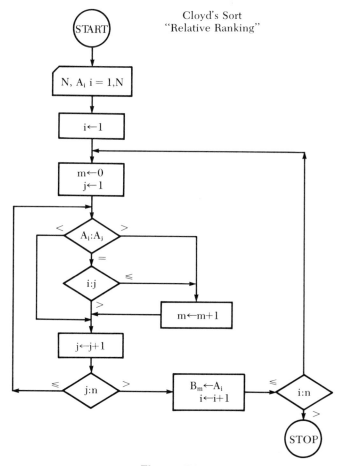

Cloyd's Sort
"Relative Ranking"

Figure 74

```
C      HENCE ONE MIGHT HAVE TO SAVE
C      ORIGINAL A SOMEWHERE ELSE.
C      B IS THE FREQUENCY VECTOR
C      THAT IS ( B(2) CONTAINS THE
C      NUMBER OF OCCURRENCES OF
C      A(2), ETC)
C      N IS THE DIMENSION OF THE ORIGINAL LIST
C      M IS THE DIMENSION OF THE DELETED LIST
          DIMENSION A(100),L(100)
C      DELETE MULTIPLE OCCURRENCES FROM A
C      INDICATING NUMBER OF TIMES IT HAS
C      OCCURRED
C      IN L AND COMPRESSING A LIST TO DIMENSION
C      M.
            S = A(1)
            J = 1
            K = 1
            DO 1000 I = 2, N
            IF(A(I)−S) 100,100,900
     100    K = K+1
            GO TO 1000
     900    L(J) = K
            A(J+1) = A(I)
            K = 1
            J = J+1
            S = A(I)
    1000    CONTINUE
            L(J) = K
            M = J
            JJ = J+1
            DO 1100 J = JJ,N
    1100    L(J) = 0.0
            RETURN
            END


C      VARYING J FROM 1 TO N
C      FOR EACH A(I)>A(J) ADD 1 TO M,IF A(I) = A(J).
C      IF I LESS OR EQUAL TO J ADD 1 TO M,
C      AFTER J IS SET EQUAL TO N SET B(M) EQUAL
C      TO A(I)
C      BY COMPARING A(I) TO A(J) FOR ALL I AND J
C      WE ESTABLISH A RANKING ALLOWING US TO
```

```
C     SORT A VECTOR, INTO ASCENDING ORDER
      SUBROUTINE CSORT(A,B,N)
      DIMENSION A(100),B(100)
      DO 1000 I = 1,N
      M = 0
      DO 900 J = 1,N
      IF(A(I)-A(J)) 900,100,800
100   IF(I-J) 800,800,900
800   M = M+1
900   CONTINUE
      B(M) = A(I)
1000  CONTINUE
      RETURN
      END
```

THIS IS THE ORIGINAL
UNSORTED DATA WITH 35 ITEMS
SORTED AND COMPRESSED LIST AND
FREQUENCY FOLLOWS

120.00	120.00	23.00	23.00
12.00	32.00	21.00	20.00
30.00	65.00	30.00	32.00
14.00	21.00	18.00	91.00
32.00	12.00	21.00	54.00
54.00	67.00	62.00	30.00
30.00	42.00	21.00	57.00
53.00	21.00	20.00	52.00
21.00	30.00	12.00	

12.00	3
14.00	1
18.00	1
20.00	2
21.00	6
23.00	2
30.00	5
32.00	3
42.00	1
52.00	1
53.00	1

54.00	2
57.00	1
62.00	1
65.00	1
67.00	1
91.00	1
120.00	2

6. JUMP SORT

Let A be a set to be sorted in ascending order. Assume that we have $A_1 \leqslant A_2 \leqslant \ldots \leqslant A_{I-1}$. We start comparing $A(I)$ with $A(J)$ for every $J > I$. If $A(J) < A(I)$, $A(I)$ and $A(J)$ are interchanged. This comparison is done for values of J from $I + 1$ to N. We illustrate this with an example. Let $A = \{6, 8, 4, 3, 11\}$. The sequence of steps necessary to implement the JUMP-UP method are shown in Figure 74.

	A					
1	6	4	3	3	3	3
2	8	8	8	6	4	4
3	4	6	6	8	8	6
4	3	3	4	4	6	8
5	11	11	11	11	11	11

Figure 74

The algorithm to the JUMP-UP method is:

(1) Get $A_1, A_2, \ldots, A_N$
(2) $I \leftarrow 1, NI \leftarrow N - 1$
(3) $J \leftarrow I + 1$
(4) Compare $A(J)$ with $A(I)$
       If $A(I) < A(J)$, $J \leftarrow J + 1$, go to (5)
       Otherwise, exchange $A(I)$ and $A(J)$, $J \leftarrow J + 1$, go to (5)
(5) Compare J with N.
       If $J > N$, go to (6)
       Otherwise, go to (4)
(6) $I \leftarrow I + 1$
(7) Compare I with NI
       If $I > NI$ go to (8)
       Otherwise, go to (3)
(8) A has been sorted

Figure 75 shows a flow-chart of the JUMP-UP algorithm.

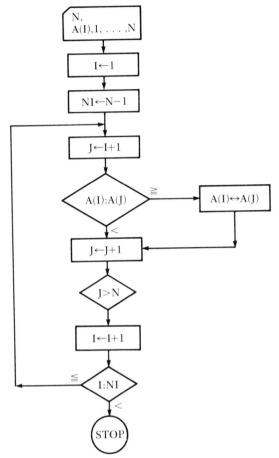

Figure 75

7. BINARY SEARCH

Assume that $A = \{a_1, a_2, \ldots a_n\}$ is a collection of numbers arranged in increasing order. For example, let us say that A is a table of numbers. Given an arbitrary number X, we wish to determine the index that corresponds to it in A; that is, we wish to find j such that $a_j = X$.

If we take a naive approach to the solution of this question, we first would have to find whether or not X is within the range of values of the set A. That is, we must check if $a_1 \le X \le a_n$ holds. After having been convinced that X falls within the range of values of A (since otherwise a solution to the problem has been found), one should start comparing X with $a_1, a_2, \ldots a_n$ one at a time. It is not difficult to see that this could become a long process. Why not divide the table into two parts by a middle index, say a_k, and then check whether $X > a_k$, $X < a_k$ or $X = a_k$. (Of course, if we were lucky enough to have $X = a_k$, our search would be over.) With this approach we would be able to find out in which half the value X might be located. Next the procedure looks at the middle of the selected half as before, and if X is not the "middle," it would be located in the "right half" or in the "left half." This procedure continues until X is found to be in the list or it is decided that X is not in the list. This decision can be made once we get a last interval containing only one point. Thus either X is that point or X is not that point. In this last case X is not a member of the set.

The procedure of dividing the members of a set A into two parts gives rise to the so-called *binary search*.

To find the middle index, we proceed as follows. The smallest integer p is found having the property that $2^p \geqslant N$. Let $M = 2^p$. Then the middle index is defined to be $M/2$. Next, compare X with $a_{M/2}$. The following three cases result:

(1) $X = a_{M/2}$
(2) $X < a_{M/2}$
(3) $X > a_{M/2}$

(A) If $X = a_{M/2}$, then the index is found and is $M/2$.
(B) If $X < a_{M/2}$, then X must be in $\{a_1, \ldots a_{M/2-1}\}$.
(C) If $X > a_{M/2}$, then X must be in $\{a_{M/2-1}, \ldots a_N\}$.

If B occurs, that is, $X < a_{M/2}$, then we must proceed as before and find the middle index, in this case, $M/4$. Now $a_{M/4}$ is compared with X and three cases result:

(4) $X = a_{M/4}$
(5) $X < a_{M/4}$
(6) $X > a_{M/4}$

(D) If $X = a_{M/4}$, then the index has been found, and it is $M/4$.
(E) If $X < a_{M/4}$, then X must be in $\{a_1, \ldots a_{M/4-1}\}$.
(F) If $X > a_{M/4}$, then X must be in $\{a_{M/4+1}, \ldots a_{M/2-1}\}$.

If C occurs, that is, $x > a_{M/2}$, we again must find the middle index. The middle index is $M/2 + M/4 = 3M/4$.

If $3M/4 > N$, then no number of A has that index. We correct this

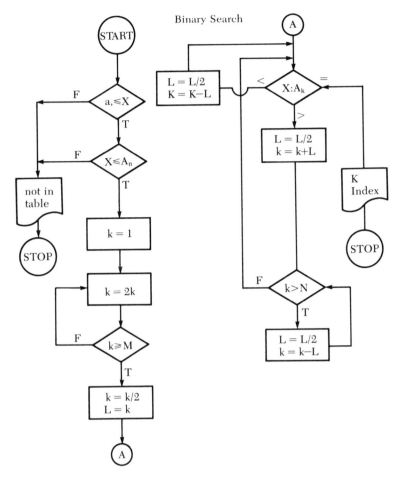

Figure 76

middle index by subtracting $M/8$, getting $5M/8$ for a middle index. Again, middle index $5M/8$ is compared with N. If middle index is greater than N, we again subtract $M/16$, getting $9M/16$. This process continues until the middle index is less than or equal to M.

We arrive at a middle index $M/2 \pm M/2^2 \pm M/2^3 \pm M/2^4 \ldots$ stopping with the first $M/2^\nu$, which makes the middle index $\leq$ to N.

For simplicity, we assume that the middle index is j. Now a_j is compared with X, and again, three cases result:

(7) $X = a_j$
(8) $X < a_j$
(9) $X > a_j$

(G)   If $X = a_j$, then the index has been found, and a is j.
(H)   If $X < a_j$, then X must be in $\{a_{M/2+1}, \ldots a_{j-1}\}$.
(I)   If $X > a_j$, then X must be in $\{a_{j+1}, \ldots a_N\}$.

This procedure will eventually terminate by finding a_j to be equal to X for some middle index j or by showing X is not in the table.

Figure 76 contains a flow chart for this algorithm.

Exercise

Given an array of numbers $A_1, A_2, \ldots, A_n$, write the necessary FORTRAN programs to implement the sorting algorithms for which programs are not provided in the text.

Part III

Chapter X

APPLICATION

This chapter contains a collection of exercises drawn from different fields. The object of this presentation is to introduce the reader to the vast number of applications of computer programming to scientific and non-scientific branches of knowledge.

At the beginning of each exercise, we introduce the concepts needed for writing a program to obtain the answer required by that exercise.

1. MATRICES

A matrix is an array of numbers, denoted by horizontal and vertical lines, called rows and columns, respectively.

$$
\begin{array}{llll}
a_{11} & a_{12} \ldots a_{1j} \ldots a_{1n} \\
a_{21} & a_{22} \ldots a_{2j} \ldots a_{2n} \\
a_{i1} & a_{i2} \ldots a_{ij} \ldots a_{in} \\
a_{m1} & a_{m2} \ldots a_{mj} \ldots a_{mn}
\end{array}
$$

Matrices are also represented in the form (a_{ij}) with $1 \leqslant i \leqslant m$, $1 \leqslant j \leqslant n$, where a_{ij} stands for that element which is located at the intersection of the ith row with the jth column.

On occasion, we shall denote matrices by a single capital letter.

The dimension of a matrix is the number $m \times n$, where m stands for the number of rows and n stands for the number of columns.

Two $m + n$ matrices

$$
A = \begin{pmatrix}
a_{11} & a_{12} & \ldots & a_{1n} \\
a_{21} & a_{22} & \ldots & a_{2n} \\
a_{m1} & a_{m2} & \ldots & a_{mn}
\end{pmatrix}
$$

and
$$B = \begin{pmatrix} b_{11} & b_{12} & \ldots & b_{1n} \\ b_{21} & b_{22} & \ldots & b_{2n} \\ b_{m1} & b_{m2} & \ldots & b_{mn} \end{pmatrix}$$

are equal if $a_{ij} = b_{ij}$ for every i and j.

There are some operations that can be performed with matrices. These are the following.

(a) Addition

Let
$$A = \begin{pmatrix} a_{11} & a_{12} & \ldots & a_{1n} \\ a_{21} & a_{22} & \ldots & a_{2n} \\ a_{m1} & a_{m2} & \ldots & a_{mn} \end{pmatrix}$$

and
$$B = \begin{pmatrix} b_{11} & b_{12} & \ldots & b_{1n} \\ b_{21} & b_{22} & \ldots & b_{1n} \\ b_{m1} & b_{m2} & \ldots & b_{mn} \end{pmatrix}$$

be $m \times n$ matrices. (Notice that the number of rows and columns of A are the same as the number of rows and columns of B.)

We define $A + B$ to be the $m \times n$ matrix obtained by adding a_{ij} and b_{ij}. That is, if c_{ij} is an element of $A + B$, then $c_{ij} = a_{ij} + b_{ij}$. ($1 \leq i \leq m, 1 \leq j \leq m$.) The matrix $A + B$ is called the sum of A and B.

Example

Given $A = \begin{pmatrix} 1 & 2 & 3 \\ 4 & 5 & 6 \end{pmatrix}$, $B = \begin{pmatrix} 3 & 2 & -1 \\ 1 & 2 & 3 \end{pmatrix}$, then

$$A + B = \begin{pmatrix} 1+3 & 2+2 & 3-1 \\ 4+1 & 5+2 & 6+3 \end{pmatrix}$$

(b) Subtraction is defined in a similar way
(c) Scalar Multiplication

Let A be an arbitrary $m \times n$ matrix.

Let c be any number, from now on called *scalar*. We define an $m \times n$ matrix cA to be the matrix whose (i, j) element is ca_{ij}.

Example

Let $A = \begin{pmatrix} 1 & 2 & 1 & 6 \\ 3 & 2 & 4 & 7 \\ 8 & 9 & 10 & 11 \end{pmatrix}$, $c = 3$, then

$$cA = \begin{pmatrix} 3 & 6 & 3 & 18 \\ 9 & 6 & 12 & 21 \\ 24 & 27 & 30 & 33 \end{pmatrix}$$

(d) Multiplication

Let $A = (a_{ij})$ be an $m \times n$ matrix and $B = (b_{ij})$ be an $n \times p$ matrix. Note that the number of columns of A is the same as the number of rows of B. We define a new $m \times p$ matrix $A \times B$ as follows:

$$c_{ik} = a_{i1}b_{1k} + a_{i2}b_{2k} + \ldots + a_{in}b_{nk},$$

where c_{ik}, as usual, denotes the element which is at the intersection of the ith row with the kth column.

Example

Let $A = \begin{pmatrix} 1 & 2 & 3 \\ 3 & 2 & 1 \end{pmatrix}$, $B = \begin{pmatrix} 2 & 3 \\ 1 & 2 \\ 0 & 1 \end{pmatrix}$, then

$$A \times B = \begin{pmatrix} 1 \times 2 + 2 \times 1 + 3 \times 0 & 1 \times 3 + 2 \times 2 + 3 \times 1 \\ 3 \times 2 + 2 \times 1 + 1 \times 0 & 3 \times 3 + 2 \times 2 + 1 \times 1 \end{pmatrix} = \begin{pmatrix} 4 & 10 \\ 8 & 14 \end{pmatrix}$$

Exercises

1. Let A and B be arbitrary $m \times n$ matrices. Draw a flow chart and write a FORTRAN program that would compute the sum of $A + B$ of these two matrices.

2. Let A be an $m \times n$ matrix (a_{ij}), and let B be an $n \times p$ matrix (b_{ij}). Draw a flow chart and write a FORTRAN program that would compute the product matrix $\{C_{ij}\} = A \times B$.

3. Given an $m \times n$ matrix A, write a FORTRAN program to compute:

(1) The maximum element on each row,
(2) the minimum of all the maximums found in (1) above.

4. Given an $m \times n$ matrix A, write a FORTRAN program to compute:

(1) The minimum element of each column,
(2) the maximum of all the minimums found in (1) above.

2. SYSTEMS OF LINEAR EQUATIONS

In that which follows we shall consider systems of linear equations with a unique solution.

Assume that we have been asked to find values of x and y such that if they were substituted in the expressions $3x + 2y$ and $x - y$, we should get the numbers 4 and 5, respectively. Finding an answer to this question is called *solving a system of linear equations.* This is written as

$$3x + 2y = 4 \tag{a}$$

$$x - y = 5 \tag{b}$$

The values of x and y so obtained are called the *solution of the linear system of equations.*

A careful look at this system shows that we could have written it as follows:

$$\begin{pmatrix} 3 & 2 \\ 1 & -1 \end{pmatrix} \begin{pmatrix} x \\ y \end{pmatrix} = \begin{pmatrix} 4 \\ 5 \end{pmatrix}$$

Before we proceed to find an answer to this question, we should rewrite (a) and (b) as follows:

$$3x + 2y - 4 = 0 \tag{a$'$}$$

$$x - y - 5 = 0 \tag{b$'$}$$

Multiplying equation (a) by A and equation (b) by B where A and B are non-zero arbitrary constants and adding the results we have:

$$A(3x + 2y - 4) + B(x - y - 5) = 0 \tag{c}$$

We claim that regardless of the values of A and B,

    (*i*)   Any values of x and y satisfying (a$'$) and (b$'$) will also satisfy (c).

    (*ii*) Any values of x and y that satisfy (c) and one of (a$'$) or (b$'$) will also satisfy the other. Why?

With the help of (*i*) and (*ii*) we can find an answer to our original question.

First, choose B so the coefficient of y (or the coefficient of x) in (c) becomes zero. To do this we regroup (c) as follows:

$$(3A + B)x + (2A - B)y - 4A - 5B = 0 \tag{c$'$}$$

and choose $B = 2A$ (or $B = 3A$). Substituting $B = 2A$ in (c) yields $5Ax - 14A = 0$. Second, we solve the system

$$5Ax - 14A = 0 \tag{a$''$}$$

$$x - y - 5 = 0 \qquad \textbf{(b'')}$$

But (a'') is an algebraic equation with one unknown, x; hence $x = \dfrac{14}{5}$. With this value of x we get

$$y = x - 5 = \frac{14}{5} - 5 = -\frac{11}{5}$$

Our original question finally has been answered: $x = \dfrac{14}{5}$ and $y = -\dfrac{11}{5}$. The method of solution used is called the Gauss elimination method.

2.1 Gauss Elimination

We can generalize the above question as follows:

For which values of $x_1, x_2, \ldots, x_n$ does the following system of linear equations hold?

$$\begin{aligned}
a_{11}x_1 + a_{12}x_2 + \ldots + a_{1n}x_n &= a_{1(n+1)} \\
a_{21}x_1 + a_{22}x_2 + \ldots + a_{2n}x_n &= a_{2(n+1)}
\end{aligned} \qquad \textbf{(1)}$$

$$\cdot$$
$$\cdot$$
$$\cdot$$

$$a_{n1}x_1 + a_{n2}x_2 + \ldots + a_{nn}x_n = a_{n(n+1)}$$

Before we try to find a *solution* to the system of linear equations (1), we are going to introduce some standard terminology. A system of linear equations with n unknowns $x_1, x_2, \ldots, x_n$ is said to be of *order n*.

Two systems of linear equations of order n are said to be *equivalent* if they have the same solution. Given two linear equations

$$c_1x_1 + c_2x_2 + \ldots + c_nx_n - e_1 = 0 \qquad \textbf{(2)}$$

$$d_1x_1 + d_2x_2 + \ldots + d_nx_n - e_2 = 0 \qquad \textbf{(3)}$$

We define a linear combination of (2) and (3) to be the following expression:

$$A(c_1x_1 + c_2x_2 + \ldots + c_nx_n - e_1) + B(d_1x_1 + d_2x_2 + \ldots + d_nx_n - e_2) = 0 \quad \textbf{(4)}$$

where A and B are different from zero.

The following result is very easy to prove:

The solution of the system of equations (1) does not change if we substitute one equation by a linear combination of itself with any other equation of the system.

Example

$$x_1 - x_2 + 3x_3 - 4 = 0$$

$$2x_1 + 3x_2 + x_3 + 5 = 0$$

$$4x_1 - 2x_2 + 4x_3 - 7 = 0$$

An equivalent system to the above is obtained if we add to the first equation the second equation obtaining:

$$3x_1 + 2x_2 + 4x_3 + 1 = 0$$

$$2x_1 + 3x_2 + x_3 + 5 = 0$$

$$4x_1 - 2x_2 + 4x_3 - 7 = 0$$

Next, we are going to proceed to find the solution to the system (1). The clue to the solution lies in the fact that we can substitute (1) by an equivalent system having the property that the coefficient of x_1 in all the equations except the first one is zero. Next, we can substitute (1) by an equivalent system having the property that the coefficient of x_2 is zero in all the equations except in the first and second equations; we can continue this process until finally we get a system of equations in which each equation has in it an unknown less than in the previous equation. The final system so obtained is called the *upper triangular form of (1)*. We also say that (1) has been reduced to an upper triangular form.

We shall show how this reduction can be accomplished using a system of equations with three unknowns.

$$a_{11}x_1 + a_{12}x_2 + a_{13}x_3 = a_{14}$$

$$a_{21}x_1 + a_{22}x_2 + a_{23}x_3 = a_{24} \qquad (5)$$

$$a_{31}x_1 + a_{32}x_2 + a_{33}x_3 = a_{34}$$

We proceed as follows:

    (*i*)   Divide all the coefficients of the first equation of the system (5) by a_{11} obtaining

$$x_1 + a'_{12}x_2 + a'_{13}x_3 = a'_{14} \tag{p}$$

where

$$a'_{12} = \frac{a_{12}}{a_{11}}, \qquad a'_{13} = \frac{a_{13}}{a_{11}}, \qquad a'_{14} = \frac{a_{14}}{a_{11}}$$

(ii)   Multiply all the coefficients of (p) by a_{21} and subtract the result from $a_{21}x_1 + a_{22}x_2 + a_{23}x_3 = a_{24}$ obtaining

$$(a_{22} - a'_{12}a_{21})x_2 + (a_{23} - a'_{13}a_{21})x_3 = a_{24} - a'_{14}a_{21}$$

(iii)   Multiply all the coefficients of equation (p) by a_{31} and subtract the result from $a_{31}x_1 + a_{32}x_2 + a_{33}x_3 = a_{34}$ obtaining

$$(a_{32} - a'_{12}a_{31})x_2 + (a_{33} - a'_{13}a_{31})x_3 = a_{34} - a'_{14}a'_{31} \tag{r}$$

(iv)   Put

$$a'_{22} = a_{22} - a'_{12}a_{21}, \qquad a'_{23} = a_{23} - a'_{13}a_{21},$$

$$a'_{24} = a_{24} - a'_{14}a_{21}, \qquad a'_{32} = a_{32} - a'_{12}a_{31}$$

$$a'_{33} = a_{33} - a'_{13}a_{31}, \qquad a'_{34} = a_{34} - a'_{14}a_{31}$$

and we obtain

$$x_1 + a'_{12}x_2 + a'_{13}x_3 = a'_{14} \tag{s}$$

$$a'_{22}x_2 + a'_{23}x_3 = a'_{24} \tag{t}$$

$$a'_{32}x_2 + a'_{33}x_3 = a'_{34} \tag{u}$$

(v)   Divide equation (t) by a'_{22} obtaining x

$$x_2 + a''_{23}x_3 = a''_{24} \tag{w}$$

where

$$a''_{23} = \frac{a'_{23}}{a'_{22}}, \qquad a''_{24} = \frac{a'_{24}}{a'_{22}}$$

(vi)   Multiply all the coefficients of equation (w) by a'_{32} and subtract from $a'_{32} + a'_{33}x = a'_{34}$ obtaining

$$(a'_{33} - a''_{23}a'_{32})x_3 = a'_{34} - a''_{24}a'_{32}$$

(vii)   Put

$$a'_{12} = a^{\ast}_{12}, \quad a'_{13} = a^{\ast}_{13}, \quad a'_{14} = a^{\ast}_{14}, \quad a''_{23} = a^{\ast}_{23}, \quad a''_{24} = a^{\ast}_{24},$$
$$a^{\ast}_{33} = a'_{33} - a''_{23}a'_{32}, \quad a^{\ast}_{34} = a'_{34} - a''_{24}a'_{32},$$

obtaining

$$x_1 + a_{12}^{\circ}x_2 + a_{13}^{\circ}x_3 = a_{14}^{\circ}$$

$$x_2 + a_{23}^{\circ}x_3 = a_{24}^{\circ}$$

$$a_{33}^{\circ}x_3 = a_{34}^{\circ}$$

which is the upper diagonal form of the system of equations (5).

Let us pause for a moment, and look back at step (*i*). We will not be able to perform this step unless a_{11} is different from zero. If $a_{11} = 0$ we must rearrange the system until we get a first coefficient that is different from zero. Figure 78 has a flow chart that would reduce a system of equations to upper triangular form. This algorithm is called REDUCE.

Before solving the system of equations (5) we will find an algorithm that we shall call BACKS, for obtaining the solution of a system of equations in upper triangular form. Let

$$a_{11}x_1 + a_{12}x_2 + \ldots + a_{1i}x_i + \ldots + a_{1n}x_n = a_{1,n+1}$$

$$a_{22}x_2 + \ldots + a_{2i}x_i + \ldots + a_{2n}x_n = a_{2,n+2}$$

$$a_{ii}x_i + \ldots + a_{in}x_n = a_{n,n+1}$$

$$a_{nn}x_n = a_{n,n+1}$$

where all the coefficients of the form a_{ii}, $i = 1, \ldots, n$ are assumed to be different from zero. To find the solution we proceed as follows:

(1)   Compute x_n from

$$x_1 = \frac{a_{n(n+1)}}{a_{nn}}$$

(2)   Compute x_{n-1} from

$$x_{n-1} = \frac{a_{n-1,n+1} - a_{n-1,n}x_n}{a_{n-1,n-1}}$$

(3)   Assume that we have computed the values of $x_n, x_{n-1}, \ldots x_{i+1}$. To compute x_i we use the *i*th equation of (7) obtaining

$$x_i = \frac{a_{i,n+1} - (a_{i,i+1}x_{i+1} + a_{i,i+2}x_{i+1} + \ldots a_{in}x_n)}{a_{ii}}$$

(4)   Set i to $i - 1$.

(5)   Compare i with 1. If $i < 1$ then a solution has been found. If $i \geq 1$ then proceed to step (3).

The figure below shows a flow chart for this algorithm.

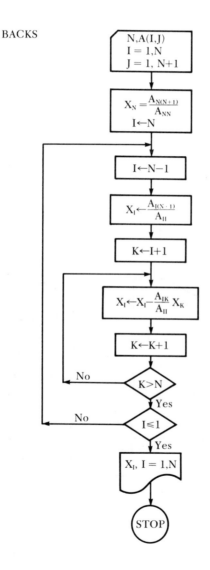

An algorithm to solve a system of equations

$$A_{11}x_1 + A_{12}x_2 + \ldots + A_{1n}x_n = A_{1,n+1}$$

.

.

$$A_{n1}x_1 + A_{n2}x_2 + \ldots + A_{nn}x_n = A_{n,n+1}$$

using the Gauss method of elimination is as follows:

Step (1)   Read the number of equations n

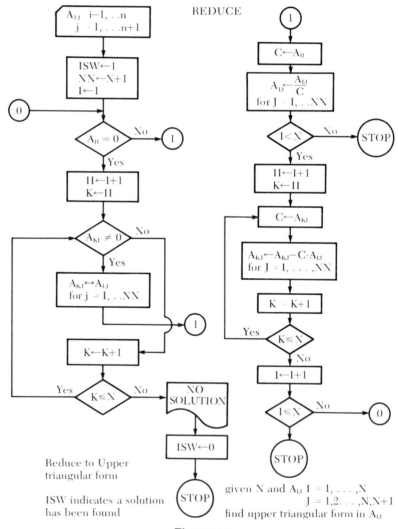

Figure 77

Step (2) Read the coefficients A_{I1}, A_{I2}, ..., A_{IN}, $A_{I,N+1}$ for $I = 1, 2, ..., N$

Step (3) Use REDUCE to form upper triangular system in A and put $ISW = 1$ in order to indicate successful completion of triangulation.

Step (4) Compare ISW to 1: if $ISW = 1$ go to step (5)
if $ISW \neq 1$ stop as no solution exists

Step (5) Use BACKS to back solve for x_n, x_{n-1}, ..., x_1

Step (6) Write x_1, x_2, ..., x_n

Figure 77 contains a flow chart for reducing a matrix to upper triangular form. Figure 78 has a flow chart for the Gauss method of elimination.

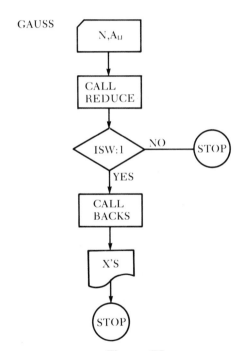

Figure 78

Exercises

1. Write a FORTRAN subroutine to reduce a matrix A to upper triangular form.

2. Using the above subroutine write a FORTRAN program to solve a system of equations using the Gauss elimination method.

2.2 Gauss-Jordan Elimination Method

We shall illustrate this method with an example. Solve for x, y, and z the following system:

$$\begin{aligned}
x - \ y + 3z &= 8 \\
2x + \ y - \ z &= 1 \\
-x + 2y + \ z &= 6
\end{aligned} \qquad (1)$$

Note that this system can be written in matrix form as follows:

$$\begin{pmatrix} 1 & -1 & 3 \\ 2 & 1 & -1 \\ -1 & 2 & 1 \end{pmatrix} \begin{pmatrix} x \\ y \\ z \end{pmatrix} = \begin{pmatrix} 8 \\ 1 \\ 6 \end{pmatrix}$$

To solve system (1) we proceed as in the Gauss elimination method. First x is eliminated from the second and third equation of (1) obtaining:

$$\begin{aligned}
x - \ y + 3z &= \ \ 8 \\
0 + 3y - 7z &= -15 \\
0 + \ y + 4z &= \ \ 14
\end{aligned}$$

Next we eliminate y from the first and the third equations obtaining

$$\begin{aligned}
3x + \ 0 + 2z &= \ \ 9 \\
0 + 3y - 7z &= -15 \\
0 + \ 0 + \ z &= \ \ 3
\end{aligned}$$

Finally we eliminate z from the first and second equation obtaining

$$\begin{aligned}
3x + \ 0 + 0 &= 3 \\
0 + 3y + 0 &= 6 \\
0 + \ 0 + z &= 3
\end{aligned}$$

From this last system of equations we get

$$x = 1, \quad y = 2, \quad z = 3.$$

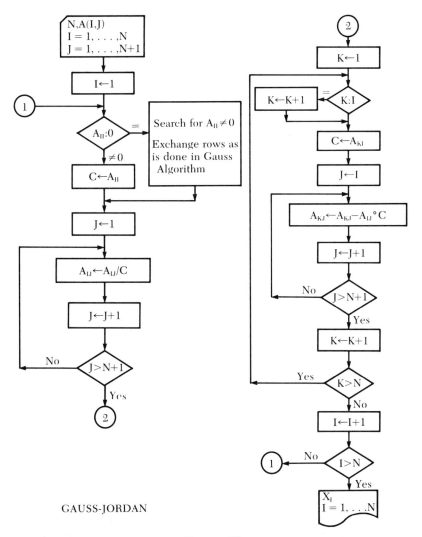

GAUSS-JORDAN

Figure 79

The Gauss-Jordan elimination method reduces a system of equations of the form

$$a_{11}x_1 + a_{12}x_2 + a_{13}x_3 = a_{14}$$
$$a_{21}x_1 + a_{22}x_2 + a_{23}x_3 = a_{24}$$
$$a_{31}x_1 + a_{32}x_2 + a_{33}x_3 = a_{34}$$

into a system of the form

$$a_{11}^{\circ}x_1 = a_{14}^{\circ}$$

$$a_{22}^{\circ}x_2 = a_{24}^{\circ}$$

$$a_{33}^{\circ}x_3 = a_{34}^{\circ}$$

This final form is called the diagonal form. To reduce a system to its diagonal form we must have, at every stage of the process, the diagonal element a_{ii}, called the *pivot* element, different from zero. The equation used at each stage of the reduction is called the *pivot row*.

If at a certain stage of the reduction the pivot element is not different from zero, then start a search from the pivot row down until an equation is found having the element located below the pivot position different from zero. Once this is found the pivot row and this row must be exchanged.

Figure 79 has a flow chart for this algorithm.

Exercise

Write a FORTRAN program to solve a system of equations using the Gauss-Jordan elimination method.

2.3 Gauss–Seidel Algorithm for Solving Systems of Linear Equations

Let

$$
\begin{aligned}
a_{11}x_1 + a_{12}x_2 + \ldots + a_{1n}x_n &= a_{1n+1} \\
a_{21}x_1 + a_{22}x_2 + \ldots + a_{2n}x_n &= a_{2n+1} \\
&\ \vdots \\
a_{n1}x_1 + a_{n2}x_n + \ldots + a_{nn}x_n &= a_{nn+1}
\end{aligned}
\tag{*}
$$

be a system of linear equations with the property that all the diagonal elements, i.e., $a_{11}, a_{22}, a_{33}, \ldots, a_{nn}$, are different from zero.

The Gauss-Seidel algorithm is an iterative procedure. Starting with an initial set of values for $x_1, x_2, \ldots, x_n$, we try to obtain a "better" approximation. Assume that

$$x_1^0, x_2^0, x_3^0, \ldots, x_n^0 \tag{0}$$

is an initial set of values for $x_1, x_2, x_3, \ldots, x_n$. Compute x_1^1 from the first equation by substituting in it the set of values (0), obtaining

$$x_1^1 = \frac{a_{1n+1} - (a_{12}x_2^0 + a_{13}x_3^0 + \ldots + a_{1n}x_n^0)}{a_{11}}$$

The exponent 1 in the unknown x_1 is used to indicate that we are performing the first iteration. In general, x_1^i would denote the value of x_1 after the ith iteration.

Next, using

$$x_1^1, x_3^0, x_4^0, \ldots, x_n^0$$

the value of x_2 is computed from the second equation of (*) obtaining x_2^1;

$$x_2^1 = \frac{a_{2n+1} - (a_{21}x_1^1 + a_{23}x_3^0 + \ldots + a_{2n}x_n^0)}{a_{22}}$$

Using

$$x_1^1, x_2^1, x_4^0, \ldots, x_n^0$$

the value of x_3 is computed from the third equation of (*) obtaining x_3^1;

$$x_3^1 = \frac{a_{3n+1} - (a_{31}x_1^1 + a_{32}x_2^1 + a_{34}x_4^0 + \ldots + a_{3n}x_n^0)}{a_{33}}$$

We proceed in this way, computing new values of the unknown, until we compute x_n^1 from the last equation of (*) using

$$x_1^1, x_2^1, x_3^1, \ldots, x_{n-1}^1$$

obtaining

$$x_n^1 = \frac{a_{nn+1} - (a_{n1}x_1^1 + a_{n2}x_2^1 + \ldots + a_{nn-1}x_{n-1}^1)}{a_{nn}}$$

Next, the "new" set of values

$$x_1^1, x_2^1, \ldots, x_n^1$$

is used to obtain

$$x_1^2, x_2^2, \ldots, x_n^2$$

If this procedure is carried out k times we will obtain

$$x_1^k = \frac{a_{1n+1} - (a_{12}x_2^{k-1} + a_{13}x_3^{k-1} + \ldots + a_{1n}x_n^{k-1})}{a_{11}}$$

$$x_2^k = \frac{a_{2n+1} - (a_{21}x_1^{k-1} + a_{23}x_3^{k-1} + \ldots + a_{2n}x_n^{k-1})}{a_{22}}$$

$$x_n^k = \frac{a_{nn+1} - (a_{n1}x_1^{k-1} + a_{n2}x_2^{k-1} + \ldots + a_{nn-1}x_{n-1}^{k-1})}{a_{nn}}$$

This algorithm ends whenever the largest of the differences

$$\frac{x_1^k - x_1^{k-1}}{x_1^k}, \quad \frac{x_2^k - x_2^{k-1}}{x_2^k}, \quad \ldots, \quad \frac{x_n^k - x_n^{k-1}}{x_n^k}$$

is smaller than a quantity that has been fixed a priori. We indicate this by saying

$$\max_{1 \le i \le n} \frac{|x_i^k - x_i^{k-1}|}{x_i^k}$$

This procedure should start with the system of equations arranged in such a way that the diagonal elements would be those with the largest absolute value. That is, in each equation the coefficient a_{ii} is the largest in absolute value. For example:

$$3x_1 + x_2 + 6x_3 = 5$$

$$x_1 + 5x_2 - x_3 = 4$$

$$6x_1 - 3x_2 + x_3 = 1$$

should be rearranged as follows:

$$6x_1 - 3x_2 + x_3 = 1$$

$$x_1 + 5x_2 - x_3 = 4$$

$$3x_1 + x_2 + 6x_3 = 1$$

It is important to observe that at some stage of the iteration the computed values might be zero! For example: Solve, using Gauss-Seidel, the following system;

$$2x_1 + 3x_2 = 6$$

$$4x_1 - 6x_2 = 0$$

Starting with $x_1 = 0$, $x_2 = 0$, we obtain: $x_1^1 = 3$, $x_2^2 = 2$; Next with these values we obtain $x_1^2 = 0$, $x_2^2 = 0$, and $er = 0$. 0 is smaller than any positive number. Hence the procedure will stop. Note that we are at the initial point.

Figure 80 shows a flow-chart to solve a system of equations by the Gauss-Seidel algorithm.

Exercise

Write a Fortran program to solve a system of equations using the Gauss-Seidel Algorithm.

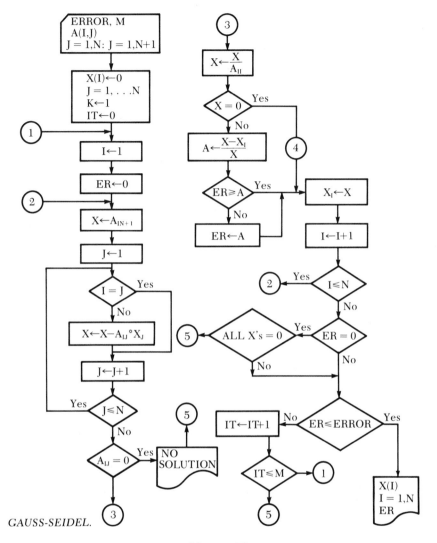

Figure 80

2.4 Jacobi's Algorithm

Let

$$a_{11}x_1 + a_{12}x_2 + \ldots + a_{1n}x_n = a_{1n+1}$$

$$a_{21}x_1 + a_{22}x_2 + \ldots + a_{2n}x_n = a_{2n+1}$$

$$\ldots\ldots\ldots\ldots\ldots\ldots\ldots\ldots\ldots\ldots\ldots\ldots\ldots\ldots\ldots$$

$$a_{n1}x_1 + a_{n2}x_2 + \ldots + a_{nn}x_n = a_{nn+1}$$

be a nonhomogeneous system of equations with all the coefficients on the diagonal different from zero. The Jacobi's algorithm is very similar to the Gauss-Seidel algorithm except for the fact that all the old values of $x_1, x_2, \ldots, x_n$ are used to compute new values of these unknowns. Starting with an initial set

$$x_1^0, x_2^0, \ldots, x_n^0,$$

new values

$$x_1^1 = \frac{a_{1n+1} - (a_{12}x_2^0 + \ldots + a_{1n}x_n^0)}{a_{11}}$$

$$x_2^1 = \frac{a_{2n+1} - (a_{21}x_1^0 + \ldots + a_{2n}x_n^0)}{a_{22}}$$

$$\ldots\ldots\ldots\ldots\ldots\ldots\ldots\ldots\ldots\ldots\ldots\ldots\ldots$$

$$x_n^1 = \frac{a_{nn+1} - (a_{n1}x_1^0 + \ldots + a_{nn}x_n^0)}{a_{nn}}$$

are computed.

Define $E_1^1, E_2^1, \ldots, E_n^n$ as follows:

$$E_1^1 = a_{1n+1} - (a_{11}x_1^0 + a_{12}x_2^0 + \ldots + a_{1n}x_n^0)$$

$$E_2^1 = a_{2n+1} - (a_{21}x_1^0 + a_{22}x_2^0 + \ldots + a_{2n}x_n^0)$$

$$\ldots\ldots\ldots\ldots\ldots\ldots\ldots\ldots\ldots\ldots\ldots\ldots\ldots$$

$$E_n^1 = a_{nn+1} - (a_{n1}x_1^0 + a_{n2}x_2^0 + \ldots + a_{nn}x_n^0)$$

With these values $x_1^1, x_2^1, \ldots, x_n^1$, can be written as follows:

$$x_1^1 = x_1^0 + E\,_1^1/a_{11}, \quad x_2^1 = x_2^0 + E\,_2^1/a_{22}, \ldots. \quad x_n^1 = x_n^0 + E\,_2^1/a_{nn}$$

Also,

$$|x_1^1 - x_1^0| \leq E\,_1^1/a_{11}, \ldots, |x_n^1 - x_n^0| \leq \,_n^1/a_{nn},$$

These values give a measure of how much the new set of values $x_1^1, \ldots x_n^1$ has improved the old set of values $x_1^0, \ldots, x_n^0$.

After $x_1^1, \ldots, x_n^1$ have been computed, a new set of values $x_1^2, \ldots, x_n^2$ is obtained. This procedure is continued until

$$E^k = \sum_{i=1}^{n} E_i^k$$

is smaller than a value E fixed a priori.

2.5 Inverse of a Matrix

A matrix having the same number of rows as columns is called a *square matrix*. A *unit matrix* is a square matrix satisfying

(*i*) $a_{ii} = 1$ for all *i* from 1 to *n*

(*ii*) $a_{ij} = 0$ if $i \neq j$.

For example

$$I = \begin{pmatrix} 1 & 0 & 0 \\ 0 & 1 & 0 \\ 0 & 0 & 1 \end{pmatrix}$$

Unit matrices have the property that

$$A \cdot I = A \cdot I = A$$

for every square matrix of the same rank as *I*. For example:

$$\begin{pmatrix} 1 & 6 & 5 \\ 2 & 3 & 5 \\ 4 & 3 & 2 \end{pmatrix} \begin{pmatrix} 1 & 0 & 0 \\ 0 & 1 & 0 \\ 0 & 0 & 1 \end{pmatrix} = \begin{pmatrix} 1 & 6 & 5 \\ 2 & 3 & 5 \\ 4 & 3 & 2 \end{pmatrix}$$

We would like to solve the following question: Given an $n \times n$ square matrix *A*, does there exist a square matrix *B* of the same rank such that $A \cdot B = I$?

We shall try to find an answer to this question by first working out an example. Let

$$A = \begin{pmatrix} 1 & 2 & 3 \\ 3 & 2 & 1 \\ 1 & 4 & 5 \end{pmatrix}$$

We want to find a matrix *B*

$$B = \begin{pmatrix} b_{11} & b_{12} & b_{13} \\ b_{21} & b_{22} & b_{23} \\ b_{31} & b_{32} & b_{33} \end{pmatrix}$$

such that if

$$I = \begin{pmatrix} 1 & 0 & 0 \\ 0 & 1 & 0 \\ 0 & 0 & 1 \end{pmatrix}$$

then

$$\begin{pmatrix} 1 & 2 & 3 \\ 3 & 2 & 1 \\ 1 & 4 & 5 \end{pmatrix} \begin{pmatrix} b_{11} & b_{12} & b_{13} \\ b_{21} & b_{22} & b_{23} \\ b_{31} & b_{32} & b_{33} \end{pmatrix} = \begin{pmatrix} 1 & 0 & 0 \\ 0 & 1 & 0 \\ 0 & 0 & 1 \end{pmatrix}$$

Computing $A \cdot B$ we get

$$A \cdot B = \begin{pmatrix} b_{11} + 2b_{22} + 3b_{31} & b_{12} + 2b_{22} + 3b_{32} & b_{13} + 2b_{23} + 3b_{33} \\ 3b_{11} + 2b_{21} + b_{31} & 3b_{12} + 2b_{22} + b_{32} & 3b_{13} + 2b_{23} + b_{33} \\ b_{11} + 4b_{21} + 5b_{31} & b_{12} + 4b_{22} + 5b_{32} & b_{13} + 4b_{23} + 5b_{33} \end{pmatrix}$$

This matrix must be equal to

$$\begin{pmatrix} 1 & 0 & 0 \\ 0 & 1 & 0 \\ 0 & 0 & 1 \end{pmatrix}$$

hence we must have

$$\begin{aligned} b_{11} + 2b_{21} + 3b_{31} &= 1 \\ 3b_{11} + 2b_{21} + b_{31} &= 0 \\ b_{11} + 4b_{21} + 5b_{31} &= 0 \end{aligned} \quad \text{(a)}$$

$$\begin{aligned} b_{12} + 2b_{22} + 3b_{32} &= 0 \\ 3b_{12} + 2b_{22} + b_{32} &= 1 \\ b_{12} + 4b_{22} + 5b_{32} &= 0 \end{aligned} \quad \text{(b)}$$

$$\begin{aligned} b_{13} + 2b_{23} + 3b_{33} &= 0 \\ 3b_{13} + 2b_{23} + b_{33} &= 0 \\ b_{13} + 4b_{23} + 5b_{33} &= 1 \end{aligned} \quad \text{(c)}$$

Therefore the problem of finding a matrix B such that $A \cdot B = I$ has been reduced to solve the three systems of equations (a), (b), and (c). We observe that the coefficients of the unknowns are the same on the three systems. These are the elements of a 3×3 matrix

$$A = \begin{pmatrix} 1 & 2 & 3 \\ 3 & 2 & 1 \\ 1 & 4 & 5 \end{pmatrix} \qquad (*)$$

We shall take advantage of this fact in trying to solve these systems using Gauss-Jordan algorithm, since to reduce a system to its triangular form the only coefficients used are those of matrix $(*)$. We shall organize the work as follows:

(1) We "augment" the matrix A by the matrix I obtaining

$$\begin{pmatrix} 1 & 2 & 3 & \vdots & 1 & 0 & 0 \\ 3 & 2 & 1 & \vdots & 0 & 1 & 0 \\ 1 & 4 & 5 & \vdots & 0 & 0 & 1 \end{pmatrix}$$

(The process of extending an $m \times n$ matrix A by an $m \times n$ matrix C having the same number of rows to obtain a new matrix with number of columns equal to $h + n$ is called *augmenting A by C*.)

(2) Multiply each element of the first row by 3 and subtract it from the corresponding elements of the second row: Subtract each element of the first row from the corresponding elements of the third row, obtaining

$$\begin{pmatrix} 1 & 2 & 3 & \vdots & 1 & 0 & 0 \\ 0 & -4 & -8 & \vdots & -3 & 1 & 0 \\ 0 & 2 & 2 & \vdots & -1 & 0 & 1 \end{pmatrix}$$

(3) Divide each element of the second row by -4 obtaining

$$\begin{pmatrix} 1 & 2 & 3 & \vdots & 1 & 0 & 0 \\ 0 & 1 & 2 & \vdots & 3/4 & -1/4 & 0 \\ 0 & 2 & 2 & \vdots & -1 & 0 & 0 \end{pmatrix}$$

(4)   Multiply each element of the second row by 2 and subtract from the corresponding elements on the first row
and from the corresponding elements of the third row,
obtaining

$$\begin{pmatrix} 1 & 0 & -1 & \vdots & -1/2 & 1/2 & 0 \\ 0 & 1 & 2 & \vdots & 3/4 & -1/4 & 0 \\ 0 & 0 & 1 & \vdots & 5/4 & -1/4 & -1/2 \end{pmatrix}$$

(5)   Add each element of the third row to the corresponding
elements on the first row: multiply by 2 each element of
the third row and subtract the results from the corresponding elements on the second row, obtaining

$$\begin{pmatrix} 1 & 0 & 0 & \vdots & 3/4 & 1/4 & -1/2 \\ 0 & 1 & 0 & \vdots & -7/4 & -1/4 & 1 \\ 0 & 0 & 1 & \vdots & 5/4 & -1/4 & -1/2 \end{pmatrix} \qquad (**)$$

(6)   The original matrix has been reduced to its diagonal
form B

$$B = \begin{pmatrix} 3/4 & 1/4 & -1/2 \\ -7/4 & 1/4 & 1 \\ 5/4 & -1/4 & -1/2 \end{pmatrix}$$

The matrix B is called the inverse of A and is denoted by
A^{-1}. The reader can see that the answer to our original
question might not be affirmative in all the cases, since it
depends on whether or not A would have a diagonal form.
Let A be an arbitrary $n \times n$ matrix

$$A = \begin{pmatrix} a_{11} & a_{12} & \dots & a_{1n} \\ a_{21} & a_{22} & \dots & a_{2n} \\ \dots & \dots & \dots & \dots \\ a_{n1} & a_{n2} & \dots & a_{nn} \end{pmatrix}$$

To find its inverse A^{-1} we proceed as follows:

(1) Augment A with $n \times n$ matrix

$$I = \begin{pmatrix} 1 & 0 & \cdots & 0 \\ 0 & 1 & \cdots & 0 \\ \cdot & \cdot & \cdots & \cdot \\ 0 & 0 & \cdots & 1 \end{pmatrix}$$

obtaining,

$$\left(\begin{array}{cccc|cccc} a_{11} & a_{12} & \cdots & a_{1n} & 1 & 0 & \cdots & 0 \\ a_{21} & a_{22} & \cdots & a_{2n} & 0 & 1 & \cdots & 0 \\ \cdots & \cdots & \cdots & \cdots & \cdot & \cdot & \cdots & \cdot \\ a_{n1} & a_{n2} & \cdots & a_{nn} & 0 & 0 & \cdots & 1 \end{array}\right)$$

(2) Apply the Gauss-Jordan algorithm of reduction to diagonal form obtaining

$$\left(\begin{array}{cccc|cccc} 1 & 0 & \cdots & 0 & c_{11} & c_{12} & \cdots & c_{1n} \\ 0 & 1 & \cdots & 0 & c_{21} & c_{22} & \cdots & c_{2n} \\ \cdot & \cdot & \cdots & \cdot & \cdots & \cdots & \cdots & \cdots \\ 0 & 0 & \cdots & 1 & c_{n1} & c_{n2} & \cdots & c_{nn} \end{array}\right)$$

(3) The inverse matrix of A is

$$I = \begin{pmatrix} c_{11} & c_{12} & \cdots & c_{1n} \\ c_{21} & c_{22} & \cdots & c_{2n} \\ \cdots & \cdots & \cdots & \cdots \\ c_{n1} & c_{n2} & \cdots & c_{nn} \end{pmatrix}$$

Note that we have obtained this result under the assumption A has an inverse; this implies that not all the elements in a row of its reduced diagonal matrix are zeros.

3. BUSINESS

3.1 Compound Interest

Assume that we have invested a certain amount of money P called *principal*, during n periods and at a rate i per period. The final amount of money C accumulated at the end of n periods is given by the formula

$$C = P(1 + i)^n.$$

Write a Fortran program that would accept P, i as input, generate n, and have as an output C. Present the result in a tabular form of the form

$$N \quad P \quad I \quad C$$

Every ten lines of output produce three blank lines.

3.2 Present Value

On occasion we have to know what is the present value of a capital C due in n periods at a rate i per period. By this we mean: What is the principal P that if i was now invested at a rate i per period will become C at the end of n periods?

Write a Fortran program that would accept C and I as input, generate n, and have as output C, P, I and N. Present this in a tabular form.

3.3 Annuity

An *annuity* is a series of equal payments made at equal intervals of time. The size of each payment is called the *periodic rent*. By *rent period* we understand the interval of time between two successive payments. The lapse of time between the beginning of the first rent period and the last rent period is called the *term of the annuity*. The *final value* of an annuity is the sum of the final values of all the periodic rents accumulated at the end of the term of the annuity. The final value can be computed using the formula

$$S_n = R \, \frac{(1 + i)^n - 1}{i}$$

where R is the periodic rent, n the number of equal payments, and i the rate per period. We assume that the payment interval coincides with the interest period.

Write a Fortran program that would accept as input R and i, generate n, and have as output N, R, C, and S. Present this in a tabular form.

3.4 Present Value of an Annuity

The *present value* A_n of an annuity after n periods is a quantity of money that if invested now at a certain rate will be equal at the end of the term of the annuity to the accumulated sum of the compound quantities of each of the payments. The present value of an annuity is given by the formula

$$A_n = R \frac{1 - (1 + i)^{-n}}{i}$$

where R is the rent per period, n, the number of periods, and i, the rate per period.

Write a Fortran program that would accept R, i as input, generate n, and have as output n, R, i, and A in tabular form.

Next we present as an example of an output in tabular form a table to compute the periodic payments to cancel a debt.

Assume that we have a debt of $\$D$ to be paid in N periods. Suppose that the interest rate per period is i. We would like to know how much the equal payments should be at the end of each period to reduce D to zero after N payments. We would like to know how much the balance is at the end of each period. To illustrate the necessary steps to be carried out to obtain this information, we use the following example.

Suppose that a debt of $\$4000$, bearing interest of 5%, is to be paid by equal payments at the end of each year for four years. Find

(a) Annual payment R
(b) The outstanding balance B_1, B_2, B_3 at the end of each year.

(a) $R = \dfrac{Di\,(1 + i)^n}{(1 + i)^n - 1} = \dfrac{4000\,(1 + .05)^4\,i}{1.05^4 - 1} = 1128.07$

(b) The outstanding balance is shown in Table I.

Table I

Year	Principal	Interest	Payment	Amount Used to Reduce Debt
1	4000.00	200.00	1128.07	928.07
2	3071.93	153.60	1128.07	974.47
3	2097.46	104.87	1128.07	1023.20
4	1074.26	53.71	1128.07	1074.36
	Total	512.18	4512.28	4000.10

3.5   State Income Tax

Consider the problem of computing a state income tax based on an employee's gross pay, tax exemptions, and a standard deduction. The standard deduction is 10% of his gross to a maximum of $9.60 per week. His exemption on a weekly basis can be found from the following table.

Married	40.00
Single	20.00
Dependents	10.00/dependent

Taxable pay, T, is computed by subtracting from gross, GROSS, the sum of tax exemptions, WKXMP, and standard deduction, D. Tax, W, is computed by

if taxable pay $\geq$ 192.00, then tax is $9.20 + (T - 192.00) \times .07$
if taxable pay is positive and less than 192.00 $\rightarrow$ tax is

$$(.00010 \times T + .0281)T$$

if taxable pay is zero or less $\rightarrow$ tax is zero.

Example

If A is married, has two children and earns $280/week, his exemptions total $(40.00 + 10.00 + 10.00) = 60.00$; his standard deduction is 9.60; his taxable pay T is $(280 - (60. + 9.80)) = 210.20$; and his tax W is $(9.20 + (210.20 - 192.00) \times .07 = 9.20 + 18.20 \times .07 = 9.20 + 1.27 = 10.47$.

Algorithm

(1)   GET GROSS, weekly gross and WKXMP, weekly exemption
(2)   Compare GROSS to 96.00
        if GROSS $\geq$ 96.00 then deduction $D \leftarrow 9.60$
        if GROSS $<$ 96.00 then deduction $D \leftarrow$ GROSS $\times .10$
(3)   Compute weekly taxable income, T by $T \leftarrow$ GROSS $- D$ $-$ WKXMP
(4)   Compare T with 192.00
        if $T \geq 192.00 \rightarrow$ set $W \leftarrow 9.20 + .07\ (T - 192.00)$
        otherwise set $W \leftarrow .00010 \times T + .0281)T$
(5)   Compare T with 0.00
        if $T < 0.00$ set $W \leftarrow 0$
        otherwise, finished with W weekly state income tax.

Draw a flow chart and write a FORTRAN program (subprogram) to implement the calculations for state income tax *W*, given GROSS and WKXMP.

3.6 Federal Income Tax

An algorithm is to be constructed that will enable one to calculate on a weekly basis the federal income tax FIT that an individual owes. The following information is to be used: the individual's gross pay GRISS, marital status MRTLS, and his exemptions NEXMS. The method to be used is to calculate the weekly exemption *D* which is 13.50 × NEXMS and subtract *D* from GROSS, getting taxable gross TGRS. Then the appropriate table is searched to find the formula for FIT.

Table for Single Taxpayers

if		then		
0 ≤ TGRS ≤ 1300	then	FIT	= .14 × TGRS −	56.
1300 < TGRS ≤ 2300	"		= .15 × TGRS −	69.
2300 < TGRS ≤ 8500	"		= .19 × TGRS −	161.
8500 < TGRS ≤ 16900	"		= .22 × TGRS −	416.
16900 < TGRS ≤ 21200	"		= .28 × TGRS −	1430.
21200 < TGRS	"		= .33 × TGRS −	2490.

Table for Married Taxpayers

if		then		
0 ≤ TGRS ≤ 2300	then	FIT	= .14 × TGRS −	56.
2300 ≤ TGRS ≤ 5800	"		= .15 × TGRS −	79.
5800 < TGRS ≤ 16900	"		= .19 × TGRS −	311.
16900 < TGRS ≤ 34000	"		= .22 × TGRS −	818.
34000 < TGRS ≤ 42300	"		= .28 × TGRS −	2858.
42300 < TGRS	"		= .33 × TGRS −	4973.

This information may be summarized to the following tables:

Upper Limits for Each Class		*Per Cents for Class*		*Corrections for Each Class*	
Single	*Married*	*Single*	*Married*	*Single*	*Married*
1300	2300	14	14	56.	56.
2300	5800	15	15	69.	79.
8500	16900	19	19	161.	311.
16900	34000	22	22	461.	818.
21200	42300	28	28	1430.	2858.
		33	33	2490.	4973.

To use these tables one proceeds thus: Suppose that GROSS = $300.00 for 1 week, NEXMS = 31 and MRTLS = married, Form D = NEXMS × 13.50 = 3 × 13.50 = 40.50, TGRS = GROSS − D = 300 − 40.50 = 259.50 per week, TGRS = 52 × 259.50 = 13494 per year. 13494 ⩽ 16900 in the 3rd row of the above table, hence % is 19% and correction is $818.00, thus FIT = .19 × TGRS − 818. = .19 × 13494.00 − 818 = 2698.80 − 818.00 = 1880.80.

   Write an algorithm and a FORTRAN program to implement the calculation for Federal Income Tax, FIT, given the variables GROSS, MRTLS, and NEXMS.

4. LINEAR PROGRAMMING

   A certain automobile company builds two different types of cars: sport and tourist. The price per unit given in thousands of dollars is 3 for the sport car and 2 for the tourist car. The company has two assembly centers, A and B. Assembly center A can be used up to 69 hours per day, while assembly center B can only be used up to 64 hours per day. The sport model requires 5 hours in assembly center A and three hours in assembly center B. The tourist model requires 3 hours in assembly center A and 4 hours in assembly center B. The management would like to find the best production schedule that will make the revenue as large as possible.

Let x_1 stand for the number of sports cars produced in one day.
Let x_2 stand for the number of tourist cars in one day.
Let z stand for the total revenue.

The following relations between x_1, x_2, and z must hold:

$$z = 3x_1 + 2x_2 \qquad 5x_1 + 3x_2 \leqslant 69$$

$$3x_1 + 4x_2 \leqslant 64 \qquad x_1 \geqslant 0, \quad x_2 \geqslant 0.$$

The problem has been reduced to find those values of x_1 and x_2 that will make z as large as possible (maximum). To accomplish this goal we proceed as follows:

   First we convert all the inequalities into equalities by adding some new variables, x_3 and x_4, called *slack variables*. We obtain

$$z = 3x_1 + 2x_2 + 0x_3 + 0x_4$$
$$5x_1 + 3x_2 + x_3 = 69$$
$$3x_1 + 4x_2 + x_4 = 64$$
$$x_1 \geqslant 0, \quad x_2 \geqslant 0, \quad x_3 \geqslant 0, \quad x_4 \geqslant 0$$

Now the problem has been reduced to find $x_1 \geqslant 0$, $x_2 \geqslant 0$, $x_3 \geqslant 0$, and $x_4 \geqslant 0$, such that

$$5x_1 + 3x_2 + x_3 = 69$$
$$3x_1 + 4x_2 + x_4 = 64 \qquad (1)$$

hold and z becomes as large as possible. The system of equations (1) has an infinite number of solutions. We can reduce this number if we assume any two of the solutions equal zero. Assume that x_1 and x_2 are equal to zero. Then $x_3 = 69$, $x_4 = 64$, and $z = 0$.

Next suppose that $x_1 = 0$ and $x_3 = 0$, then we have

$$3x_2 = 69$$
$$4x_2 + x_4 = 64,$$

which once solved gives $x_2 = 13$, $x_4 = 12$ and $z = 26$. Now suppose that $x_1 = 0$, $x_4 = 0$, then

$$3x_2 + x_3 = 69$$
$$4x_2 = 64$$

Solving for x_2 and x_3, we get $x_2 = 16$, $x_3 = 53/3$, and $z = 32$. Put $x_2 = 0$, $x_3 = 0$ in (1) and we get

$$5x_1 = 69$$
$$3x_1 + x_4 = 64$$

From this system we obtain: $x_1 = 69/5$, $x_4 = 113/5$, and $z = 207/5$. with $x_2 = 0$ and $x_4 = 0$, we obtain

$$5x_1 + x_3 = 69$$
$$3x_1 = 64$$

Solving for x_1 and x_3 we get: $x_1 = 64/3$, $x_3 = -113/3$. This solution is not feasible since $x_3 < 0$. Now put $x_3 = 0$ and $x_4 = 0$, then we have

$$5x_1 + 3x_2 = 69$$
$$3x_1 + 4x_2 = 64.$$

Solving for x_1 and x_2 we obtain $x_1 = 84/11$, $x_2 = 113/11$, and $z = 478/11$. Now from all the values of z that we have obtained, that is 26, 32, 207/5, 478/11, we select the largest, which is $z = 478/11$. We have the solution 84/11 sport cars, 113/11 tourist cars and the revenue is 478/11.

Assume now, that we are trying to find an answer to the following problem: Find $x_1 \geqslant 0$, $x_2 \geqslant 0$, $x_3 \geqslant 0$ such that $z = px_1 + qx_2 + rx_3$ would be as large as possible while x_1, x_2 and x_3 satisfy the following inequalities:

$$a_{11}x_1 + a_{12}x_2 \leqslant b_1$$

$$a_{21}x_1 + a_{22}x_2 \leqslant b_2$$

$$a_{31}x_1 + a_{32}x_2 \leqslant b_3$$

To find an answer to this problem we proceed as follows:

(1) Introduce slack variables $x_3 \geqslant 0$, $x_4 \geqslant 0$, $x_5 \geqslant 0$, so the above inequalities would become equalities

$$a_{11}x_1 + a_{12}x_2 + x_3 = b_1$$

$$a_{21}x_1 + a_{22}x_2 + x_4 = b_2$$

$$a_{31}x_1 + a_{32}x_2 + x_5 = b_3$$

(2) Assign, arbitrarily, to two of the unknowns the value zero. Note that we can choose two variables from x_1, x_2, x_3, x_4, x_5 in ten different ways:

$$
\begin{align}
(x_1, x_2), (x_1, x_3), (x_1, x_4), (x_1, x_5)& \\
(x_2, x_3), (x_2, x_4), (x_2, x_5)& \qquad \textbf{(1)}\\
(x_3, x_4), (x_3, x_5)& \\
(x_4, x_5)&
\end{align}
$$

As an example take $x_2 = 0$ and $x_3 = 0$ then we have

$$a_{11}x_1 = b_1$$

$$a_{21}x_1 + x_4 = b_2$$

$$a_{31}x_1 + x_5 = b_3$$

Solving for x_1, x_4, and x_5 we obtain a *basic solution*. If we do this for each pair in (1) we shall obtain 10 basic solutions.

(3) Next, check to see whether or not the basic solutions satisfy the relations $x_1 \geq 0$, $x_2 \geq 0$, $x_3 \geq 0$, $x_4 \geq 0$, $x_5 \geq 0$, rejecting those that do not satisfy the above relations. The solutions that have passed the test are called *feasible solutions*.

(4) Compute the value of z by substituting each feasible solution in

$$z = px_1 + qx_2 + rx_3$$

(5) Select the largest z.

Write a FORTRAN program that would accept as data:

(1) p, q, r

(2)
$$\begin{pmatrix} a_{11} & a_{12} & b_1 \\ a_{21} & a_{22} & b_2 \\ a_{31} & a_{32} & b_3 \end{pmatrix}$$

The output should be the values of x_1, x_2, x_3, and the largest possible value of z.

5. STATISTICS

Mean. Given a collection of N numbers, $x_1, x_2, \ldots, x_n$ their *Mean* is defined to be

$$M = \frac{x_1 + x_2 + \ldots + x_n}{n}$$

An algorithm to compute M follows:

(1) Get $x_1, x_2, \ldots, x_n, N$
(2) Set $M \leftarrow 0$
(3) Set $I \leftarrow 0$
(4) Set $M \leftarrow M + x_I$
(5) Set $I \leftarrow I + 1$
(6) Compare I with N.
   If $I > N$ go to (8)
   otherwise go to (4)
(7) Set $M \leftarrow M/N$
(8) Stop. The mean has been obtained.

Standard deviation. On occasion, one needs to know how the data separates from its mean value. A measurement of this deviation is obtained by computing the standard deviation "*s*." The standard deviation is defined by

$$s = \sqrt{\frac{(x_1 - M)^2 + (x_2 - M)^2 + \ldots + (x_N - M)^2}{N}}$$

Where M is the mean of $x_1, x_2, \ldots, x_n$. In order to facilitate the computation of s the following formula can be used:

$$s^2 = \frac{1}{N}(x_1^2 + x_2^2 + \ldots + x_n^2) - \frac{(x_1 + x_2 + \ldots + x_n)^2}{N^2}$$

Next we shall use an example to introduce some terminology used in Statistics. Suppose that Table II contains the scores obtained by 50 students taking Math. 141.

Table II

87	58	81	68	91	54	64	71	82	93
83	18	93	70	49	87	65	78	58	65
75	28	29	72	57	78	77	45	32	83
67	65	45	54	67	65	72	75	34	66
64	75	67	83	69	54	93	98	65	47

We would like to know

(1) The smallest score, 18.
(2) The largest score, 98.
(3) The difference between the largest and the smallest score (*range*) 80.
(4) The most common score, (*mode*).
(5) How often (*frequency*) each different score appears in the table.

For example, score 83 appears twice. We would like these frequencies to be presented in a table with two entries. (Table III)

Entry (a) contains the score.
Entry (b) contains the frequencies.

A table of this type is called a *frequency distribution.*

Table III

(a)	(b)	(a)	(b)	(a)	(b)
18	1	64	2	77	1
28	1	65	2	78	2
29	1	66	1	81	1
32	1	67	3	82	1
45	2	68	1	83	3
47	1	69	1	84	1
49	1	70	1	87	2
54	3	71	1	91	1
57	1	72	2	93	3
58	2	75	3	98	1

To show "how" the scores tend to cluster around certain values, Table III is rearranged in Table IV.

Table IV

Class Intervals	Frequency	Class Intervals	Frequency
0– 9	0	50–59	6
10–19	1	60–69	13
20–29	2	70–79	10
30–39	1	80–89	8
40–49	4	90–100	5

The end-points of the class-intervals are called upper and lower boundaries. The data in Table III can be represented graphically as is shown in Figure 81, obtaining what is called a *histogram.*

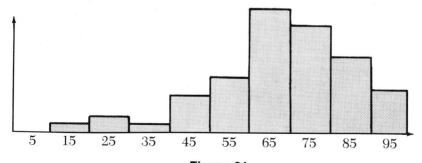

Figure 81

The points 5, 15, 25, . . . , 85, 95, are called *class-marks* (class representatives).

To see how the data is distributed, statisticians often compute the "quartile points," Q_1, Q_2, Q_3. These points divide the frequency scale into 4 equal parts. The points Q_1, Q_2, Q_3, satisfy the following conditions:

> (*i*)   One fourth of the items (data) considered falls below Q_1. That is, their value is less than or equal to Q_1.
>
> (*ii*)   Half of the items considered falls below Q_2.
>
> (*iii*)   Three-fourths of the items considered falls below Q_3.

To compute the quartile points, first we must find in which class-interval they are located. To accomplish this, start computing $N/4$, $N/2$, and $3N/4$. Since each class-interval C_I has a frequency f_I associated with it, we accumulate each f_I until the sum is greater than or equal to $N/4$. When this happens the quartile Q_1 is in class C_I. Where in class C_I is Q_1? This depends on 1) how much data is in this class, 2) how much $N/4$ exceeds the accumulation of frequencies from all the previous classes, and 3) how wide is class C_I. A formula for accomplishing this follows:

$$Q_1 = L_I + \frac{N/4 - S_I}{f_I} \cdot W$$

where L_I represents the lower boundary of C_I, S_I represents the accumulation of frequencies for all classes below C_I, f_I represents the frequency of class C_I, and W represents the class width.

In the example under consideration, Q_1 is in class C_6, $L_6 = 50$, $N/4 = 12.5$, $S_6 = f_1 + f_2 + f_3 + f_4 + f_5 = 0 + 1 + 2 + 1 + 4 = 8$ and $f_6 = 6$, and $W = 10$. Therefore

$$Q_1 = 50 + \frac{(12.5 - 8)10}{6}$$

Q_2 and Q_3 are derived similarly by using $N/2$ and $3N/4$, respectively. To find Q_I we have the following procedure:

> (1)   Set $A \leftarrow I*N/4$.
>
> (2)   Set $SS \leftarrow 0, S \leftarrow 0, I \leftarrow 1$.
>
> (3)   Put $SS \leftarrow SS + f_I$
>
> (4)   Compare SS to A
>
> > If $SS < A$ go to (5)
> >
> > If $SS \geq A$ go to (6)
>
> (5) $S \leftarrow S + f_I, I \leftarrow I + 1$, go to (3).
>
> (6) $Q_I \leftarrow L_I + \dfrac{(A - S)*W}{f_I}$

To show how the class-intervals are found we shall use the data given in Table II.

Letting the class width W be 10, we find that 18 yields 1 when integer divided by W, and the maximum value 98 yields 9 when integer divided by W. (This suggests that our classes run from min. W to max. W + 1, where min. and max. are the largest and the smallest element in the frequency table). Hence the first class will be from 10.1 to 10.1 + 9, second class from 10.2 to 10.2 + 9, . . . , and the ninth class from 10.9 to 10.9 + 9. That is, C_1 ranges from 10–19, C_2 ranges from 20–29, . . . , and C_9 ranges from 90–99.

Next, we give a procedure to find the class intervals and the number of elements in each class interval. Let W stand for class width.

(1) Let MIN be equal to the minimum of all the elements obtained using the MINA subalgorithm.

(2) Let MAX be the largest of all the elements obtained using a subalgorithm that we are calling MAXA.

(3) Let IMIN be the integer part of MIN/W.

(4) Let IMAX be the integer part of MAX/W.

(5) Let NCLASS = IMAX−IMIN+1, number of classes

(6) Set K←1

(7) A_K←(IMIN+K−1)*W

(8) B_K←A_K+(W−1)

(9) K←K+1

(10) Compare K with NCLASS
  If K≤NCLASS go to (7).
  If K>NCLASS STOP.

NCLASS is the number of intervals and (A_1, B_1), (A_2, B_2), . . . (A_{NCLASS}, B_{NCLASS}) are the class boundaries.

Once the class intervals have been determined then a counter, C_I, is set up for each interval (A_I, B_I). These counters are zeroed out and the observations are talleyed by incrementing the appropriate counter. This is done by comparing an observation X_J to successive end-points $A_1, A_2, . . . , A_{NCLASS}$ to determine into which interval it falls. When it has been decided that X_J falls in the interval A_I to B_I, then C_I is replaced by $C_I + 1$. The X's are thus ranked by continuing this comparison and associated tallying for $J = 1, 2, . . . , N$.

We have the following algorithm:

(1) Set K←1

(2) Set C_K←0

(3) Set K←K+1

(4) Compare K with NCLASS
  If K≤NCLASS go to step (2)
  If K>NCLASS go to step (5)
(5) Set J←1
(6) Set K←1
(7) Compare K with NCLASS
  If K = NCLASS go to step (11)
  If K≤NCLASS go to step (8)
  If K>NCLASS impossible as we have no points outside all intervals
(8) Compare A_K with X_J and X_J with A_{K+1}
  If A_K≤X_J and X_J<A_{K+1} go to step (11)
  If either A_K>X_J or X_J≥A_{K+1} go to step (9)
(9) Set K←K+1
(10) Go to (7)
(11) Set C_K←C_K+1
(12) Compare J with N
  If J≤N go to step (6)
  If J>N STOP, job finished

5.1 Histogram

We have all seen charting techniques for graphically displaying data. These include pie charts, bar charts, line graphs, etc. We would like to display a frequency distribution over class intervals in a bar chart or histogram. Since we will chart by using the printer, let us place the intervals on the vertical axis and the plotting symbols across the page.

We are to write an algorithm to construct a histogram. Let NCLASS be the number of intervals $(A_1, B_1), (A_2, B_2), \ldots, (A_{NCLASS}, B_{NCLASS})$ and $f_1, \ldots, f_{NCLASS}$ the frequencies on each interval class. The output form would be as follows.

A_1
F_1 ✱✱✱   ✱ F_1 symbols
B_1
A_2
F_2 ✱✱✱✱✱✱   ✱ F_2 symbols
B_2

....

A_{NCLASS}
F_{NCLASS}✱✱✱✱✱✱✱✱✱ F_{NCLASS} symbols
B_{NCLASS}

Let NPRINT stand for the number of print positions on a line. Let X stand for print positions of line. Note that there are NPRINT X's.

(1) Set I = 1 ⎫
(2) Print A$_I$
(3) Set K=1
(4) X$_K$←blank   Blanking out
(5) Set K←K+1   of a print line
(6) Compare K with NPRINT
      If K≤NPRINT go to (4)
      If K>NPRINT go to (7) ⎭

(7) Compare F$_1$ with 0 ⎫
      If F$_1$>0 go to (8)
      If F$_1$≤0 go to (12)
(8) Set K = 1
(9) X$_K$←* (or any other symbol)   Printing of
(10) Set K←K+1   a line
(11) Compare K with F$_1$
      If K≤F$_1$ go to (9)
      If K>F$_1$ go to (12)
(12) Print F$_1$ and X$_K$ for K = 1, 2,. . .NPRINT ⎭
(13) Print B$_1$
(14) Set I←I+1
(15) Compare I with NCLASS
      If I≤NCLASS go to 2
      If I>NCLASS, stop.

Exercises

1. In a certain statistical experiment two variables X and Y are measured and their values are punched on a card. Let (X_1, Y_1), $(X_2, Y_2) \ldots$, (X_n, Y_n) be the different values of X and Y so obtained. With these values numbers A and B are calculated as follows:

$$A = \frac{(X_1^2 + X_2^2 + \ldots + X_n^2)(Y_1 + Y_2 + \ldots + Y_n) - (X_1 + X_2 + \ldots + X_n)(X_1Y_1 + \ldots + X_nY_n)}{n(X_1^2 + X_2^2 + \ldots + X_n^2) - (X_1 + X_2 + \ldots + X_n)^2}$$

$$B = \frac{n(X_1Y_1 + X_2Y_2 + \ldots + X_nY_n) - (X_1 + X_2 + \ldots + X_n)(Y_1 + Y_2 + \ldots + Y_n)}{n(X_1^2 + X_2^2 + \ldots + X_n^2) - (X_1 + X_2 + \ldots + X_n)^2}$$

In order to know when the last card has been read into the computer, three numbers, X, Y, and Z, are punched on each card. The values of X and Y are arbitrary. The values that Z can take are 0 or 1. If the value of Z is 0, this indicates that the last card has been read in. Write a FORTRAN program to compute A and B. The output should be in the form

Y = AX+B

Note. The above equation is called the line of regression Y on X.

2.   The coefficient of correlation r for n pairs of observations of two variables X and Y is given by the formula:

$$r = \frac{n(X_1Y_1 + \ldots + X_nY_n) - (X_1 + \ldots + X_n)(Y_1 + \ldots + Y_n)}{\sqrt{n(X_1^2 + \ldots + X_n^2) - (X_1 + \ldots + X_n)^2} \cdot \sqrt{n(Y_1^2 + \ldots + Y_n^2) - (Y_1 + \ldots + Y_n)^2}}$$

Write a FORTRAN program to compute r. The data is read in the computer as in the previous exercise. The output should be r and the number of observations n.

3.   The probable error of the coefficient of correlation r is given by the formula

$$PER = 0.6745(1 - r^2)/\sqrt{n}$$

Using exercise 2 as a subroutine, write a FORTRAN program to compute the value of PER.

4.   On occasions, we have to rank individuals or observations according to certain criteria. Assume that the rank of n individuals according to two criteria are given in pairs of observations (X_i, Y_i), $i = 1, \ldots, n$. The Spearman's rank correlation is given by the formula

$$RS = 1 - \frac{6((X_1 + X_2 + \ldots + X_n) - (Y_1 + Y_2 + \ldots + Y_n))}{n(n^2 - 1)}$$

Write a FORTRAN to compute RS. In order to know when the last card has been read in, use the same procedure as in the previous exercises.

5.   The results of an experiment are entered in an $N \times M$ array A called a *contingency table*. From this array A the following totals are computed:

TR(I) = A(I,1)+A(I,2)+. . .+A(I,M), (I = 1, . . . , N).
TC(J) = A(1,J)+A(2,J)+. . .+A(N,J), (J = 1, . . . , M).

A new $N \times M$ array 0 is formed as follows:
0(I,J) = TR(I)×TC(J)/TOTAL, I = 1, . . . , N. J = 1, . . . , M.

where

TOTAL = TC(1)+TC(2)+. . . .+TC(N) = TR(1)+TR(2)+. . . .+TR(M).

Using A(I,J) and 0(I,J) the value CHISQ is computed as follows:

$$\frac{(A(1,1) - 0(1,1))^2}{0(1,1)} + \frac{(A(1,2) - 0(1,2))^2}{0(1,2)} + \ldots + \frac{(A(1,M) - 0(1,M))^2}{0(1,M)} +$$

$$\frac{(A(2,1) - 0(2,1))^2}{0(2,1)} + \frac{(A(2,2) - 0(2,2))^2}{0(2,2)} + \ldots + \frac{(A(2,M) - 0(2,M))^2}{0(2,M)} +$$

....

$$\frac{(A(N,1) - 0(N,1))^2}{0(N,1)} + \frac{(A(N,2) - 0(N,2))^2}{0(N,2)} + \ldots + \frac{(A(N,M) - 0(N,M))^2}{0(N,M)}$$

The degrees of freedom D for the contingency table A are computed using the formula $D = (N - 1)(M - 1)$. To each value of D we associate a number $P(D)$ as follows:

$P(1) = 3.84$	$P(5) = 11.07$	$P(9)\ = 16.92$
$P(2) = 5.99$	$P(6) = 12.59$	$P(10) = 18.31$
$P(3) = 7.82$	$P(7) = 14.07$	$P(11) = 19.68$
$P(4) = 9.49$	$P(8) = 15.51$	$P(12) = 21.03$

For example, if $D = 5$, $P(D) = P(5) = 11.07$

Write a FORTRAN program that will accept the array A, $P(1)$, ..., $P(12)$ as data. The output should be CHISQ, D (degrees of freedon). If the value of CHISQ exceeds the corresponding value of P (say if $D = 6$ then CHISQ $= 12.59$), then print out the message

REJECT HYPOTHESIS

If the computed value of CHISQ is less than or equal to the corresponding value of P, print out the message

ACCEPT HYPOTHESIS.

6.   Write a FORTRAN program to compute the mean and the standard deviation of a collection of numbers, $x_1, x_2, \ldots, x_n$.

6. PHYSICS

6.1 Ohm's Law

If the intensity of the current through a metallic circuit is I, the source voltage is E, and the resistance R is constant, then the Ohm's law states that

$$E = R \cdot I$$

Assume that current flows from a point 1 to a point 2. The voltage dropped between these two points will be denoted by E_{12}. We have

$$E_{12} = E_1 - E_2$$

An ideal resistor is a circuit element that opposes the flow of current. If between points 1 and 2 an ideal resistor is inserted and if the intensity of the current is I, then we have

$$E_{12} = I \cdot R$$

where the current flows from the point of higher voltage to the point of lower voltage.

Resistors can be placed in a circuit in two different ways:

(*a*) Series connection
(*b*) Parallel connection

Figure 82 represents a series connection of four resistors, R_1, R_2, R_3, and R_4. Occasionally it is convenient to substitute several resistors connected in series by an ideal resistor, R_e, which would produce the same effect as R_1, R_2, R_3, and R_4. To accomplish this, it is assumed that the drop of voltage E_{14} between points 1 and 4 is the sum of the drop of voltage between the intermediate points, that is

$$E_{14} = E_{12} + E_{23} + E_{34} = E_1 - E_4$$

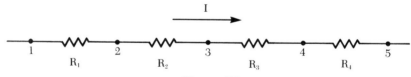

Figure 82

Applying Ohm's law to each individual resistor, we get

$$E_{14} = I \cdot R_e = I(R_1 + R_2 + R_3 + R_4)$$

where R_e is the equivalent resistor. We have

$$R_e = R_1 + R_2 + R_3 + R_4.$$

If there were n resistors R_1, R_2, ... , R_n, the formula to compute R_e would be

$$R_e = R_1 + R_2 + \ldots + R_n. \tag{1}$$

Next, assume that the current flowing from point 1 to point 2 splits

in three branches as shown in Figure 83. This connection of resistors is said to be a parallel connection. The relation between
I, and I_1, I_2, I_3 is given by

$$I = I_1 + I_2 + I_3. \tag{2}$$

The drop of voltage between 1 and 2 is the same for the three
branches. We get the following formulas:

$$E_{12} = L_i(R_{11} + R_{12}) = I_2 \cdot R_{21} = I_3(R_{31} + R_{32} + R_{33}).$$

Next

$$I_1 = \frac{E_{12}}{R_{11} + R_{12}}, \quad I_2 = \frac{E_{12}}{R_{21}}, \quad I_3 = \frac{E_{12}}{R_{31} + R_{32} + R_{33}}$$

Substituting the values of I_1, I_2, and I_3 in

$$E_{12} = I \cdot R_e$$

we get

$$R_e = \frac{1}{\dfrac{1}{R_{11} + R_{12}} + \dfrac{1}{R_{21}} + \dfrac{1}{R_{31} + R_{32} + R_{33}}}$$

This formula can be generalized as follows: Assume that a current
of intensity I splits into n branches with intensities I_1, I_2, $\ldots$, I_n.
Assume that several resistors are inserted in each branch in the
following way:

Branch 1. R_{11}, R_{12}, $\ldots$, R_{1h_1} total h_1
Branch 2. R_{21}, R_{22}, $\ldots$, R_{2h_2} total h_2
....
Branch n. R_{n1}, R_{n2}, $\ldots$, R_{nh_n} total h_n.

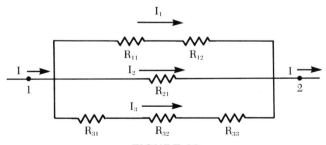

FIGURE 83

R_e can be computed using the formula

$$R_e = \cfrac{1}{\cfrac{1}{R_{11} + \ldots + R_{1h_1}} + \cfrac{1}{R_{21} + \ldots + R_{2h_2}} + \ldots + \cfrac{1}{R_{n1} + \ldots + R_{nh_n}}}$$

Write a FORTRAN program that would compute the ideal resistor R_e in

    (a) Series connection.
    (b) Parallel connection.

The program should have as an input:

    (1) Intensity of the current I.
    (2) Number of branches N.
    (3) Number of resistors in each branch and their values R_{IJ}.
    (4) What kind of connection the circuit has. For this purpose the program should have a built-in switch that will allow the computing of R_e in series or in parallel. For example a variable called ISW would have the value 0 for series connection or would have the value 1 for parallel connection.

6.2   Transient in Electric Circuit

Consider the circuit shown in Figure 84. The capacitor C is initially charged to a voltage V_0. At time $t = 0$, let the switch K be closed. The current $I(t)$ can be one of three different types, depending upon the relative magnitude of R, L and C. Let us define the quantity ζ called the damping factor:

$$\zeta = \frac{R}{2} \sqrt{\frac{L}{C}}$$

and the quantity W_n, called the undamped natural frequency

$$W_n = \frac{1}{\sqrt{L\,C}}$$

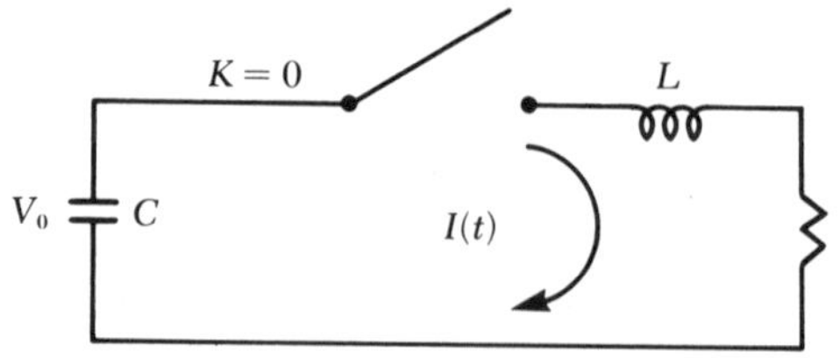

Figure 84

Then, depending on the magnitude of ζ there will be three cases:

Case 1. $\zeta > 1$. Overdamped case.

$$I(t) = \frac{V_0}{2W_n L\sqrt{\zeta^2 - 1}} \, e^{\zeta W_n t} \, (e^{W_n \sqrt{\zeta^2 - 1} t} - e^{-W_n \sqrt{\zeta^2 - 1} t}) \tag{1}$$

Case 2. $\zeta = 1$. Critically damped case.

$$I(t) = \frac{V_0}{L} \, te^{-W_n t} \tag{2}$$

Case 3.   1. Underdamped or oscillatory case.

$$I(t) = \frac{V_0}{W_n L \sqrt{1 - \zeta^2}} \, e^{-\zeta_n W_n t} \sin{(W_n \sqrt{1 - \zeta^2} t)} \tag{3}$$

Knowing the initial voltage on the capacitor and the circuit elements values R, L, and C, we can compute the transient current $I(t)$ as a function of time.

Write a program such that after reading the initial voltage, the element values, the increment DT, and the final time TF will compute the damping factor ζ and the natural frequency W_n. The program should have as output which case the computed value of ζ gives rise to. After the value of ζ has been produced, the value of $I(t)$ should be computed according to one of the three expressions given above. The program should provide a print out for the time T and the corresponding value of $I(T)$. The time should be increased by one step, and $I(T)$ is computed until the final time, TF, is passed.

6.3 Heat Conduction Through Composite Walls

It is known (Fourier's Law) that the steady state heat flow, Q, through a plane wall (Figure 85) of thickness L is given by

$$Q = \frac{k}{x} (t_1 - t_2)$$

where Q is the amount of heat per unit of surface, x is the width of the wall, t_1 and t_2 are the temperature of the outside walls, and k is a constant, the thermal conductivity, that depends on the material used to build the wall. The number $\dfrac{k}{x}$ is called the *thermal resistance*.

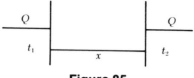

Figure 85

Now, assume we have a composite wall made up of three layers of *d* different materials (Figure 86).

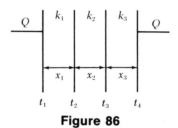

Figure 86

Assume, also, that each wall is at a uniform temperature. We want to compute the heat flow Q per unit of surface. First we compute the heat flow through each of the layers, obtaining

$$Q = \frac{k_1}{x_1}(t_1 - t_2) = \frac{k_2}{x_2}(t_2 - t_3) = \frac{k_3}{x_3}(t_3 - t_4),$$

the heat flow Q being equal because we are assuming the heat flow is steady.

$$t_1 - t_2 = \frac{Qx_1}{k_1}, \quad t_2 - t_3 = \frac{Qx_2}{k_2}, \quad t_3 - t_2 = \frac{Qx_3}{k_3}$$

Adding the above equalities we obtain:

$$t_1 - t_4 = Q\left(\frac{x_1}{k_1} + \frac{x_2}{k_2} + \frac{x_3}{k_3}\right)$$

Q can be obtained from the formula

$$Q = \frac{t_1 - t_4}{\frac{x_1}{k_1} + \frac{x_2}{k_2} + \frac{x_3}{k_3}}$$

This formula can be generalized to obtain the best flow of a composite wall with *n*-layers as follows:

$$Q = \frac{t_1 - t_n}{\displaystyle\sum_{i=1}^{n} \frac{x_i}{k_i}}$$

where x_i is the width of the ith layer $t_1, \ldots t_{n+1}$ are the temperatures of the outside walls, and k_i is the thermal conductivity of the ith layer.

Let $\bar{t}_1, \bar{t}_2, \bar{t}_3$ be the mean temperature of the different layers of the composite wall on Figure 86. Assume that the thermal conductivities k_1, k_2, k_3, k_4 are given by the formulas

$$k_1 = a_1 \bar{t}_1 + b_1 \quad k_2 = a_2 \bar{t}_2 + b_2 \quad k_3 = a_3 \bar{t}_3 + b_3$$

where

$$\bar{t}_1 = \frac{1}{2}(t_1 + t_2) \quad \bar{t}_2 = \frac{1}{2}(t_2 + t_3) \quad \bar{t}_3 = \frac{1}{2}(t_3 + t_4)$$

Assuming that t_1 and t_4 are known, we can compute t_2 and t_3 using the formulas

$$t_3 = t_4 + \frac{\dfrac{x_3}{k_3}(t_1 - t_4)}{\dfrac{x_1}{k_1} + \dfrac{x_2}{k_2} + \dfrac{x_3}{k_3}} = t_4 + \frac{x_3}{k_3} Q$$

$$t_2 = t_1 - \frac{\dfrac{x_1}{k_1}(t_1 - t_4)}{\dfrac{x_1}{k_1} + \dfrac{x_2}{k_2} + \dfrac{x_3}{k_3}} = t_1 - \frac{x_1}{k_1} Q$$

To compute the values of t_2 and t_3 we can proceed as follows:

(1)   Assume initial values of t_2 and t_3 to be

$$t_2 = t_1 + \frac{2(t_1 - t_4)}{3} \qquad t_3 = t_4 + \frac{t_1 - t_4}{3}$$

(2)   Compute $\bar{t}_1, \bar{t}_2, \bar{t}_3$
(3)   Compute k_1, k_2, k_3

(4)   Compute $Q = \dfrac{t_1 - t_4}{\dfrac{x_1}{k_1} + \dfrac{x_2}{k_2} + \dfrac{x_3}{k_3}}$

(5)   Compute t_2 and t_3 using $t_3 = t_4 + \dfrac{x_3}{k_3} Q \quad t_4 = t_1 - \dfrac{x_1}{k_1} Q$

Repeat steps (2), (3), (4), and (5) until we obtain consecutive values of Q that differ in a preassigned equality, $\epsilon > 0$. Write a FORTRAN program that will compute t_1 and t_2. The input should consist of:

(1) x_1, x_2, x_3
(2) $a_1, a_2, a_3, b_1, b_2, b_3$
(3) T_1, T_4
(4) ϵ. (Error)

Draw a flow chart.

Chapter XI

SIMULATION

As we mentioned in Chapter II, DATAS is a three address machine language simulator. Machine language is generally formed as output from assembly language. However machine language is important on its own as it may determine computer organization and structure and help in its understanding. In this section we will look at a pseudo or simulated machine language, as it may be simulated on a computer.

We assume that we have a machine with 99 memory positions, each of which contains eight decimal digits. Therefore, with these design constraints, we have usually up to sixty or seventy instructions and perhaps up to twenty or thirty data locations. With each location containing eight digits we shall allocate these digits in the following ways. Digits 1–2 will be the operation code such as addition, subtraction, etc.; digits 3–4, 5–6, and 7–8 will, respectively, represent the locations in which operands 1, 2, and 3 reside. Therefore if 01 is addition, 01 12 75 84 could mean ADD what is in location 12 to what is in location 75, and place in location 84.

What type of operations should our simulator possess? Certainly we need the basic operations of addition, subtraction, multiplication, and division. The coding for these will be 01, 02, 03, and 04, respectively. Also needed is logical testing ability for branching purposes; the code for it will be 05. Stop is the operation represented by 06, while 07 and 08, respectively, represent read and write. Completing the operations of DATAS are 09 and 10 which allows us to use square root and absolute value operations. What we are planning to do is investigate each operation, decide what are desirable options of these operations, implement these operations with both flow charts and FORTRAN coding, and finally, integrate all these subsections of coding into a program that will allow us to simulate these operations on any computer possessing certain very basic properties.

A brief program shall be examined next. Suppose an integer A is stored in memory location 17, B in location 25, and C in location 45. Add A to B and divide by C, placing the result in location 60.

$$01\ 17\ 25\ 60 \qquad A + B \text{ in } 60$$
$$04\ 60\ 45\ 60 \qquad (A + B)/C \text{ in } 60$$

The first instruction says add (01) quantity in 17 (A) to quantity in 25 (B) and place result in location 60. The second instruction says divide (04) what is stored in 60, ($A + B$), by what is stored in 45, (C), and place the result in 60, thus replacing the temporary answer, ($A + B$), in 60.

Each instruction is composed of four two digit integers. The first two digit number is the operation. The last three two digit pairs are the first, second, and third operands. For convenience we shall compress the four pairs into one eight digit number. Each may be stored in a memory location as each has an eight digit capacity. Then the data in a location can be treated as an instruction by decoding the eight digits into the digits representing operation and operands. After the operations and operands are decoded, the instruction may be executed.

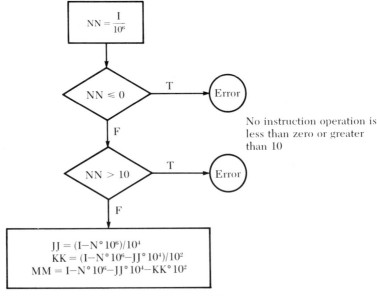

Figure 87

Now let us consider the problem of decoding an instruction. That is, given an instruction I in the form NNJJKKMM stored in one location as eight decimal digits, find NN, JJ, KK, and MM, the operation code, and the first, second, and third operands, respectively. We shall first divide by 10^6, saving the integer quotient NN. Next by subtracting $10^6 \times$ NN from I, we have JJKKMM; divide JJKKMM by 10^4 getting the integer quotient JJ. Continue the process indicated above to get KK and MM. A flow chart is shown in Figure 87.

In order to execute each instruction, we shall use the computed go to with ten arguments, one for each of add, subtract, multiply, divide, branch, halt, read, write, square root, and absolute value. This is shown in Figure 88.

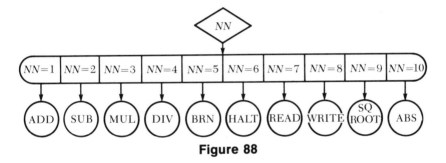

Figure 88

ADD

In addition 01JJKKMM indicates that the data at location JJ is to be added to data at location KK and the result stored in location MM

$$I_{MM} = I_{JJ} + I_{KK}$$

SUB

The instruction 02JJKKMM indicates that the data at location KK is to be subtracted from the data at location JJ and the results stored in location MM.

$$I_{MM} = I_{JJ} - I_{KK}$$

MULT

03JJKKMM instructs the computer to multiply the data at location JJ by the data at location KK and place the product in location MM.

$$I_{MM} = I_{JJ} * I_{KK}$$

DIV

04JJKKMM is our divide instruction. The quantity at location JJ is integer divided by the data at location KK, and the quotient is stored in location MM.

$$I_{MM} = I_{JJ}/I_{KK}$$

BRANCH

We desire a four-way branch, or we need an unconditional branch. Also needed are three branches, one for negative testing, one for positive testing, and one for zero testing. As a convention, we shall always use the third operand for the branch address. Since we are to have four branches, we shall use the first operand to denote the particular one. We shall use 00, 01, 02, and 03 for unconditional branch, negative branch, positive branch, and zero branch. In the case of the negative, positive, or zero branch, we need some quantity to test. For this purpose operand two is used as the address of the location to be tested. That is, if $operand_1 = 0$ we unconditionally branch to address in $operand_3$; if $operand_1 = 1$, we branch to address at $operand_3$ if $operand_2$ is the address of a negative number; if $operand_1 = 2$, a conditional branch to address at $operand_3$ if $operand_2$ is the address of a positive operand; and finally, if $operand_1 = 3$, then a branch to address in $operand_3$ if $operand_2$ is the address of a zero quantity.

Examples

Branch	Kind of Branch	Location to Be tested	Location to Branch to	
05	00	00	73	unconditional branch to 73
05	02	35	73	if quantity at location 35 is positive branch to 73
05	01	43	73	branch to 73 if quantity at 43 is negative
05	03	70	73	branch to 73 if quantity at 70 is zero

To implement the above we must test JJ, operand$_1$, for a value between 0 and 3; we must find the value (positive, negative, or zero) at location I_{KK} where KK is operand$_2$; we must branch to location MM according to the test of value in I_{KK}.

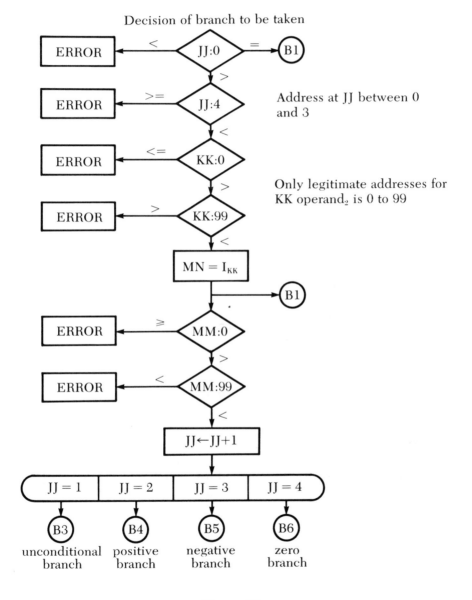

Decision of branch to be taken

Address at JJ between 0 and 3

Only legitimate addresses for KK operand$_2$ is 0 to 99

Figure 89

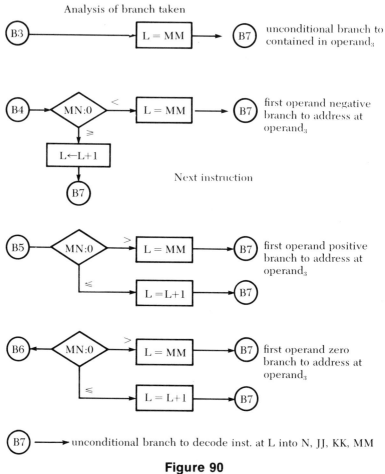

Figure 90

HALT

To implement a halt command we issue the FORTRAN STOP

Figure 91

READ

In order to read information we use an operation code of 07 and operand 1 called JJ, which causes an eight-digit number to be read and inserted into location I_{JJ}.

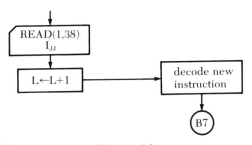

Figure 92

WRITE

In using the printer we desire to either print after single spacing, double space, or space to a new page. The second operand KK will contain a zero, one, or two to accomplish single spacing, new page, or double spacing, respectively.

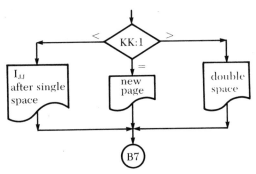

Figure 93

SQUARE ROOT

Take the square root of the quantity whose address is in first operand and place it in the location indicated by operand three.

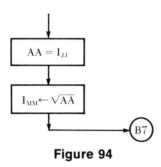

Figure 94

ABS VALUE

Here we desire to take the square root of quantity whose address is in operand 1 and place it in location indicated in operand 3.

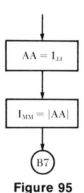

Figure 95

ERROR

On errors we might desire to have a *dump* of the computer memory, that is, a display of the current contents. As there are 99 storage locations, we might want three columns of 33 items each. In conclusion, write the location L of the instruction that caused the error.

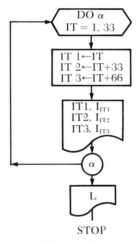

Figure 96

Several other points remain in this simulation. One is initialization of the "computer memory," the next the "loading the program," and the last the start of execution.

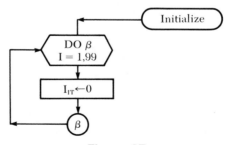

Figure 97

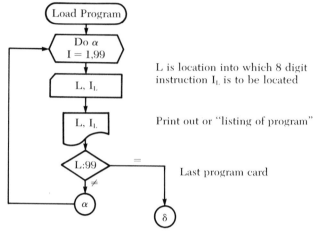

L is location into which 8 digit
instruction I_L is to be located

Print out or "listing of program"

Last program card

Figure 98

EXECUTION

We make the assumption that the program shall always start in location 1.

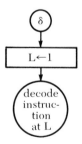

Figure 99

Therefore we must always have a valid instruction in location 1 and after that within the sequential flow or branch flow of the program.

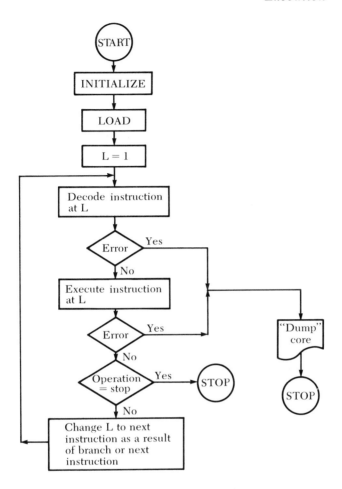

Figure 100

Flow Chart of Simulator

To trace a small program through DATAS, consider the problem of reading two numbers, A and B; if A is as large as B, then form D = A*B, otherwise put D = B−A. Print the result D.

An algorithm to do this follows:

(1)   Read A
(2)   Read B

(3) Compare A:B
     If A≥B go to step (7)
     If A<B go to step (4)
(4) Form D = B—A
(5) Print D
(6) STOP
(7) Form D = A°B
(8) Print D
(9) STOP

A flow chart to do this is shown in Figure 101.

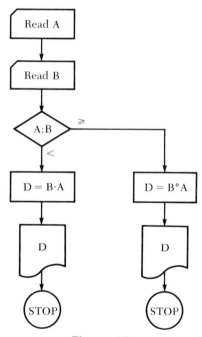

Figure 101

A program that will accommodate this is

0107500000
0207570000
0302505751
0405025709
0505035709
0602575058
0708580000

0806000000
0903505758
1008580000
1106000000
99
       8
       5

Separating this we have

	Loader	Operation	Op1	Op2	Op3
P	01	07	50	00	00
R	02	07	57	00	00
O	03	02	50	57	51
G	04	05	02	57	09
R	05	05	03	57	09
A	06	02	57	50	58
M	07	08	58	00	00
	08	06	00	00	00
	09	03	50	57	58
	10	08	58	00	00
	11	06	00	00	00

End of   99
Program

D   8
A   5
T
A

Figure 102

Under DATAS, let us trace the program's execution. Of course, the initialization of the information array I is done first. All ninety-nine locations of I are set to zero. Next, each line of the program is read and assigned to the location of I prescribed by the "loader" (first two digits of each instruction line). As the first line is 0107500000, the quantity 07500000 is placed in I_{01} or I_1. Line two, 0207570000, causes 07570000 to be placed in line 2, and so forth through line 11. However, before any instruction is loaded the loader number is compared to 99. If the loader is 99, DATAS assumes that no more program steps are to be loaded and as always, begins execution at location 01. Hence, for the line following line 11, 99 is sensed and control is passed to instruction one.

Now each instruction is decoded into operation, operands one, two, and three. For example, 07500000 is decomposed into 07, 50, 00, and 00. This is done by successive divisions and multiplications by powers of 10. To demonstrate first, 07500000 is integer divided by 10^6 getting 07. By multiplying the quotient 07 by 10^6 and subtracting from the original, we get $07500000 - 07000000 = 500000$. Next the difference is integer divided by 10^4 getting 50. This quotient 50, when multiplied by 10^4 and subtracted from 500000, leaves 0000. Therefore, following the above procedure by dividing by 10^2 and subtracting, we get a quotient of 00 and a remainder of 00. Summarizing 07500000 gives an operation of 07, operand one of 50, operand two of 00, and operand three of 00.

Now beginning with instruction at 01, we have NN, an operation code whose value is seven, JJ operand 2 whose value is 50, KK operand two whose value is 0, and MM operand three whose value is also zero. Immediately after decoding it goes to decision area where control is passed to READ routine. This decision is implemented via a computed go to. The read routine reads eight digits off the current card and assigns this value to I_{JJ}, that is, 8 is read into I_{50}. Next, L, the location counter, is advanced by one, making it two, and the decoder decodes instruction I_L or I_2. As I_2 is also a read instruction, the value 5 is read into I_{57} in a manner previously described. Again L is incremented by one getting 3 and I_3 is decoded. I_3 is 02505751, hence NN is 02, JJ is 50, KK is 57 and MM is 51. The instruction decision routine senses this is a subtract and control passes to the subtract routine. Here I_{MM} is formed by subtracting I_{KK} from I_{JJ}. That is, I_{51} is computed and stored by evaluating $I_{50} - I_{57}$. Control passes to location four. I_4 is 05025709; decoded NN = 5, JJ = 02, KK = 57, and MM = 09. Forced to go to the BRN routine at NN is 5. Here JJ is compared to zero and four to insure that JJ has value of 0, 1, 2, or 3 (the only legitimate numbers). Next, KK is examined to insure its value being between 1 and 99. This is necessary as KK is an address used as a testing number. Since our machine has only 99 locations, only positive addresses less than 99 are legitimate. Next, MM is replaced by the value of I_{KK} or I_{57} whose value is 5. MM, the branch address, is then examined to insure that it is a number between 1 and 99. Having legitimate addresses, by using JJ whose value is 02, we go to the area where the 02 modification of instruction 05 is handled. In 05 we look at MM whose current value is 5. If MM > 0 then L is set to MM, otherwise L is incremented by one. As MM is 5, L is set to MM or 09. Hence control is passed to instruction at I_9 which is 03505758. Decomposition of this instruction yields NN of 03, JJ of 50, KK of 57, and MM of 58. The instruction decision sends us to a multiply area where I_{MM} is computed by $I_{JJ} \times I_{KK}$ or $I_{58} = I_{50} \times I_{57} = 8 \times 5 = 40$, hence I_{58} is set to 40, L is incremented by one, and now has value 10. When I_{10} is decomposed NN = 08, JJ = 58, KK and MM = 00. Going to the write routine KK, whose value is zero, is compared to 1. The proper logical test indicates that I_{JJ} or I_{58} is to be printed after single spacing. Therefore, our answer of 40 is printed. Again L is incremented and we find that I_{11} is 06000000 and that NN is 06 while JJ, KK, and MM are all zero. The instruction decision routine sends us to Halt area where a STOP command is issued and the program terminates.

Exercise

Write a FORTRAN program to simulate the arithmetic operations performed with an abacus as they are stated in Chapter I.

A FORTRAN Program for the DATA simulator follows.

```
C     . .
C     SIMPLE ASSEMBLER
C     99 STORAGE WORDS. EACH WORD HAS AN
C     A LOCATION FROM 1 TO 99.
C
C     A LOADER CARD WITH 99 AS LOADER
C     TERMINATES LOADING. EACH WORD HAS AN
C     OPERATION AND THREE OPERANDS, EACH
C     TWO DIGITS LONG. EACH INSTRUCTION IS
C     LOADED BY A LOCATION CODE OF I2 IN
C     THE FIRST TWO COLUMNS. WORD IS
C     LOCATION ADDRESS, OPERATION, OP1, OP2,
C     OP3, READ BY I2,I8 FORMAT. NORMAL FORMAT
C     IS OP1 OPERATION OP2 STORE IN OP3.
C     CODES FOR OPERATION ARE
C     0001 = ADD
C     0002 = SUBTRACT
C     0003 = MULTIPLY
C     0004 = DIVIDE
C     0005 = BRANCH
C        OP1 = 0     UNCOND.
```

```
C       OP1 = 1    COND TO ADDRESS OP3,
C                  IF OP2 = NEGATIVE.
C       OP1 = 2    COND TO ADDRESS OP3,
C                  IF OP2 = POSITIVE.
C       OP1 = 3    COND TO ADDRESS OP3,
C                  IF OP2 = ZERO.
C    0006 = HALT
C    0007 = READ INTO LOCATION ADDRESS OP1
C    0008 = WRITE FROM LOCATION ADDRESS OP1
C    0009 = WRITE A NEW PAGE IF OP2 = 1,
C           NO PRINTING OF DATA
C    0008 = WRITE A DOUBLE SPACE BLANK LINE
C           IF OP2 = 2, NO PRINTING OF DATA
C    0009 = SQRT FROM LOCATION OP1 AND STORE
C           IN OP3
C    0010 = ABSOLUTE VALUE FROM LOCATION OP1
C           AND STORE IN OP3.
C
C
        DIMENSION I(99)
        DIMENSION TT(17)
        WRITE (3,32)
        DO 4 IT = 1,99
        I(IT) = 0
    4   CONTINUE
        DO 3 IT = 1,99
        READ (1,1) L,I(L),(TT(JACK),JACK = 1,17)
        WRITE(3,31) L,I(L),(TT(JACK),JACK = 1,17)
        IF(L-99) 3,33,33
    3   CONTINUE
   33   L = 1
    5   N = I(L)/1000000
        IF(N) 1500,1500,111
  111   IF(N-11) 112,1500,1500
  112   JJ = (I(L)-N*1000000)/10000
        KK = (I(L)-N*1000000-JJ*10000)/100
        MM = I(L)-N*1000000-JJ*10000-KK*100
  400   GO TO (110,120,130,140,500,600,700,800,900,1000),N
  110   I(MM) = I(JJ)+I(KK)
        GO TO 1200
  120   I(MM) = I(JJ)-I(KK)
        GO TO 1200
```

```
 130   I(MM) = I(JJ)*I(KK)
       GO TO 1200
 140   I(MM) = I(JJ)/I(KK)
1200   L = L+1
       GO TO 5
 500   IF(JJ) 1500,507,2500
2500   IF(KK) 1500,1500,506
 506   MN = I(KK)
       IF(JJ−4) 507,1500,1500
 507   IF(MM) 1500,1500,1508
1508   JJ = JJ+1
       GO TO (501,502,508,512),JJ
 501   L = MM
       GO TO 505
 502   IF(MN)504,503,503
 503   L = L+1
       GO TO 505
 504   L = MM
       GO TO 505
 508   IF (MN) 510,510,509
 509   L = MM
       GO TO 505
 510   L = L+1
       GO TO 505
 512   IF(MN) 514,513,514
 513   L = MM
       GO TO 505
 514   L = L+1
 505   GO TO 5
 600   STOP
 700   READ (1,38) I(JJ)
       GO TO 510
 800   IF(KK−1) 801,802,803
 801   WRITE (3,2) I(JJ)
       GO TO 510
 802   WRITE (3,32)
       GO TO 510
 803   WRITE (3,34)
       GO TO 510
 900   AA = I(JJ)
       I(MM) = SQRT(AA)
       GO TO 510
```

```
1000   AA = I(JJ)
       I(MM) = ABS(AA)
       GO TO 510
1500   DO 1501  IT = 1,33
       IT1 = IT
       IT2 = IT+33
       IT3 = IT+66
1501   WRITE(3,1136)IT1,I(IT1),IT2,I(IT2),
    1  IT3,I(IT3)
       WRITE(3,30) L
       GO TO 600
    1  FORMAT(I2,I8,1X,17A4)
    2  FORMAT(1X,I8)
   38  FORMAT(I8)
   30  FORMAT(' ERROR IN STATEMENT ',I3)
   31  FORMAT(1X,I2,1X,I8,10X,17A4)
   32  FORMAT('1')
   34  FORMAT('0')
   36  FORMAT(1X,I2,I8)
 1136  FORMAT(10X,I2,I8,20X,I2,I8,20X,I2,I8)
       END
```

1	7510000		READ A
2	7520000		READ B
3	7530000		READ C
4	5025306		
5	6000000		STOP
6	1515254	A+B	INTO D
7	4545355		D DIVIDED BY C
8	8550000		WRITE ANS
9	5000005		
99	0		
	19		
1	7510000		READ A
2	7520000		READ B
3	7530000		READ C
4	5025306		
5	6000000		STOP
6	1515254	A+B	INTO D
7	4545355		D DIVIDED BY C
8	55000000		WRITE ANS
9	5000005		

99	0				
1	7510000	34	0	67	0
2	7520000	35	0	68	0
3	7530000	36	0	69	0
4	5025306	37	0	70	0
5	6000000	38	0	71	0
6	1515254	39	0	72	0
7	4545355	40	0	73	0
85	5000000	41	0	74	0
9	5000005	42	0	75	0
10	5000000	43	0	76	0
11	0	44	0	77	0
12	0	45	0	78	0
13	0	46	0	79	0
14	0	47	0	80	0
15	0	48	0	81	0
16	0	49	0	82	0
17	0	50	0	83	0
18	0	51	53	84	0
19	0	52	5	85	0
20	0	53	3	86	0
21	0	54	58	87	0
22	0	55	19	88	0
23	0	56	0	89	0
24	0	57	0	90	0
25	0	58	0	91	0
26	0	59	0	92	0
27	0	60	0	93	0
28	0	61	0	94	0
29	0	62	0	95	0
30	0	63	0	96	0
31	0	64	0	97	0
32	0	65	0	98	0
33	0	66	0	99	0

ERROR IN STATEMENT 8

Data has a built-in "dump." When there is an error, upon request of the operator, it will produce a memory dump. The above example shows a program with an error in statement 8.

Review Exercises

In this section we present a collection of exercises with different degrees of difficulty. We think practice is the best teacher. Try to solve as many exercises as possible. Do not disregard the elementary exercises. We hope that something can be learned from each problem.

Review Exercises

1. The radius of curvature of a highway is determined by using the formula

$$R = 0.258 \ V^2$$

where

R is the radius of a circular curve,
V is the velocity in mph,
0.258 is a constant factor that takes into consideration gravity, tire friction, and a maximum super elevation slope of 0.10.

Write a FORTRAN program that would output R for different values of V.

2. Let $V = X_1 i + X_2 j$ be a two-dimension vector. The length L of this vector is given by

$$L = X_1^2 + X_2^2$$

The angle that it makes with the X-axis is given by

$$\tan \theta = X_2/X_1$$

Write a FORTRAN program that would accept X_1 and X_2 as data and would have as output L and θ.

3. Let (X_1,Y_1), (X_2,Y_2), . . . , (X_n,Y_n) be a collection of two-dimension vectors. Form

$$X = X_1 + X_2 + \ldots + X_n$$
$$Y = Y_1 + Y_2 + \ldots + Y_n$$

Write a FORTRAN program that would accept (X_1,Y_1), . . . , (X_n,Y_n) as data and will have X and Y as output.

4. Let (X_1,Y_1), (X_2,Y_2), . . . , (X_n,Y_n) be a collection of points with masses m_1, m_2, . . . , m_n, respectively. The center of gravity of this set is defined to be the point (X, Y) given by the formula

$$X = (m_1X_1 + m_2X_2 + \ldots + m_nX_n)/(m_1 + m_2 + \ldots + m_n)$$
$$Y = (m_1Y_1 + m_2Y_2 + \ldots + m_nY_n)/(m_1 + m_2 + \ldots + m_n)$$

Write a FORTRAN program that would accept as data (X_1, Y_1, m_1), ..., (X_n, Y_n, m_n) and will have as output the center of gravity (X, Y).

5.   A body is released from rest and falls freely. The distance s in feet traveled after t seconds is given by

$$s = -16t^2$$

Write a FORTRAN program that will output in a tabular form the distance traveled after 1, 2, ... , 10 seconds.

6.   The centripetal force F acting on a particle of mass m revolving in a circle is given by

$$F = mV^2/R$$

where

   $m =$ mass of the particle,
   $V =$ velocity of the particle,
   $R =$ radius of the circle.

Write a FORTRAN program that will accept m, V, R as input. Keeping fixed m and R modified V by V (i.e., if the initial value of V is five and if $V = .5$ then $V + V = 5.5$) until V reaches a final value FV. Print a table showing m, V, R and the values of F from initial V to final FV.

7.   When a projectile is launched, its horizontal and vertical position, X and Y, may be given as a function of time T. Assuming that the projectile has an initial velocity V_0 and an initial angle of launch α, the position of the projectile at each time T is given by

$$X = (V_0 \cos \alpha)T$$

$$Y = -\frac{1}{2}gT^2 + (V_0 \sin \alpha)T$$

The relation between the coordinates of the projectile is given by

$$Y = -\frac{1}{2}\left(\frac{X}{V_0} \cos \alpha\right)^2 + \tan \alpha \cdot X$$

The highest point reached by the projectile is given by

$$Y = (V_0 \sin \alpha)^2/2g$$

The distance that the projectile travels horizontally is

$$\text{RANGE} = (V_0^2 \sin 2\alpha)/g$$

Using the subroutine GRAPH plot the trajectory of a projectile for different values of α and V_0.

8. Each student of a certain college uses his (her) Social Security number for identification purposes. The grade of each student in Math. 121 is punched on a card in columns 11–25 in the form xx.xx. Sex is recorded as a zero for males and 1 for females in column 10. Write a FORTRAN program that will count the number of A, B, C, D, and F according to the following scale:

> If grade $\geqslant 80$, A
> If $70 \leqslant$ grade < 80, B
> If $60 \leqslant$ grade < 70, C
> If $50 \leqslant$ grade < 60, D
> If grade less then 50, F

A false card with negative grade, say -1.00, would indicate that the last card has been used.

Count the number of students and give the percentage of students getting A, B, C, D, and F. If 5% of the students have grade A print "TEST WAS TOO EASY." If 20% of the students have grade F and the percentage of A's is less than 5%, then print "TEST WAS TOO DIFFICULT." In any other case print "NO COMMENT."

9. Define X, Y and Z as follows:

$$X = 1 - T^2, \quad Y = 2T, \quad Z = 1 + T^2$$

It is easy to check that $X^2 + Y^2 = Z^2$. This shows that X, Y and Z can be the sides of a right triangle.

Write a FORTRAN program to produce a table with output X, Y and Z for integer values of T ranging from $T = 2$ to $T = 40$.

10. Given two points (X_1, Y_1) and (X_2, Y_2), the parametric equations of the line joining them are given by

$$X = \frac{X_1 + \lambda X_2}{1 + \lambda}$$

$$Y = \frac{Y_1 + \lambda Y_2}{1 + \lambda}$$

Write a program to compute the values of (X, Y) for values of $\lambda = 0, 1, \ldots, 10$. Print them in tabular form.

11.   A function is a set f of ordered pairs $f = \{(X_1, Y_1), (X_2, Y_2), \ldots, (X_n, Y_n)\}$ such that no two pairs have the same first element.

For example, $f = \{(1, 1), (2, 3), (5, 7)\}$ is a function. $h = \{(3, 1), (2, 3), (3, 4)\}$ is not a function, since there are two pairs $(3, 1)$ and $(3, 4)$ and $1 \neq 4$.

Write a FORTRAN program that will read in $X_1, X_2, \ldots, X_n$ and their corresponding values $Y_1, Y_2, \ldots, Y_n$ in two vector arrays, X and Y, respectively. The program should check if the set $\{(X_1, Y_1), (X_2, Y_2), \ldots, (X_n, Y_n)\}$ is a function or not. The output should be

(1) F is a function.

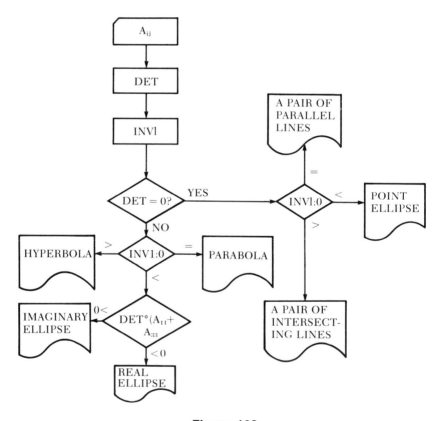

Figure 103

or (2) *F* is not a function, showing the pairs that violate the rules for *f* to be a function.

12. Find all positive integers *m* and *n* such that $\dfrac{1}{m} + \dfrac{1}{n} = \dfrac{p}{q}$ where *p* and *q* are fixed positive numbers.

13. An equation of the form

$$A_{11}X_1^2 + 2A_{12}X_1X_2 + A_{22}X_2^2 + 2A_{13}X_1 + 2A_{23}X_2 + A_{33} = 0$$

is called a *conic*.

Let $T1 = A_{11}A_{22}A_{33}$, $T2 = 2A_{12}A_{23}A_{13}$, $T3 = A_{13}^2A_{22}$, $T4 = A_{12}^2A_{33}$, $T5 = A_{23}^2A_{11}$. With $T1$, $T2$, $T3$, $T4$ and $T5$ we compute DET and INVI using

DET = T1+2·T2−(T3+T4+T5)
INV1 = $A_{12}^2 - A_{11}A_{22}$

Conics can be identified using the flow chart of Figure 103.

Write a FORTRAN program that would accept as data A_{11}, A_{12}, A_{13}, A_{22}, A_{23} and A_{33} and will have as output the identification of the conic represented by equation (1). The output should be in the form,

THE CONIC
A11*X1+2*A12*X2+A22*Y2+2*A13*X1+2*A23*X2+A33 = 0
REPRESENTS...................

14. The equation of second degree $ax^2 + bx + c = 0$ can be solved exactly using the formula

$$x_1 = \frac{-b + \sqrt{b^2 - 4ac}}{2a}$$

$$x_2 = \frac{-b - \sqrt{b^2 - 4ac}}{2a}$$

provided $b^2 - 4ac > 0$.

Write a FORTRAN program to compute x_1 and x_2 for different values of *a*, *b*, and *c*. Check whether or not $b^2 - 4ac > 0$. If $b^2 - 4ac < 0$, print "EQUATION HAS NO REAL SOLUTIONS."

15. Write a program to generate the first one hundred numbers. Print them in groups of 20, separating each group by three blank lines. For example:

1	2	3	4	5
6	7	8	9	10
11	12	13	14	15
16	17	18	19	20

21	22	23	24	25
26	27	28	29	30

16.   Cards are read into a computer with three numbers X, Y, Z punched on them. Compare the value of X with the value of Y in the same card; Compute A as follows:

$$\text{If } X < Y \quad \text{then } A = X^2 - Y^2,$$
$$\text{If } X > Y \quad \text{then } A = X^2 + Y^2,$$
$$\text{If } X = Y \quad \text{Then } A = 0.$$

In order to know that the last card has been read in, each card has punched a zero except for the last card that would have punched a -1. Write a program to find the value of P where

$$P = \Sigma(A) \cdot \Sigma(Z)$$

where the summation symbol Σ extends to all the cards read into the computer.

17.   Let $X = (X_1, X_2, \ldots, X_n)$ and $Y = (Y_1, Y_2, \ldots, Y_n)$ be n-dimensional vectors. The inner product of X and Y is defined to be

$$X_1 Y_1 + X_2 Y_2 + \ldots + X_n Y_n = \sum_{i=1}^{i=n} X_i Y_i$$

Write a FORTRAN IV program that will read in the vectors X and Y, compute their inner product, and print the result. Assume that the X_i's are real variables. Read $10X_i$'s per card with a FORM at F 5.3.

18.   Modify the above exercise so it will be possible to compute the inner product of a vector X with itself. Once the inner product is computed obtain its square root. The number obtained is called the length of the vector X.

19. Let (X_1, Y_1), (X_2, Y_2), . . . , (X_n, Y_n) be a set of n pairs of observations. Write a program to compute

$$P = \sum_{i=1}^{i=n} X_i Y_i^2 = X_1 Y_1^2 + X_2 Y_2^2 + \ldots + X_n Y_n^2$$

Punch 5 observations per card with F 7.3. Print P with F 10.3.

20. Let (X_1, Y_1), (X_2, Y_2), . . . , (X_n, Y_n) be a set of n observations. Let

$$P_j = \sum_{i=1}^{i=n} X_j Y_i^2 = X_j Y_1^2 + X_j Y_2^2 + \ldots + X_j Y_n^2$$

Define

$$P = \frac{1}{n} \Sigma P_j = \frac{P_1 + P_2 + \ldots + P_n}{n}$$

Write a program which will accept 7 observations per card with a F 3.2 format. This program will print P_j for every j and will compute and print P.

21. Given c sets of n plates $p_1, p_2, \ldots, p_n$ where each plate p_i has measurements x_i and y_i. For each plate calculate $H_i = \frac{x_i}{y_i}$. For every value H_i, the following F_i is computed.

$$F_i = H_i^2 + 2 \cdot H_i \qquad \text{if } H_i > 5$$

$$F_i = \frac{H_i + 5}{2} \qquad \text{if } H_i \leqslant 5$$

Write a program that will accept n, the number of plates, and the pairs (x_1, y_1), . . . , (x_n, y_n). The columns 1–3 will contain n; the x_i's and y_i's will alternate on the same card, each punched as FS.3 fields. In the calculation for H_i, set $H_i = 1$, if $y_i \leqslant .01$. Choose a format for printing that will accommodate your answers F_i, assuming that the values of x_1 and y_i are between 0.000 and 5.000.

22. All students entering a certain college must submit their high school English average to the admissions office. A table is constructed that assigns a one digit code for the averages.

Average	Code
0– 49	0
50– 59	1
60– 69	2
70– 79	3
80– 89	4
90–100	5

Each student's record is contained on an accounting card. Columns 78 and 80 contain the students' average, recorded to the nearest percent. For example, 82% is recorded as 082 in columns 78, 79, and 80. Write a program that will accumulate the numbers of students with code 0, code 1, . . . , code 5. Write the six answers with I5 Format. In order that the program can sense the last card, enter into columns 78–80 the number 105. This artificial mark can be placed after the data and used to stop the counting.

23. Let $(x_1, y_1), (x_2, y_2), \ldots , (x_n, y_n)$ be a set of n observations. For each observation $H = \dfrac{x_i}{y_i}$ is computed. For every value of H the following value of F is computed.

$$F = H + 2H \qquad \text{if } H > 5$$

$$F = \frac{H + 5}{2} \qquad \text{if } H \leq 5$$

Write a program which will accept 5 observations per card with a F 3.2 Format and will compute F.

24. The sieve of Eratosthenes is an algorithm to form a table of prime numbers smaller than a certain integer N. We illustrate the algorithm by constructing a table for $N = 50$.

Writing 1 and 2 and all odd numbers smaller than 50, we have:

```
  1,   2,   3,   5,   7,   9,  11,  13,  15,  17,  19
 21,  23,  25,  27,  29,  31,  33,  35,  37,  39,  41
 43,  45,  47,  49.
```

Delete all the multiples of 3 that remain in the table getting

```
  1,   2,   3,   5,   7,  11,  13,  17,  19,  23,  25,  29
 31,  35,  37,  41,  43,  47,  49.
```

Next delete all multiples of 5 (first prime has not been used so far).

Next we delete all multiples of 11, which is the next prime that has not been deleted. We have the following situation in summary.

$$
\begin{array}{cccccccccc}
1 & 2 & 3 & \not{4} & 5 & \not{6} & 7 & \not{8} & \not{9} & \not{10} \\
11 & \not{12} & 13 & \not{14} & \not{15} & \not{16} & 17 & \not{18} & 19 & \not{20} \\
\not{21} & \not{22} & 23 & \not{24} & \not{25} & \not{26} & \not{27} & \not{28} & 29 & \not{30} \\
31 & \not{32} & \not{33} & \not{34} & \not{35} & \not{36} & 37 & \not{38} & 39 & \not{40} \\
41 & \not{42} & 43 & \not{44} & \not{45} & \not{46} & 47 & \not{48} & 49 & \not{50}
\end{array}
$$

The numbers left are all prime and less than 50. Write a FORTRAN program that will produce a table containing prime numbers less than 500.

Appendix

APPENDIX

Table A.1

FORTRAN IV Compiler		Range of Integers	Number of Decimal Digits
CDC	1604,3600	$-(2^{47}-1)$ to $(2^{47}-1)$	14
GE	635	$-(2^{35}-1)$ to $(2^{35}-1)$	10
HW	1800	$-(2^{44}-1)$ to $(2^{44}-1)$	13
IBM	1130,1800	$-(2^{15}-1)$ to $(2^{15}-1)$	4
	360	$-(2^{31}-1)$ to $(2^{31}-1)$	9
	1401,1410,1440	-99999 to $+99999$	5
	1460,7010	-99999 to $+99999$	5
	7040,7044	$-(2^{35}-1)$ to $(2^{35}-1)$	10
	7090,7094	$-(2^{35}-1)$ to $(2^{35}-1)$	10
Philco	2000	$-(2^{39}-1)$ to $(2^{39}-1)$	12
RCA	Spectra 70	$-(2^{31}-1)$ to $(2^{31}-1)$	9
SDS	9300	$-(2^{23}-1)$ to $(2^{23}-1)$	7
Univac	1107,1108	$-(2^{35}-1)$ to $(2^{35}-1)$	10

Table A.2

FORTRAN IV Compiler		Precision of Real Numbers Approximate Number of Significant Digits
CDC		10
GE		8
HW		12
IBM	1130,1800	7
	360	7
	1401,1410,1440,1460	8
	7010,7040,7044	8
	7090,7094	8
Philco	2000	10
RCA	Spectra 70	7
SDS	9300	12
Univac	1107,1108	8

Table A.3

FORTRAN IV Compiler		Range of Exponents for Real Numbers
CDC	1604,3600	−308 to 308
GE	635	−38 to 38
HW	1800	−78 to 78
IBM	1130,1800	−38 to 38
	System 360	−75 to 75
	1401,1410,1440,1460	−100 to 99
	7010	−100 to 99
	7040,7044,7090,7094	−38 to 38
Philco	2000	−616 to 616
RCA	Spectra 70	−75 to 75
SDS	9300	−77 to 77
Univac	1107,1108	−38 to 38

Table A.4

		Maximum Number of Characters Allowed in Naming an Integer or Real
FORTRAN IV Processor		*Variable*
CDC	1604,3600	8
GE	635	6
HW	1800	6
IBM	1130,1800	5
	360	6
	1401,1410,1440,1460	6
	7010,7040,7044,7090,7094	6
Philco	2000	6
RCA	Spectra 70	6
SDS	9300	8
Univac	1107,1108	6

Table A.5

FORTRAN IV Processor		*Statement Number Range*
CDC	1604,3600	1 to 99999
GE	635	1 to 32767
HW	1800	1 to 32767
IBM	1130,1800	1 to 99999
	360	1 to 99999
	1401,1410,1440,1460	1 to 99999
	7010,7040,7044	1 to 99999
	7090,7094	1 to 32767
Philco	2000	1 to 32767
RCA	Spectra 70	1 to 99999
SDS	9300	1 to 99999
Univac	1107,1108	1 to 32767

Table A.6 — Statements

	RCA	CDC 3100–3500	IBM D Level	IBM F Level
Assign	x			x
Backspace	x	x	x	x
Call	x	x	x	x
Character		x		
Common	x	x	x	x
Common/Data	x	x		x
Complex	x	x		x
Continue	x	x	x	x
Data	x	x		x
Do	x	x	x	x
Double precision	x		x	x
End	x	x	x	x
Endfile	x	x	x	x
Entry	x	x		x
Equivalence	x	x	x	x
External name	x	x	x	x
Format I	x	x	x	x
F	x	x	x	x
E	x	x	x	x
D	x		x	x
H	x	x	x	x
O		x		x
L	x			x
A	x	x	x	x
G	x			x
C				x
X	x	x	x	x
T	x		x	x
Function name	x	x	x	x
Go to n	x	x	x	x
Go to i, $(n_1, n_2 \ldots)$	x		x	x
Go to $(n_1, n_2, \ldots)$, i	x	x		x
If (arit. exp) n_1, n_2, n_3	x	x	x	x
If (log exp) S	x	x		x
Integer	x	x	x	x
Logical	x			x
Pause, pause n	x	x	x	x
Real	x		x	x
Read (i,j) list	x	x	x	x

	RCA	CDC 3100–3500	IBM D Level	IBM F Level
Read (i) list	x	x	x	x
Return	x	x	x	x
Rewind i	x	x	x	x
Subroutine name $(a_1, \ldots)$	x	x	x	x
Write (i,j) list	x	x	x	x
Write (i) list	x	x	x	x

Index